Martin Luther King, Jr. ....
To The Mountaintop

Martin Luther King, Jr. ...
To The Mountaintop

Wm. ROGER WITHERSPOON

DOUBLEDAY & COMPANY, INC.   GARDEN CITY, NEW YORK   1985

Grateful acknowledgment is made for permission to reprint the following: "Letter from a Birmingham Jail," April 16, 1963, in *Why We Can't Wait*, by Martin Luther King, Jr. Copyright 1963 by Martin Luther King, Jr. Reprinted by permission of Harper & Row, Inc.

"I Have A Dream," by Martin Luther King, Jr. Copyright 1963 by Martin Luther King, Jr. Reprinted by permission of Joan Daves.

"I've Been to the Mountaintop," by Martin Luther King, Jr. Copyright 1968 by Martin Luther King, Jr., Estate. Reprinted by permission of Joan Daves.

"The Drum Major Instinct," by Martin Luther King, Jr. Copyright 1968 by Martin Luther King, Jr., Estate. Reprinted by permission of Joan Daves.

Selections from *My Life with Martin Luther King, Jr.* by Coretta Scott King. Copyright 1969 by Coretta Scott King. Reprinted by permission of Joan Daves.

Frontispiece: (PAUL SCHUTZER/LIFE MAGAZINE.)

Library of Congress Cataloging in Publication Data

Witherspoon, William Roger.
    Martin Luther King, Jr.—to the mountaintop.

    Includes index.
    1. King, Martin Luther.   2. Afro-Americans—Biography.   3. Baptists—United States—Clergy—Biography.   4. Afro-Americans—Civil rights.
I. Title.
E185.97.K5W58   1985   323.4'092'4 [B]
ISBN 0-385-19883-3
Library of Congress Catalog Card Number 84-28723

Copyright © 1985 by Wm. Roger Witherspoon/Wordsmith, Inc.

Designed by Judith Neuman

First Edition

Contents

This book is for Kir.

Author's Note

If this book succeeds, it will be because of the collective efforts and devotion of a number of people who coaxed, coached, worked, and worried with me from its conception to its conclusion.

First and foremost is Gerald Gladney, my editor at Doubleday, who conceived this project, serving as both boss and friend so we would each have something to be proud of; executive editor Loretta A. Barrett; and my agents, Marie Dutton Brown and Carol Mann, who brought the project to me and taught me the intricacies of the publishing business.

This is, essentially, three books in one: an oral history, an academic biography, and a photo essay on a man and his times. The melding of the first two into a text was the most comfortable for me, but I owe a debt to two historians I have never met, who showed me the possibilities of each genre. They are Stephen B. Oates, who wrote *Let the Trumpet Sound: The Life of Martin Luther King, Jr.* and illustrated just how academic research should be done, and journalist Howell Raines, whose *My Soul Is Rested: The Story of the Civil Rights Movement in the Deep South* is the most superb oral history I have ever come across.

The photo essay portion of this tribute would not have been possible without the diligence of nine disparate colleagues who culled photos from archives, newspapers, and private collections around the country to find unique and representative shots from which I could make a selection. Many of these people served dual functions, however, locating sources for me and, sometimes, conducting interviews.

Anne Fischel, in New York, one of my oldest friends, located more than half the photos in this collection and devised the cataloguing system we followed. Sunni Smith, in Washington, D.C., culled the archives there and tracked down a number of former SNCC members. Mary Gaines, in Montgomery, located and interviewed most of the former members of the Montgomery Improvement Association, as well as Alabama officials from that period. Diana Clyne tracked down photos in Birmingham, Alabama, and braved the ire of the Ancient City Gun Club tracking down participants in the St. Augustine, Florida, campaign. Rose Ragsdale, in Jackson, Mississippi, and Nanette Baker in Memphis, Tennessee, located photos in those cities. Garland Thompson, in Philadelphia, Pennsylvania, tracked down associates of Mike King, the Crozer theological student. And Hermene Hartman, in Chicago, provided photos from the civil rights leader's only Northern campaign and located the principals involved. My wife, Cynthia Bedford, handled the Atlanta research and coordinated the efforts of all the others.

I owe an obvious debt to many of the participants in a heroic time in America, for taking hours to patiently share with me, in some cases, extremely painful memories. First and foremost is Coretta Scott King, who was there at the beginning and who is doing her best to ensure that the movement doesn't fade into oblivion.

Revs. Ralph David Abernathy, Joseph Lowery, James Lawson, Fred Shuttlesworth, Hosea Williams, Bernard Lee, and James Bevel of SCLC, and John Lewis, Julian Bond, and Bob Moses of SNCC are people whose courage, sacrifice, and pain made the movement. They were never more than a telephone call away, and I am grateful for their guidance and assistance. And there are the lesser known but equally key figures, such as E. D. Nixon and Joann Robinson in Montgomery, Judge Bryan Simpson in St. Augustine, and Dr. William Anderson from Albany.

I would be remiss in not acknowledging Alabama Supreme Court Justice John Patterson, who was the embattled attorney general and then governor of that state during the early days of the movement. Mr. Patterson spent several hours explaining the opposite side of the civil rights struggle and opened doors to some of his former colleagues.

A special thanks to Steve Klein and archivist Louise Cook of the Martin Luther King, Jr., Center for Nonviolent Social Change in Atlanta for their invaluable assistance.

There are my friends Oretha Pope, Diana Clyne, and Doug Lyons, who read parts of the manuscript and provided advice and support throughout.

Finally, there is my wife, Cynthia, an active participant in this project whose encouragement, advice, and love sustained me and the household. As always.

WM. ROGER WITHERSPOON
Atlanta, Georgia
1984

Martin Luther King, Jr. ...
To The Mountaintop

*The King family home on
Auburn Avenue, in the heart
of Atlanta's black district*
(ATLANTA CONSTITUTION).

1
GENESIS

THE RIDE TO MONTGOMERY, ALABAMA, WAS A PLEASURE.

It was a clear, cold Saturday in January 1954, and the young Martin Luther King, Jr.—just days shy of his twenty-fifth birthday—was to preach the following day at the Dexter Avenue Baptist Church. It wouldn't be the first time he'd preached. King had made a reputation as an erudite orator when he was associate pastor of his father's church in Atlanta—Ebenezer Baptist Church—and at a host of churches in Pennsylvania and Boston as a guest minister while continuing his education. Stop Here

But this was different. He had completed the coursework for his doctorate at Boston University the preceding August and now spent the bulk of his time working on his dissertation. He wanted to end the student life and begin supporting himself and his young wife, Coretta. He'd had tentative offers of a deanship, an administrative post, and a teaching position at three Northern colleges. While the academic world appealed to him, his main interest was in preaching, and he eagerly accepted the invitation from Dexter to deliver a trial sermon while he was home for the Christmas holidays.

The church was small, and it had an elitist reputation. Its ministers usually had advanced degrees, and the bulk of the three hundred middle-class parishioners were teachers, either in public schools or at the predominantly black Alabama State College. King wasn't sure whether he should try to dazzle the parishioners with a display of his considerable intellectual range or preach in a more familiar style. Impressing the congregation was important, for this time he was auditioning for a job and not just practicing for his future career.

The drive to Montgomery was a lighthearted one. The radio provided an enjoyable backdrop for the trip by playing one of his favorite operas, Donizetti's *Lucia di Lammermoor*, performed by the Metropolitan Opera. Accompanying him on the trip was Dr. Vernon Johns, who had just retired as minister of Dexter.

Dr. Johns was something of a legend in the South. One story has it that Dr. Johns refused to give up his seat on a Montgomery bus. The driver stormed up to him and hollered, "Nigger, didn't you hear me tell you to get the hell out of that seat?"

The young Reverend King was a personable young man, quiet in his speech and manner . . . (MOREHOUSE COLLEGE).

. . . yet forceful and animated when standing in the pulpit (P. H. POLK).

The good Christian minister, who was wearing his clerical collar at the time, said, equally loudly, "And didn't you hear me tell you that I'm going to sit right goddamned here?"

The driver, stunned by that reply from the clergyman, retreated. Dr. Johns told that story himself during the following Sunday's sermon and said that rather than being offended by the use of His name, God probably smiled and said, "I'd better keep an eye on that boy: he's going to do a lot for Christianity down South."

Dr. Johns was hitching a ride to Montgomery to preach a guest sermon at the First Baptist Church, headed by Rev. Ralph David Abernathy, before continuing on to New Orleans to conduct a series of lectures at Dillard University. Dexter had spun off from First Baptist years ago, and the two congregations were traditionally close, with Dexter regarded as the daughter church.

Abernathy, just two years older than Martin, had been a part-time preacher for eighteen months at an Eastern Star Church in Demopolis, Alabama, while teaching social studies and serving as the dean of men at Alabama State. When he took over the helm of First Baptist in 1952 at age twenty-five, it was his first full-time pastorate.

The church, as its name implied, was the oldest black Baptist church in the city, having been spun off by a white First Baptist Church in 1867. In Abernathy's view, Dexter and First Baptist "were of the same order, though First Baptist does not have as many professional people as Dexter does."

King had planned to drop off Dr. Johns at Abernathy's house and go to Dexter. But it had been a long drive, and when he smelled the aroma of smothered steak wafting through the Abernathy household he readily accepted an invitation to dinner. It was the start of a lifelong friendship between the two ministers, though it was not their first encounter.

Abernathy kidded King about their first meeting, in 1951, when King was known to the college crowd as Mike and had a reputation for his natty dress, his oratorical skills, and his popularity with young women. Mike had been studying at Crozer Theological Seminary in Chester, Pennsylvania, while Abernathy was a graduate student in sociology at Atlanta University. Abernathy saw a notice that the younger King was home for a few days and would be preaching that Sunday at his father's church.

"I went over to hear him," said Abernathy, "and was surprised that he was so profound and provocative and good."

That afternoon, Abernathy walked over to Spelman, the women's college at Atlanta University, to pick up his date for a play, but was informed that she was not feeling well.

"I was later standing outside the dormitory talking to some young men when who should come by but my date, with Martin Luther King, Jr. She was terribly embarrassed.

"But it ended well. He didn't marry her, and neither did I."

King took his leave, to find his host for the night and take a look at Dexter. It was a stately red brick church across the street from the Alabama State Capitol, whose gleaming white columns were erected in 1851, just a decade before Alabama seceded from the Union. From the church, one could see the statehouse steps where Jefferson Davis took the oath of office as president of the Confederate States of America, an event that led to Montgomery being labeled the Cradle of the Confederacy.

King still had to decide about his sermon for the following morning. He solved the problem about his approach to the congregation by polishing up a sermon he first delivered at the Twelfth Street Baptist Church in the Roxbury section of Boston, two years earlier, called "The Three Dimensions of a Complete Life." He decided to let divine inspiration guide his method of delivery.

"I said to myself," he later wrote, "keep Martin Luther King in the background and God in the foreground and everything will be all right. Remember, you are a channel of the gospel, and not the source."

The sermon was more than all right. Dexter's elders spent some time telling King about the church's structure and finances and then promised to contact him shortly with their decision. He spent the rest of his Sunday afternoon dining and talking with Abernathy before driving back to Atlanta and then flying on to Boston.

A month later, Dexter's elders sent him an airmail letter formally offering him the pastorate. That posed a problem.

Both he and Coretta were products of the South, and they weren't at all sure that they wanted to leave the relative racial ease of the North to go back below the Mason-Dixon Line, with what King termed "all the tragic implications of segregation."

King hated discrimination and all its ramifications. Until the time he was five, his "inseparable playmates" were two white boys whose parents owned a store across the street from the King family home. Then they suddenly stopped playing with him, and his mother, Alberta King, had the painful task of sitting the child on her knee and telling him the facts of black life in America. She told him about the horrors of slavery and the Civil War. She told him about Reconstruction and the end of that brief period of progress. She told him about segregated theaters and housing and restaurants and schools and the ubiquitous signs pointing to white or colored water fountains, white or colored bathrooms. She told him all about the separate way of life black people were forced to lead, and then added, "But you are as good as anyone."

He remembered that. But it still hurt.

"I could never adjust to the separate waiting rooms, separate eating places, separate rest rooms," he said later, "partly because the separate was always unequal and partly because the very idea of separate did something to my sense of dignity and self respect."

He remembered traveling with his father through Atlanta one day. Daddy King drove past a stop sign and was flagged by a policeman on a motorcycle, who said, "All right, boy, pull over and let me see your license."

The elder King indignantly pointed at his son and said, "This is a boy. I'm a man, and until you call me one, I will not listen to you."

In that instance, the startled white man quickly wrote the ticket and left. But it was not uncommon in the South for that same type of situation to take a nastier turn.

"I grew up abhorring not only segregation," King said later, "but also the oppressive and barbarous acts that grew out of it. I had passed spots where Negroes had been savagely lynched, and had watched the Ku Klux Klan on its rides at night. I had seen police brutality with my own eyes, and watched Negroes receive the most tragic injustice in the courts.

"I had come perilously close to resenting all white people."

As a youth, Daddy King, the son of a southern Georgia sharecropper, had seen a black man beaten and hanged for no reason at all. He was called Mike in those days, a compromise between his mother, Delia Lindsey, who wanted to name him Michael, and his father, James, who wanted to name him Martin Luther. He didn't straighten it out until 1933, when his dying father asked him to officially make his name Martin Luther. He obliged, and changed the name of his four-year-old son, Mike Jr., as well. But people still called him either Daddy King or Mike, and his firstborn was known as M.L. at home and Mike to his friends.

The elder King had earned a minor reputation as a country preacher before turning his back on his sharecropping days in Stockbridge at age sixteen and traveling to Atlanta to make his fortune in the big city. He quickly learned that his country ways were no asset here, so he went to school at night to obtain the high school education he lacked. Then he earned degrees at Morehouse College, the prestigious men's college at Atlanta University.

He married Alberta Williams, the daughter of Rev. Adam Daniel Williams, then one of the most prominent black ministers in the region. Reverend Williams was a tireless fighter for civil rights and was one of the first presidents of the fledgling National Association for the Advancement of Colored People shortly after its founding in 1906. He was constantly involved in legal challenges to the Southern way of life and encouraged his son-in-law to be an activist minister as well.

Daddy King took his advice. He preached about voter rights and voter responsibility at a time when few blacks were allowed to go near the polls because of economic or physical intimidation, and in 1935 led a thousand blacks on a voter registration march to Atlanta city hall. The following year, he led a protest march by black teachers and began an eleven-year court fight that eventually equalized the payment for white and black public school teachers.

It was in this environment that the young Mike King developed: born in the church, infused with a sense of social responsibility, and detesting the Southern way of segregated life.

Yet the younger Mike did not inherit his father's distrust of whites. He was a precocious youth and skipped his last year at Washington High School to enter Morehouse College as a fifteen-year-old freshman. That wasn't an easy move.

Professor Louis Chandler, who taught Mike public speaking and freshman and sophomore English at Morehouse, said the lad "was a hard worker, but did not distinguish himself as a student.

"He came in at the eleventh-grade level and had certain handicaps coming out of the Atlanta public schools. He had deficiencies in English and had to work pretty hard."

Chandler gave him a C+ in English, though "he would have had an A based just on interest."

Daddy King was a trustee of Morehouse and always watched his son's progress closely. He once called Chandler and said, "If at any time you find Martin is not working up to his capacity you tell me. He's not too big for me to still strap him and whip him."

That may not have been an idle boast, for the elder King, a strict disciplinarian, took a switch to Mike and his brother, A.D., until they were fifteen.

In his junior year he joined the interracial Intercollegiate Council, a move that touched off a heated row with his father.

Daddy King said he did not like his son attending these integrated meetings on various college campuses in the area because "you don't need to risk any betrayals from them, and that's mainly what you'll get."

M.L. answered, "I know I could resent every person in the white race, and it would be easy. That's the point. It would be too easy, and I know the answer to so much of this is more complicated."

To forget that many whites were fundamentally decent would be to eliminate the moral difference between bitter blacks struggling for freedom and equality and racist whites fighting to hold them back.

At this, Daddy King relented, impressed at his son's moral conviction though dubious about its efficacy in 1947. Mike kept that fervor throughout his tenure at Morehouse. He was looking for more, however: a system to combat the oppression he saw around him, and a theology that embraced that effort.

This was also a year of closeness for the elder and junior Kings. Mike said he wanted to enter the ministry and obtained a license to preach. He became an assistant to his father at Ebenezer, and the following February was ordained into the Baptist ministry.

He applied to Crozer in 1948, stating on his application that he had "an inescapable urge to serve society" and that his background had imbued him with a "sense of responsibility which I could not escape."

Crozer was a different world for Mike King. It was situated in Chester, then an industrial city with a population of about sixty-six thousand. Much of the city was physically off-limits to blacks, who basically stayed in the western part of town. King and a long-time friend and fellow Morehouse graduate, Walter McCall, were among the few blacks out of a student body of about fifty students, taught by an all-white faculty.

He was not despondent about the abrupt shift from an all-black Southern environment to a nearly all-white Northern one. He did state later, though, "I was well aware of the typical white stereotype of the Negro, that he is always late, that he's loud and always laughing, that he's dirty and messy, and for a while, I was terribly conscious of trying to avoid identification with it. If I were a minute late to class, I was almost morbidly conscious of it and sure that everyone else noticed it."

So he paid meticulous attention to his dress and his deportment and applied himself to his studies and to the lectures of two of his professors, George W. Davis and Kenneth L. Smith. Davis taught systematic and historical theology, philosophy and psychology of religion, and comparative religion. King took a third of his 110 hours of coursework toward his Bachelor of Divinity from Davis, an exponent of Christian liberalism, which held that religion is active and the church has an active role in both the faith and daily life.

Martin Luther King, Jr. (front row, seventh from right) *entered Morehouse College at age fifteen, skipping his senior year in high school* (MOREHOUSE COLLEGE).

(AP/WIDE WORLD).

He had matured into a confident young preacher by the time he graduated in June 1948 (front row, second from left) (MOREHOUSE COLLEGE).

This was crystalized in his readings with Davis and Smith of the work of theologian Walter Rauschenbusch. King would later say that reading Rauschenbusch's *Christianity and the Social Crisis* provided the theological basis for his social activism, giving him real hope that the church could play a pivotal role in correcting the inequities of 1948 American society.

Rauschenbusch insisted that the gospel required the church to concern itself with the whole man, not just his spirit. King said, "It has been my conviction ever since reading Rauschenbusch that any religion which professes to be concerned about the souls of men and is not concerned about the social and economic conditions that scar the soul, is a spiritually moribund religion only waiting for the day to be buried. It well has been said: 'A religion that ends with the individual, ends.' "

Smith, a Virginian who taught an Introduction to Christian Ethics and a History of Christian Ethics, lived in the same dormitory with King, and they would hold nearly nightly discussions about the role of religion in solving social problems, with McCall occasionally joining in.

"We discussed the problem of race quite a bit," Smith recalled. "Sometimes I initiated them [the discussions] and sometimes he did. What I taught in class was that racial patterns had to be changed in light of Christian ethics. He wanted to find the best strategy to go about doing something about it. He always took the form of nonviolent direct action, but he didn't know if it could work. Neither did I."

He also studied the great philosophers: Locke, Mill, Rousseau, Hobbes, Aristotle. During his sophomore year he analyzed Marxist thought, rejecting its atheism and its premise that the end justifies the means. But he accepted the fact that Marxism and communism grew out of a protest against the economic injustice against the poor. He felt that Christianity ought to be challenged by communism and try to find better ways to redress these injustices rather than just dismiss Marxist thought because of its lack of moral fiber.

King rejected standard pacifist thought, contending that war can, at times, serve as a "negative good" in stopping the spread of an evil, like nazism. That left him in a quandary. If pacifism didn't work, what nonviolent alternatives were left?

King rejected Jesus's "turn the other cheek" and "love your enemies" philosophies as unrealistic when dealing with separate races or nations. He attended a guest lecture in Philadelphia one Sunday by Mordecai Johnson, then president of Howard University, on the life of Mohandas K. Gandhi of India.

"His message was so profound and electrifying," King later wrote, "that I left the meeting and bought a half-dozen books on Gandhi's life and works.

"My skepticism concerning the power of love gradually diminished, and I came to see for the first time its potency in the area of social reform. . . . I came to feel that this was the only morally and practically sound method open to oppressed people in their struggle for freedom."

He came to believe that nonviolent action is not the same as simply ignoring an evil. Instead, it is a "courageous confrontation of evil by the power of love, in the faith that it is better to be the recipient of violence than the inflictor of it."

Crozer was the cauldron in which the young King's desire for social activism and social reform bubbled and boiled and formed the basis for the philosophy with which he was to live. But there was more to graduate school than just academics, and King had two lives. By day, he was the studious, impeccably dressed young scholar who would become senior class president and valedictorian of the 1951 graduating class. After classes, things were different. It was time to unwind.

King and Walter McCall spent a good deal of time entertaining the ladies in the area, whom they met either on Edwards Street, the social center of the black community, or in one of the many churches where the young ministers conducted guest sermons.

The largest block of their free time, however, was spent at the home of Rev. J. Pious Barbour, pastor of the imposing Calvary Baptist Church on West Second Street and a friend of Daddy King. Young black ministers were always welcome in the Barbour home, where they could relax, soak up Mrs. Barbour's home cooking, and discuss both social events and the ministry. It was a training ground for many, and Mike took what he could from the elder preacher.

After dinner dishes were removed, Reverend Barbour and his guests would repair to the living room, where they would practice sermons. They discussed the choice of the texts and the content of the sermon. Then Reverend Barbour would have them give a sermon, insisting that they get up in front of a mirror and see how they looked when they spoke.

They would work on style and content, and "everyone would pitch in with comments or criticisms," said Reverend Barbour's daughter, Almanina. "A person who doesn't have a very melodious voice may try moaning at times in a sermon. But that doesn't work for everyone. Mike had a very resonant, melodious voice, and he toyed for a while with moaning. But he didn't like it very much. And since black churches like a certain amount of passion along the way, you have to develop other methods for getting the passion up.

"So Mike developed this poetic literary style, where he could dance through all sorts of pieces of literature and put it together with a cadence and rhythm which moves people. That was his style."

The Barbour household was also a place of refuge and guidance. It was Reverend Barbour who counseled Mike in his first year to break off his growing love affair with the daughter of Crozer's white superintendant of buildings and grounds. On a lighter note, the clergyman consoled a couple of young ladies who erroneously thought they were to become engaged to young King upon his graduation.

On one occasion, Mike and Walter McCall stormed into Reverend Barbour's home after returning from a date. The young ministers had taken two young women to a restaurant in Maple Shade, a suburb of Camden, New Jersey, and were denied service. When they refused the proprietor's request to leave, he brandished a pistol and forced them out.

"Mike was furious when he got home," Almanina Barbour said. "I was in law school at the time and told him he didn't have to take that. They have laws against that sort of thing. Take them to court."

So he and McCall returned with New Jersey policemen and filed a complaint. They obtained the names of three University of Pennsylvania students who agreed to testify as witnesses, if necessary. The Camden branch of the NAACP agreed to handle the case for the two men, but when it came time to actually go to court, the three white students declined to testify. The publicity gave the restaurant a bad image in the neighborhood, however, and it eventually shut down.

That experience taught him an important lesson about the North—there was discrimination, but it wasn't legal and was not publicly acknowledged.

When King was growing up, discrimination against blacks was rampant throughout the nation. Then, in 1941, a young minister fresh out of Howard University's theological school, James Farmer, took a job with the Fellowship of Reconciliation, an old-line pacifist organization. During King's studies, he had read the criticism of the FOR and its brand of pacifism by the theologian Reinhold Niebuhr, who felt pacifism was a mere acquiescence to evil.

Farmer, like the student King a decade later, was acquainted with Gandhi's movement, and he began organizing nonviolent sit-ins and protests throughout Chicago in 1941 to force downtown restaurants and other businesses to serve blacks. Farmer started a group called CORE—the Committee on Racial Equality—to organize nonviolent protests in the North.

Its makeup was about two-thirds white, primarily middle-class college students and ministers. "It was difficult to find blacks who were willing to go through that," Farmer said. "We found more whites who were cued in to the idealism of the technique and thus willing to do it."

In Peoria, Illinois, a year later, a young black minister named C. T. Vivian organized a series of demonstrations and sit-ins that opened up all the lunch counters there by 1945.

"There was a tremendous difference between the North and the South. The North said it was always integrated, but in fact, its practices were against it. The laws were in our favor, but the mores were against us. So we could sit in in a restaurant and didn't have much worry about the police driving us out or beating us. And we knew if they didn't serve us, we could take them to court.

"There were a number of people all around the country who were doing the same thing we were doing in Peoria and Farmer was doing in Chicago. But it didn't spread. We never could get a movement."

They did get results. King had to wonder how the same type of approach could work in the South.

At graduation from Crozer in 1951, King, as top student in the class, received the Pearl M. Plafker Citation for the most outstanding student and the J. Lewis Crozer Fellowship of thirteen hundred dollars for graduate study. That came in handy, as King then went to Boston University to pursue his doctorate in systemic theology. Here he continued polishing and refining the theoretical base for his belief in the nonviolent approach to solving social problems. He borrowed Gandhi's phrase: "If cowardice is the only alternative to violence, it is better to fight."

Nonviolence was not synonymous with cowardice or the passive acceptance of evil. A victory won through nonviolence was preferable to one earned through violent means. "The aftermath of nonviolence," he wrote, "is the creation of the beloved community, while the aftermath of violence is tragic bitterness."

Mike King pursued something else in Boston: a wife. He and his roommate, Morehouse graduate Philip Lenud, who was attending the divinity school at nearby Tufts University, enjoyed the nightlife in Boston's extensive black community. The two of them had started a philosophy club, which met each Friday at their apartment. It began as a black intellectual gathering to discuss the issues of the day, but as word of the caliber of the discussions circulated throughout Boston's academic community, it evolved into an interracial cultural forum.

King wanted more, and one day in 1952 he confided to Mary Powell, an Atlantan then living in Boston, that "I wish I knew a few girls from down home to go out with." She suggested Coretta Scott, an attractive woman attending the New England Conservatory of Music.

Coretta was a strong-willed young woman from Marion, Alabama, a rural community about eighty miles south of Montgomery. She grew up in the two-room, unpainted wooden home her father, Obadiah Scott, built in 1920 after marrying her mother, Bernice McMurry.

She was a farm girl—feeding hogs, picking cotton, tending crops, and carrying water from the well in the back yard. At that, she and her sister, Edythe, and brother, Obie, were lucky—during drought seasons, many of the poorer blacks in the area had to walk long distances to find streams that were still running and then tote the water back home. In that region, she was considered well off.

Both sets of grandparents had carved niches for themselves in Alabama's rural Black Belt. They owned three-hundred-acre farms rather than sharecropping. Coretta still had to walk four miles to the African Methodist Episcopal Zion Church on Sunday, and a bit farther each day to school, but at least the Scott kids didn't have to carry their one set of shoes and walk barefoot, like many of the other blacks in the region.

In addition to farming, her father hauled lumber with his own truck—something the poor whites in the area who could not afford trucks bitterly resented.

"Sometimes they would stop him on a lonely road and curse him and threaten to kill him—and there was always a good chance they might do it," Coretta recalled. "But he used to say, 'If you look a white man in the eye, he can't hurt you.'"

Still, he carried a pistol, and when he went into the woods to find lumber he often told Bernice, "I may not get back." Coretta grew up learning to live in fear for the lives of her family.

Hauling lumber proved profitable, as long as he was hauling for whites. He eventually bought his own sawmill, which local whites asked him to sell to them. He refused; that night it burned down.

At home, Coretta developed a love of music, which was, at first, to be her career. In her two-room house with the open hearth was a Victrola, and Coretta learned to appreciate good gospel and to jitterbug to the strains of Clara and Bessie Smith and other black jazz singers of the day.

King knew after his first date that he wanted to marry Coretta Scott, the vivacious young singer from Marion, Alabama. But it took awhile to convince her to become a preacher's wife (MARTIN LUTHER KING, JR., CENTER).

She admired Paul Robeson and resolved that she would be politically active, never "just an artist," although she didn't really know how she would go about doing that.

The Scott children went to a private high school in Marion with an integrated faculty, where they were both instructed in voice and instruments. From there, Edythe, in 1943, became the first black student accepted at Antioch College. Coretta followed her two years later, but even black private schools in the South were educationally disadvantaged, and it took her six years to complete the five-year program.

In 1951, when she entered the New England Conservatory as a voice major, she was eager to make a name for herself in the music world, away from the stifling world in which she had grown up. That life did not include marriage.

It came as a surprise, therefore, when at the end of her first date with young Martin King, he said, "You have everything I ever wanted in a wife," and began talking of marriage.

That was the last thing she wanted to hear, for she was interested neither in getting married nor in marrying a minister. "I had a stereotype of ministers," she said, "and it wasn't very positive. I thought ministers were narrow-minded, overly pious people. I just didn't feel that that kind of person could challenge me."

Being immersed in the entertainment world, she had an idea what life at the top could be like—and did not want to sacrifice that or her career for the relative poverty of a minister's wife.

Coretta couldn't disregard Martin's intellect or his personal magnetism, however. The voice had rounded out to a rich baritone, and through his weekly sessions in his philosophical club, he had become enchantingly conversant in a wide range of topics.

A year later, on a sunny June 18, 1953, Coretta and Martin were married by Daddy King on the lawn of the Scott home in Marion. She had resigned herself to being a minister's wife only because Martin, she said, "was unlike anyone else I had ever met. And he was committed to making changes in society. We both were."

She was not pleased, either, with the offer the following year from the Dexter Avenue Baptist Church. She, even more than Martin, knew the stifling pressures of racism in Montgomery, which still gloried in its Civil War role. She knew that in Montgomery she would assume the role of a minister's wife: the opportunities available for a black classical singer in the North simply vanished in Dixie.

Then there was the problem of raising a family. Did they really want to have their children raised under the heel of segregation, as they had been? The answer was no.

Yet they couldn't avoid the feeling that taking a pastorate in the North was, somehow, running away. They were Southerners, and if they lived anywhere else, they would be spectators. The South was home, and they missed its warmth and its homey pace. And if any place needed social change, the South, with its violently imposed, all-encompassing racism, needed it most.

"We came to the conclusion that we had the moral obligation to return," said King, "at least for a few years."

GEORGIA

ROADSIDE
PARK

STATE HIGHWAY
DEPARTMENT

ENTRANCE →

GEORGIA
US
278

GA.
12

WHITE
ONLY

It was not easy to leave the relative racial freedom of Boston's academic community to return South (COSTA MANOS/MAGNUM).

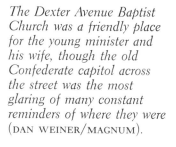

So Martin flew back to Montgomery in March 1954 and accepted the pastorate, though he would not officially take over until September because he had not finished his dissertation. In the meantime, he agreed to commute between Montgomery and Boston at least once a month. He preached his first sermon as Dexter's pastor in May. It was an auspicious beginning. The sermon was delivered just days before the U.S. Supreme Court issued a ruling in the protracted *Brown v. Board of Education of Topeka,* declaring that "separate but equal" facilities were inherently unequal and therefore unconstitutional.

That decision was thought to usher in a new era for Southern blacks: change was in the offing and it was a good time to be back home.

"We had the feeling that something remarkable was unfolding in the South," said King, "and we wanted to be on hand to witness it. The region had marvelous possibilities and, once it came into itself and removed the blight of racial segregation, it would experience a moral, political, and economic boom hardly paralleled by any other section of the country."

The Kings moved to Montgomery in July, and on October 31, 1954, Martin Luther King, Jr., was officially installed as the head of Dexter Avenue Baptist Church.

They were home.

The Dexter Avenue Baptist Church was a friendly place for the young minister and his wife, though the old Confederate capitol across the street was the most glaring of many constant reminders of where they were (DAN WEINER/MAGNUM).

WHITE

2
MONTGOMERY
Birth of a Movement

THE CITY THAT CRADLED THE CONFEDERACY DID NOT PRO-
vide much in the way of comfort to the fifty thousand blacks who called Montgomery home in 1954.

Montgomery was a major marketplace for cotton, livestock, and lumber,
but it lacked significant heavy industry. For that reason, 63 percent of the black
women in Montgomery were domestics, and 48 percent of the men were laborers
or domestic workers. The median income for the seventy thousand whites was
nearly twice the $970 earned annually by the city's black workers, which was one
reason that 31 percent of the black homes had indoor toilets while only 6 percent
of the whites were so inconvenienced.

Fourteen percent of the city's work force was employed by the Air Force
at either Maxwell or Gunter Air Force Bases, but the government had a hands-
off policy when it came to the South. Although the military was fully integrated,
segregation was rigidly enforced outside military property.

There were separate schools, despite the Supreme Court decision. There
were eighteen black taxi companies, which could only pick up blacks, and even
the clergymen were segregated into separate white and black ministerial alli-
ances.

Fewer than two thousand of the thirty thousand blacks of voting age in
Montgomery were registered to vote because of the formidable barriers placed
before blacks with the temerity to seek to register and the economic sanctions
placed on them afterward.

Barriers like the poll tax were adopted throughout the South in 1901 in
an effort to combat the Populist movement, which had attracted a lot of blacks
and poor whites. It was part of a series of acts written into Southern state
constitutions to disenfranchise these potential allies. In Alabama, the poll tax
amounted to only $1.50 per year. But if you registered to vote, you had to pay it
retroactively to when you first came of voting age.

The black community itself was fragmented and weak. The NAACP
came to Alabama before 1920, but its influence was negligible. The agency felt
that integration would come slowly, if at all, only through the courts. There were
frequent suits challenging police brutality, but they did little more than provide a
constant annoyance to the city administration.

There was the Citizens Committee, headed by Rufus Lewis, a parishioner

These were good times. The young Reverend King had time for the occasional sermon in Atlanta with the elder Reverend King (CHARLES MOORE/ BLACK STAR).

at Dexter, which was open only to blacks who had registered to vote. In that regard, it was an activist organization, but its influence was limited by its size. Yet these were blacks who had already proven they were willing to risk their livelihood to assert their rights.

There were the Progressive Democrats, headed by E. D. Nixon. Nixon was a living legend in Montgomery for his willingness to challenge the white power structure and his ability to get away with it. He was a Pullman porter and an organizer for A. Philip Randolph (founder of the Brotherhood of Sleeping-Car Porters, the nation's largest black union), a position that rendered Nixon economically untouchable by the powers that be because his salary came from outside the state.

In the 1930s he organized the city's Welfare Rights Organization, and in 1944 he led 750 blacks on a voter rights march around Montgomery city hall.

"Only a few of them got registered," said Nixon, but the very idea was unheard of in those days.

He had headed the NAACP for a decade, and he hired a young seamstress named Rosa Parks as its secretary before turning over the leadership of that organization to R. L. Matthews.

In late 1953 Nixon persuaded those blacks who were registered to throw all their votes behind Dave Birmingham for police commissioner. In return, after winning a close election, Birmingham came through with his promise to provide black policemen in black areas. A pistol was part of his wardrobe, and a Winchester hung near the door of his home during tense periods. In Montgomery, people believed that if there were ever to be changes in the city's racial patterns, Nixon would be in the forefront of the effort.

Then there was the Women's Political Council, founded by Jo Ann Robinson and Dr. Mary Fair Burks. This was a quiet group, composed primarily of the women among the two hundred members of the faculty at Alabama State College and other professional women. They had one purpose: to end segregation of the city's buses.

Like most places in the South, the city buses were segregated. In this case, blacks had to pay their money at the front of the bus, like whites, and then get off and walk to the rear entrance, climb on again, and sit down. It was not uncommon for a jeering bus driver to pull off and leave a black person on the street after the dime had been paid. A reserved section for whites in the front extended past the first five rows usually reserved for whites in most other cities. In many cities in the South, if there were no whites on the bus, blacks could sit anywhere.

In Montgomery, if those reserved seats were filled, blacks in the following seats had to get up to give their seats to whites if the bus driver told them to. To ensure obedience, bus drivers had quasi-police powers and could carry guns and arrest blacks who defied the seating law.

Robinson began teaching English literature at Alabama State in 1949. She joined Dexter, as most of the teachers there did because they felt it was a "high-class church."

She discovered the more rigid Montgomery bus rules at Christmas, after putting her car in a garage and heading to the airport to join relatives in Cleveland.

"I sat down after the fifth seat," she said, "and the next thing I knew, the bus had stopped and the driver stood over me with his hand balled in a fist, waiting to strike me. He said to get up. I jumped out of that seat and ran to the front door and got out. I was crying uncontrollably.

"I vowed if ever I got a chance, I would put everything I had into fighting segregation in Alabama."

After the holidays, she began talking to other teachers about her bus experience, and the stories came out. They had all suffered indignities and heard of even worse. Blacks had been shot for refusing to move.

She and Dr. Burks, another English professor, organized the Women's Political Council that January. Between them, they recruited most of the teachers into cadres that met regularly to discuss the latest legal developments in the fight against segregation—and the latest outrages.

They were an independent group, though they did provide support services for other organizations. They would draw up leaflets and mimeograph the flyers when there were voter rights campaigns. By 1955 they were pushing E. D. Nixon to help them boycott the buses. He agreed, if the right candidate to rally around could be found.

There were changes on the other side of town. Early in 1954 John Patterson won election to the office of attorney general of Alabama. Patterson had a reputation as an honest crime buster. His father had been district attorney in Phenix City, Alabama, and was murdered after tangling with the gambling and prostitution rackets there.

John took over his father's position and completed the cleanup, earning a national reputation for law and order in the process. His move in January 1955 to the capitol complex across the street from Dexter was another step in an ambitious career that would encompass a run for the governor's chair in 1958 and hopes for national office four years after that.

His major obstacle—and ally—was segregation. To become governor he would have to be on the "right" side of the segregation issue. He started making his moves early.

The fight then was over school integration, and Patterson had the sense to see that the Supreme Court's 1954 decision could cause problems for the South. He had the sense to see that its implications could affect virtually all other areas of segregation. He had the sense to see that fighting desegregation in the courts was a losing proposition.

He also had the sense to see that a rearguard legal action could delay the inevitable for perhaps a decade. So he met with prominent Southern constitutional lawyers and convened meetings of other Southern attorneys general to plot the "Southern Strategy" to stall desegregation in the South as long as legally possible.

"The consensus of the groups was that from a legal point of view we would ultimately lose," he said. "Our course was to legally fight a delaying action to give people time to adjust to the changes that were coming and avoid confrontation. It wasn't a moral issue at all."

So he moved to decentralize the state: virtually every single school system would have to be taken to court individually to force compliance with the 1954 Supreme Court decision banning separate schooling. The state's highest justice official began seeking blocking mechanisms for other segregated facets of Alabama life.

Patterson wasn't alone in these sentiments. The Alabama legislature met and voted to "nullify" the U.S. Supreme Court decision, and the state board of education voted unanimously to continue segregated facilities through the 1954–55 school year.

In Mississippi, a former Mississippi State football star named Robert Patterson got together with several Mississippi politicians and bankers in Indianola, Mississippi, on July 11 and organized the White Citizens Council to fight for the segregated way of life. In 1955 they published a book by state judge Tom Brady of Brookhaven called *Black Monday.*

It was a diatribe against the 1954 Supreme Court decision and blacks, stating, "Whenever and wherever the white man has drunk the cup of black hemlock, whenever and wherever his blood has been infused with the blood of the negro, the white man, his intellect and his culture have died."

Often dubbed the white-collar Klan, the Citizens Council became a power throughout the South. Within two years it had eighty-five thousand members in Mississippi and more than sixty thousand in Alabama.

There was rising antiblack violence and resistance across the South. The Georgia legislature established the Georgia Education Commission, dedicated to the preservation of segregation. In neighboring Mississippi, Rev. George W. Lee led a voter registration drive in Belzoni for thirty blacks in early 1955. Whites told the minister to persuade his parishioners to take their names off the roles. He refused, and the day before Mother's Day he was gunned down as he left the tailor's downtown after picking up the suit he planned to preach in the next day.

That summer, fourteen-year-old Emmett Till was shopping in a Greenwood department store and allegedly whistled as a white woman passed by. Two white men grabbed him, took him to a barn outside of town, beat and mutilated him, tied a seventy-pound gin fan around his neck with barbed wire, and tossed him in the Tallahatchie River. None of the whites who saw the youth hauled out of town or heard the screams from the barn intervened.

The two killers were acquitted in a travesty of a trial, punctuated by jokes about a "crazy nigger" who stole a fan from a gin mill and drowned while trying to swim away with it.

This was the Montgomery the young minister Martin Luther King entered in 1954, telling Coretta, "I like this church." After seeing the spacious, if run-down, seven-room parsonage and meeting the congregation, Coretta responded, "If this is what you want, I'll make myself happy in Montgomery. You will perfect your preaching and improve yourself in the ministry at Dexter, and I will learn to be a good minister's wife."

His was an orderly existence: getting up at five-thirty so he could devote at least three hours in the morning to writing his dissertation and spending the rest of the day tending to the needs of his church. One day each week was allotted to visiting the sick and shut-in, and he attended five to ten auxilliary meetings each week in an effort to get to know the active members of his congregation better. King usually spent a total of fifteen hours on a sermon, conducting most of his research on Wednesday and writing it on Friday.

He wanted to give Dexter more of an identity in the city and rid it of its silk-stocking image. To that end, he created a social service committee to provide outreach services to the sick and needy, a committee to raise scholarship funds for worthy high school graduates, and a social and political action committee. This group included both Lewis and Robinson and was intended to stress the importance of the NAACP and voter registration. It was an effort by Reverend King to forge a permanent alliance between the three more important black groups in the city.

Strengthening the NAACP was a pet project of King's. He and Abernathy had become fast friends and had a mutual drive to become "the most outstanding preacher in the city, with the most dynamic social programs."

Abernathy was membership chairman of the NAACP in 1955, and during the latter part of the year the two ministers competed to see who could bring in the most members. Between them, they brought in five thousand new members, though the "Abernathy team" won the interchurch rivalry with thirty-five hundred of those. Many people supported Abernathy to take over the presidency of the organization, but he declined because he intended to take a leave of absence from First Baptist in 1956 and go to Colgate to get his doctorate. King turned it down also, because he wanted to run a different type of organization, one that was much more activist than the staid NAACP. One that did not exist in the fall of 1955.

It appeared that something would be needed soon. In March 1955 fifteen-year-old Claudette Colvin was arrested, handcuffed, pulled off a bus, and taken to jail for refusing to relinquish her seat to a white passenger. This infuriated the black community in general and the Women's Political Council in particular, and there was talk of a bus boycott.

They formed a committee, including E. D. Nixon and Reverend King, to meet with Police Commissioner Birmingham and J. E. Bagley, then manager of the Montgomery City Lines. The officials were pleasant at that March meeting, even going so far as to admit that the bus driver had been wrong and promising to reprimand him.

But they didn't, and Colvin was convicted of violating the segregation ordinance and given a suspended sentence.

The women wanted to boycott the buses then and there. "We worked with her," said Robinson. "We really did. But we had to have somebody who was strong enough to take the weight, and Claudette went to pieces on us.

"The only way we could break up segregation on the bus lines was to have somebody get arrested who would be able to stand whatever they threw against them."

Not only was the young woman afraid to go against the system, but Nixon vetoed the idea of using her as a rallying point, saying, "We need someone who is independent and respected, someone people can identify with.

While there was disappointment, King noticed a change in what had been an apathetic black community. For the first time, there was open talk of a bus boycott. It did not occur, but it was a start.

Another woman was arrested that summer for violating the bus segregation ordinance and the subject was revived. But Nixon, who was considered crucial to any such effort, vetoed it because he felt the woman did not come from an upstanding family.

"The Women's Political Council was really mad at me," said Nixon. "But we had never rallied around anything like this before, and I felt if we did, it would have to be around someone beyond reproach."

Nixon vetoed another potential boycott in October, and that's where matters stood through the fall. Coretta gave birth November 17 to the Kings' first child, Yolanda Denise, who was generally called Yoki.

Then came December.

A storm was brewing. On December 1, 1955, Rosa Parks was arrested for refusing to vacate her seat for a white man and was found guilty four days later (AP/WIDE WORLD).

The evening temperature in Montgomery dropped below freezing for the third day in a row. Rosa Parks, Nixon's former NAACP assistant, stepped on the thirty-six-seat Montgomery Avenue bus and headed for her home on Cleveland Avenue. At the Court Square stop, the bus filled with twenty-two blacks and fourteen whites, and driver J. F. Blake asked a row of blacks to vacate their seats and move to the rear. Three of the blacks did. Parks said, "I don't think I should have to move," and didn't.

Blake put her under arrest and then called two policemen to come and take her to jail. One of the officers asked, "Did you hear this man ask you to get up?"

"Yes."

"Did you refuse?"

"Yes."

"Why?" asked the officer.

She looked him in the eye and said, "Why do you all have to push us around all the time?"

"I don't know, lady," he replied with a shrug. "But the law is the law and it says you're not supposed to sit here."

She again refused to move and was taken to jail. Word immediately went out to the Women's Political Council, and they called Nixon and told him to "get her out."

"I called down to the jail," he said, "and they wouldn't tell me why she had been arrested or why she was being held. They said it was none of my goddamned business, which is the way they usually spoke to us."

So he called Clifford Durr, a former attorney in the Roosevelt administration and part of Alabama's white aristocracy. Durr had returned to the South in 1951, and Nixon, then head of the NAACP, brought him many of his first clients. He was the only white lawyer in town who would represent blacks in complaints against the city or police departments.

Rosa Parks had often helped Virginia Durr with her sewing, and the attorney's wife had counseled the Women's Political Council at a meeting in the Parks home on the Colvin case.

Clifford Durr contacted the police and called Nixon back, telling him that "she was arrested for violating the bus segregation law."

Nixon drove the Durrs to the jail and made bond for Parks. She was released just as her husband and mother arrived.

That night, the telephone lines burned between the Nixon home and members of the Women's Political Council. Robinson insisted that this was the case to rally around, and it was time for a boycott. Nixon concurred and agreed to spearhead the move Friday morning, December 2.

Nixon got little sleep that night. He took a map of the city and measured out the distances between the white and black neighborhoods. He crisscrossed these areas with various routes from black areas to white business and residential areas and measured them with a ruler.

"We can break the buses," he told his wife. "There is no place in Montgomery blacks can't get to easily enough, if they agree to it."

"You expect them to walk, as cold as it is?" asked his wife.

"Yes, I do," Nixon replied.

"I doubt it," she said.

He made a list of eighteen people: ministers who were influential in Montgomery and whose support was necessary if there was to be a successful boycott.

He first called Abernathy, who had not heard of the arrest—indeed, he had just gotten out of bed—and said, "We have taken this stuff long enough. I am calling people together to try and organize a bus boycott."

"I'll go along with you," Reverend Abernathy responded and then suggested that Nixon call Michael King, the new minister in town who headed Dexter Avenue Baptist Church.

"He's third on my list," Nixon replied, after Rev. H. H. Hubbard, president of the Baptist Ministerial Alliance. King was busy preparing for a church conference and, not sure he had the time that day to attend a meeting, asked Nixon to call him back in a few minutes.

Nixon went through his list and then called King, who said, "Mr. Nixon, I think I'll go along with you, and you can use the church basement for the meeting."

"That's good," Nixon replied, "because that's where I've been telling people to come."

King then called Abernathy (whom he referred to as David) and they began tracking down the rest of the black ministers, with Abernathy taking the Methodists and King contacting the Baptists. Nixon spent the rest of his time tracking down the civic leaders, particularly Lewis and Robinson.

They agreed that Abernathy would convene the meeting and Rev. L. Roy Bennett, president of the Interdenominational Ministerial Alliance, would preside.

Jo Ann Robinson, after conferring with Nixon, grabbed two of her students and ran off fifty-two thousand fliers on the college's mimeograph equipment. The fliers stated:

Another Negro woman has been arrested and thrown into jail because she refused to get up out of her seat on the bus and give it to a white person. . . . This must be stopped. Negroes are citizens and have rights.

Until we do something to stop these arrests, they will continue. The next time, it may be you. This woman's case will come up Monday. We are, therefore, asking every Negro to stay off the buses on Monday in protest of the arrest and trial. Don't ride the buses to work, to town, to school, or anywhere on Monday. . . .

The fliers were tied into bundles, and members of the women's group picked them up and dropped all of them off at churches and other distribution centers within two hours.

Nixon was working that weekend and had to leave town in midafternoon. Before he left, he called Joe Azbell, the city editor of the Montgomery *Advertiser*, the predominant white paper in town, and asked Azbell to meet him at the train station at 2 P.M. Azbell had covered many of Nixon's civil rights activities, including the recent protest against two policemen who had raped a black woman and were not disciplined because officials said she was just a "nigger gal."

Azbell worked for a segregated daily newspaper, but he had earned the respect of the black community. It was Azbell who became incensed when he heard of a black infant dying from a gangrenous leg and forced the white hospital to admit the baby and operate to save her life and leg. It was Azbell who raised money to air-condition the pediatric ward in the hospital. It was Azbell who had the paper organize a charity to collect food and clothing for blacks whose homes were burned, serving the function the Red Cross did for whites. And it was Azbell who had taken a black waiter, trained him, and made him editor of the segregated "black page" in the *Advertiser.*

Azbell and Nixon respected each other's integrity, if not always their views.

"I've got a good story for you," said Nixon, giving Azbell one of the mimeographed sheets. "We're going to boycott the buses. We're going to do it through the churches. I don't know if it will be successful, but it's something we have got to do. We can't have any more abuse of our women."

At that time, only the White Citizens Council conducted economic boycotts, and those were against integrationists. Azbell wrote a story for the Sunday paper, December 4, and marked it for the front page.

Abernathy and King, who were usually inseparable, went to the meeting together. About seventy-five civic and religious leaders crowded into the meeting room at Dexter that Friday evening, but the strategy session did not get off to a good start. Reverend Bennett, who had organized a brief boycott in North Carolina, stated at the outset that "this is a time for action, not talk."

He wouldn't recognize anyone who had a question. After more than a half hour of this, some people started to leave in disgust. Abernathy calmed them down and then persuaded Bennett to yield the floor.

They discussed the logistics of a boycott: how long should it last, how would people get around, what were the legal ramifications to everyone, and how much support could they get from the black community? There had been a successful bus boycott in Baton Rouge in 1953, but blacks in Montgomery had not previously shown an inclination to stick together.

They decided to have a boycott for at least one day, Monday, and then meet Monday night at the Holt Street Baptist Church to discuss the disposition of Rosa Parks's court case and decide how much longer the protest would last. They also decided to contact the eighteen black taxi companies in the city, with 210 cabs, on Saturday and ask them to cooperate by charging only a dime for fares.

No one questioned the idea of the boycott itself, and the ministers agreed to ask their congregations Sunday to stay off the buses Monday.

Sunday was a busy day. Azbell's front-page story included a verbatim transcript of the Robinson boycott leaflet and succeeded in spreading the word about the boycott to virtually every black person in Montgomery.

King was troubled, however, by the comparison of the proposed boycott to past actions of the White Citizens Council. He finally decided that boycotts could be used for good or evil, and their action was justified. Blacks, he said, can "no longer lend our cooperation to an evil system.

"He who passively accepts evil is as much involved in it as he who helps to perpetuate it. In order to be true to one's conscience and true to God, a righteous man has no alternative but to refuse to cooperate."

News of the pending boycott triggered an angry reaction from the city. Clyde Sellers was the new police commissioner, having ousted Birmingham with a campaign pledge not to "sell his Southern heritage for a single nigger vote." He announced that he would assign two policemen to follow each bus to prevent "Negro goon squads" from enforcing the boycott. His televised announcement also helped get the message out. One black woman who had not attended church Sunday or bought a paper said she knew nothing of the boycott, but "when she heard Sellers saying on the radio it was all right [to ride the buses] she knew something was wrong."

King was excited Sunday night, and he and Coretta stayed up late discussing the pending protest. They were not sure how much support they could muster and went to bed agreeing that if 60 percent of the seventeen thousand blacks who rode the buses daily stayed away, the boycott would be a success.

King awoke at five-thirty, a half hour before the first bus was to pass his home, and began getting dressed. At 6 A.M. he was in the kitchen, making coffee, when Coretta shouted from the living room, "Martin! Martin, come quickly!"

King ran to the front room as Coretta pointed out the window at the first bus on the South Jackson line—the heaviest black route—and yelled, "Darling! It's empty!"

King finished dressing, got in his car, and began cruising around town, peering at the buses. He saw only eight black riders during the morning rush hour and realized that the boycott was nearly total.

Nixon said later, "There were still some people who didn't know about the boycott that day, or weren't sure if they were going to support it. But when they saw the policemen, they thought the policemen would bother *them*, so they stayed off and walked."

People cheerfully walked, car-pooled, and even rode mules and buggies to work. There was also some help from the other side of town: many white housewives drove to the black community to pick up their maids and nannies rather than do without their services for the day.

At nine-thirty King went to court to watch the proceedings. The city had made a tactical error. Instead of charging Parks with the misdemeanor of disobeying a police officer, they had charged her with violating the 1947 segregation law. When Rosa Parks was declared guilty and fined ten dollars and four dollars for court costs, blacks had a clear-cut challenge to segregation that they could appeal all the way to the U.S. Supreme Court.

Following the hearing, Nixon, Abernathy, and Rev. E. N. French of the Hilliard Chapel A.M.E. Zion Church discussed the need for an organization to guide the protest and an agenda. Abernathy suggested the name Montgomery Improvement Association, and the others agreed.

They also decided to offer a few tentative demands: black bus drivers for predominantly black routes; seating on a first-come, first-served basis, with blacks being seated from the back to the front, and more courteous bus drivers.

At 3 P.M., the original organizers met with Reverend Bennett to plan for the night's mass rally at the Holt Street Baptist Church. The group readily adopted the MIA as its name, and then Bennett asked for nominations for officers. Lewis nominated King, and though it caught him by surprise, he accepted the nomination and was unanimously elected. King, as the new man in town, was one of the few who could deal with all the factions in the black community.

Bennett was elected vice president, but he was transferred to Los Angeles a few months later, and Abernathy took his place.

There were nagging doubts. Many of those present were not sure what the repercussions might be and wanted all their decisions—and the names of officers—to be kept secret.

Nixon protested vehemently, charging that they were "acting like little boys" and that they should have the courage to "stand up like men." There was no more talk of secrecy.

There was talk of ending the boycott, quitting while they were ahead. The boycott had been nearly 100 percent successful that day, and they had proved their point to the white community. There was fear that if they decided to continue the protest, it would just fizzle out as blacks got tired of walking and filtered back to the buses. They decided to play it by ear: if there was a large crowd at the mass meeting, and if they wanted to continue the boycott, then they would continue. If not, it would end as just a footnote in the city's history.

King didn't get home until nearly 6 P.M., an hour before the meeting, and talked to Coretta about the day's events. He was hedging. Finally, he told her he had accepted the call to be president of the new MIA and was gratified when she said he had no alternative but to accept it once it was offered.

King picked up Abernathy and drove to the church. More than a dozen blocks away, he noticed a lot of cars parked on lawns. King asked Abernathy if somebody important had died or if there had been a big accident in the black area that afternoon. It was awhile before they realized that this was overflow parking from the crowd at the church, which had been filled since 5 P.M.

The church was packed with more than five thousand people and another seven thousand more were standing on the lawn and sidewalk listening to the meeting over hastily set-up loudspeakers. King had to park more than five blocks away, and it took a half hour to work their way through the crowd to the pulpit inside.

King spoke without notes to the crowd, reciting the litany of insults they had endured and adding, "We have sometimes given our white brothers the feeling that we liked the way we were being treated. But we come here tonight to be saved from that patience that makes us patient with anything less than freedom and justice."

He said they had the right as Americans to stand up for justice. But he wanted to be sure that the throng was aware of the distinction between the protests of the White Citizens Council and their ongoing protest. Those racist groups, he said, "are protesting for the perpetuation of injustice in the community. We are protesting for the birth of justice in the community.

"Their methods lead to violence and lawlessness. But in our protest, there will be no cross burnings. No white person will be taken from his home by a hooded Negro mob and brutally murdered. . . . We will be guided by the highest principles of law and order."

He spoke of Christian love and Jesus's command to love thine enemy. He spoke of the need to accept mistreatment from whites along the way without becoming bitter. "If we fail to do this," he said, "our protest will end up as a meaningless drama on the stage of history, and its memory will be shrouded with the ugly garments of shame. . . .

"If you will protest courageously, and yet with dignity and Christian love, when the history books are written in future generations, the historians will have to pause and say, 'There lived a great people—a black people—who injected new meaning and dignity into the veins of civilization.' "

The sixteen-minute address drew a thunderous ovation, and there was no question of calling off the boycott. The meeting closed with the adoption of a set of demands presented by Abernathy that were to be met before the boycott would end. These were the same three demands tentatively drafted by Nixon, Reverend Abernathy, and Reverend French earlier in the day.

They took up the first of what would become a long series of collections to support the boycott and raised $785. Nixon, who was treasurer of the organization, walked up to Police Commissioner Sellers and said he needed police protection. Sellers, dumbfounded, ordered one of his officers to drive Nixon home in a squad car, and Mrs. Nixon drove the family car home by herself.

The fight was on.

Reverend King accepted the mantle of leadership and agreed to head the fledgling protest movement called the Montgomery Improvement Association (CHARLES MOORE/BLACK STAR).

3
A TASTE OF FREEDOM

NOW WAS THE TIME TO ORGANIZE IN EARNEST.

If there was to be a workable boycott, the MIA had better be prepared to meet the physical and psychological needs of Montgomery's black community for a long time.

The boycott had stunned white Montgomery, but the consensus seemed to be that given time, the blacks would trickle back to the buses and it would be business as usual. Mayor W. A. "Tacky" Gayle and officials of the bus company requested a meeting with the MIA leaders for Thursday, December 8, ostensibly to see if their differences could be ironed out. Black riders provided 75 percent of the bus company's revenues, and a protracted boycott would hurt. The company signed a new contract with its bus drivers Wednesday and was wondering where it would get the money to finance the pay raises.

King called a board meeting for Wednesday. There was a need for a transportation committee to figure out the best way to get 17,500 blacks to and from their jobs. Rufus Lewis was to chair that committee, though it was clear from the start that everyone was going to have to do some walking, no matter what system was set up.

He immediately began work on a car-pooling system with dispatch points in the black community and pickup points in the white community and downtown. They had been relying on the eighteen black-owned taxi companies. But King feared the city would find some ways to kill that relationship.

Rev. R. J. Glasco, head of the Alabama Negro Baptist Center, was elected to head the finance committee and raise money on an ongoing basis for the MIA. Money would be needed for legal fees, transportation, and, if the strike dragged on long enough, a staff person to handle the MIA's internal affairs full time. In the end, their expenses amounted to more than $250,000.

King also decided they needed a permanent strategy committee to deal with crises as they occurred. This committee contained a dozen people, including their attorney, Fred Gray, Nixon, Abernathy, and Robinson.

King added one other person to the executive committee—Rev. Robert Graetz, the white minister of the Negro Trinity Lutheran Church, whom King

had met on the Council on Human Relations, the city's ineffectual but only interracial body. Reverend Graetz was the only white minister to oppose the segregation system.

The meeting Thursday was a farce. Mayor Gayle, Police Commissioner Sellers, and Commissioner Frank Parks acted as if they were seriously considering the delegation's proposals, laid out by King. But Bagley and the bus company's lawyer, Jack Crenshaw, were openly hostile.

Crenshaw said the request for driver courtesy was something that could be looked into, but adamantly rejected the rest. The seating arrangement the MIA asked for was not new. It was already used on buses in Mobile, Alabama, and the buses in both cities were owned by the same parent company. In fact, Rev. Joseph Lowery, the leader of Mobile's black community, had called King the day before and said, "You are settling for too little. We already have that kind of seating arrangement down here. You should demand an end to segregated seating altogether."

Daddy and Alberta King enjoyed visiting Coretta and their granddaughter, Yoki. The calm at the home of the younger Kings would be shattered by a bomb at the end of January ("LEVITON-ATLANTA"/BLACK STAR).

Parks said he thought the seating arrangement requested could be accommodated. But Crenshaw said acquiescence would be impossible, "in view of the segregation law." Besides, he added, "If we granted the Negroes these demands, they would go about boasting they had won a victory over the white people, and this we will not stand for."

King was taken aback and said they were not looking for a victory "over" anyone. They just wanted fair treatment. He said blacks should also be hired because it "made good business sense" to hire representatives from the largest block of the company's customers.

Crenshaw was unmoved by this argument, responding, "We do not contemplate and have no intentions of hiring Negro drivers. The time is not right in Montgomery, but who can say what will happen in ten years?"

"We don't mean ten years," snapped attorney Gray. "We mean this year."

As they left the meeting, Commissioner Sellers mentioned to King in passing that there was a city ordinance setting minimum fares for cabs at 45 cents. King knew then that it was only a matter of time before they lost the use of the taxis.

Sure enough, the next day the bus company canceled the routes in black areas because they were "underutilized," and the police department announced that taxis had to charge at least the minimum fare to passengers.

That didn't daunt the boycotters or the leaders of the MIA. King stopped on one occasion to ask an elderly woman, who was walking with difficulty, if she would like a ride.

"No," she replied. "I'm not walking for myself. I'm walking for my children and my grandchildren."

Abernathy was waved off by another elderly woman, who said, "My feets are tired, but my soul is rested."

King placed a phone call to Rev. T. J. Jemison in Baton Rouge, who had led a successful bus boycott there the year before. Reverend Jemison told him how they had set up a car pool, and King relayed the details to Lewis and Glasco. At the mass meeting that night, they outlined their plans for a car-pool system, and 150 people volunteered the use of their vehicles for the effort.

By Tuesday, December 13, the entire car-pool system was laid out, with most of the forty-eight dispatch points being in black churches, which provided the advantage of seating and warmth on cold mornings. There were another forty-two pickup points in white areas, and mimeographed maps of the city showing the locations of each were circulated through the black community.

King, Robinson, and many of the leaders with cars participated in the car pool fairly regularly, and a number of students volunteered to drive cars virtually full time.

Fifteen of the black churches bought station wagons and painted the name of their church on the side so they officially became church vehicles, which were constantly picking up people for "church business."

The young boycott was having a dramatic effect on the divided black community of Montgomery. For the first time, the poor and uneducated worked together in a common effort with the black professionals. Blacks who never rode the buses now shared cars and long walks with those who had never owned automobiles. Pharmacists and physicians used their stores and waiting rooms as pickup points, their phones as dispatch centers. Black morticians transported the living to their places of work before taking the dead to their place of rest. And the MIA employed twenty-five people as full-time drivers.

The MIA expanded to a full-time staff of ten, just to handle the transportation dispatching and calls from people who had missed rides or had to make a sudden trip and needed one in a hurry, and they set up shop in space rented from the black Bricklayers Union.

King issued a statement on behalf of the MIA that "there is no issue between the Negro citizens and the Montgomery City Lines that cannot be solved by negotiations between people of good will."

But it was clear that there was no good will involved, and the boycott was going to be a long one. A meeting was scheduled with the city on December 17 with city officials and K. E. Totten of Chicago, vice president of the National City Lines, which owned the bus company. Totten had been in town for two days, but had not tried to get in touch with the MIA.

The meeting was unproductive. The mayor had invited three white ministers to come to the meeting as well: Rev. Henry Russell of the Trinity Presbyterian Church, Rev. Henry Parker of the white First Baptist Church, and Rev. Stanley Frazier of the St. James Methodist Church.

Totten simply mouthed the rejections already enunciated by Crenshaw, and King became angry.

He jumped to his feet and blasted Totten's statements as unfair and biased. "In spite of the fact that he was asked to come to Montgomery by the MIA, he has not done the Negro community the simple courtesy of hearing their grievances. The least that all of us can do in our deliberations is to be honest and fair."

Then there was to be a religious challenge. Reverend Frazier stood up and delivered an eloquent defense of segregation and the status quo. The blacks were wrong, he said, to boycott the buses. The ministers were wrong to be involved in such a project. A minister's job, he said, "is to lead the souls of men to God," not to get involved in social issues.

He told the ministers to leave the meeting, go back to their pulpits, end the boycott, and prepare their congregations to celebrate that most "glorious experience of the Christian faith," Christmas.

He smugly sat down, and the mayor and council relaxed. They were sure that a group of blacks could not possibly challenge the learned Reverend Dr. Frazier.

But this was King's area, the social gospel. He didn't hold back. "We too know the Jesus that the minister just referred to," he said. "I can see no conflict between our devotion to Jesus Christ and our present action. In fact, I see a necessary relationship.

"If one is truly devoted to the religion of Jesus he will seek to rid the earth of social evils. The gospel is social as well as personal. We are only doing in a minor way what Gandhi did in India, and certainly no one referred to him as an unrepentant sinner; he is considered by many a saint."

King went on to deride Frazier's assertion that the boycott challenged "cherished customs" in what had been a harmonious city. If those customs are wrong, said King, "We have every reason in the world to change them. The decision now is whether we will give our allegiance to outmoded and unjust customs or to the ethical demands of the universe. As Christians, we owe our ultimate allegiance to God and His will, rather than to man and his folkways."

The wind temporarily taken from his sails, Mayor Gayle appointed a committee to try and work out a solution and scheduled a new meeting for Monday, December 19.

It was to be a confrontation, not a conference. The blacks entered the room and immediately noticed that Gayle had invited Luther Ingalls of the White Citizens Council to the meeting. King jumped up and called for adjournment of the meeting right then and there, saying the mayor had been "very unfair" to add someone like Ingalls to the group, that their differences would never be settled "so long as there are persons on the committee whose pronouncements are anti-Negro" and whose minds were already made up.

But the whites jumped on King, saying his mind was already made up and if Ingalls shouldn't be on the committee, King shouldn't either.

Gayle then said, "King, you've talked long enough. You have dominated this conversation and I am going to ask Reverend Abernathy to speak because he has been here a long time and he is respected by everybody on this council."

It was an obvious move to divide the black leadership, but Abernathy didn't fall for it. "I have nothing to say as long as Dr. King wishes to speak," said Abernathy. King, he said, spoke for all the blacks involved in the boycott, and "I yield the floor to Dr. King."

The meeting ended with bad feelings all around. It was now a waiting game.

On January 4, 1956, the city commission granted the bus company a 50 percent fare increase that was "subject to review" once the emergency was over. They tried to divide the black community with a hoax. King was informed by Carl T. Rowan, an editorial writer for the Minneapolis *Tribune*, that there was a wire story saying the boycott was over.

The city commission said it had met with three "prominent Negro ministers" and worked out an agreement including segregated seating with the first ten seats from the front reserved for whites and the last ten seats reserved for blacks. During rush hour, special all-black buses would be added to the predominantly black routes. And the bus drivers would endeavor to be more courteous to black patrons.

King was dumbfounded and quickly called a meeting of the MIA leaders at his home. By midnight, they had tracked down the three ministers, who were not members of the MIA and not prominent, and they denied having agreed to any deal. They said they had been invited to city hall to talk about insurance and had not agreed to anything.

Sunday morning, January 22, a week after King's twenty-seventh birthday, the ministers told their congregations that the story in the day's papers about a settlement was a hoax. They had no intention of settling for more of the status quo.

That effort by the city commission failed, and then things got vicious. Mayor Gayle went on television and said it was time "to get tough" with the boycotters. He said the white community didn't care if blacks never rode the buses again.

All three city commissioners publicly joined the White Citizens Council. The police began harassing black car drivers, giving them tickets for real or faked infractions, sometimes taking them to jail for allegedly running red lights. Blacks waiting for rides were threatened with arrest for vagrancy.

Many of those in the car pools dropped out under the constant intimidation. King was arrested one afternoon for speeding—supposedly doing thirty miles an hour in a twenty-five-miles-per-hour zone. He was placed into a police car, which sped off toward the outskirts of town. King, who had thought the jail was downtown, became frightened, believing they were taking him to some out-of-the-way place where he would be turned over to a mob and lynched. But as he finished asking God for strength to endure whatever lay ahead, he saw a sign saying CITY JAIL and was relieved.

King was booked and thrown into a cell with drunks and thieves. Abernathy arrived, was told that he could pay a cash bond to get King released, and left to get the funds from his church. While he was gone, however, hundreds of blacks gathered in front of the jail, and the panicky police released King in his own custody, pending trial.

Ever since the start of the boycott, whites had been making hundreds of threatening telephone calls to the King household and the MIA. Hate mail was common. Martin and Coretta found they could not avoid the phone calls—they could not leave their telephone off the hook because important calls about the boycott were coming in at all hours. But the wear and tear took its toll.

During one of the biweekly mass meetings, King startled the crowd by stating that "if one day you find me sprawled out dead, I do not want you to retaliate with a single act of violence. I urge you to continue protesting with the same dignity and discipline you have shown so far."

Later, Abernathy asked him what had prompted that statement, and King confided about the threats and his nagging fear that some violence might soon occur. That night, he looked at Coretta and their sleeping child and suddenly realized, "They can be taken away from me at any moment; I can be taken away from them at any moment."

The thought depressed him. A few days later, he got a call saying, "Listen, nigger, before next week you'll be sorry you ever came to Montgomery."

He could no longer sleep. The threats, the strain, the doubts about the ability to keep up the boycott forever were taking a toll. He prayed. He said, "I am at the end of my powers. I have nothing left. I've come to the point where I can't face it alone."

He said he felt the Lord's presence and heard a voice saying, "Stand up for righteousness, stand up for truth, and God will be at your side forever."

He stopped being afraid.

Which was good, for three nights later, the terrorists struck.

King was at a mass meeting in Abernathy's church on January 30, the anniversary of Gandhi's assassination, when the sound of a bomb explosion was heard. A few minutes later King saw people rush into the church and go to

Abernathy; and whisper. Abernathy did not tell King about it at first, but ordered people to go find out what condition Coretta and Yoki were in.

They were safe. A friend, Lucy Williams, was visiting Coretta—someone usually stayed with her when Martin was out—and they heard something land on the front porch.

The quick-thinking Coretta had yelled for Lucy Williams to run with her to the rear of the house. That saved their lives. Had they waited to see what happened, or gone to the door to see what the loud thud was, the several sticks of dynamite would have blown up in their faces. Yoki was still sleeping peacefully in her bassinet in the rear of the house. Within moments, the house was surrounded by concerned blacks from all over the city.

At the church, King noticed the commotion and finally asked Abernathy what was wrong.

"I want to share something with you," said Abernathy. "Something has happened in the movement, and nobody has been injured. Coretta is all right and the baby, Yoki, is all right. But your house has been bombed."

They immediately went to King's house, where thousands of people were milling around, many of them angry, and many of them armed. One black man, being pushed back by a policeman, said, "I ain't gonna move nowhere. You white folks is always pushing us around. Now you got your .38 and I got mine, so let's battle it out."

Mayor Gayle and Commissioner Sellers were already there, expressing their regrets, but C. T. Smiley, chairman of Dexter's board of trustees, retorted, "Regrets are all very well. But you are responsible. It is you who created the climate for this."

Coretta had been expecting violence and was now relieved that it had finally occurred and they were all unscathed. Her calmness was infectious, and reassured Martin that God was with him.

He went onto the shattered porch and addressed the crowd. Ours is a nonviolent movement, he reminded them. We cannot solve this problem through retaliatory violence. "We must love our white brothers," he said. "No matter what they do to us. We must make them know that we love them.

"If I am stopped, this movement will not stop because God is with the movement. Go home with this glowing faith and this radiant assurance."

They did, but it was difficult. King devoted many of his addresses to the mass meetings to the nonviolent teachings of Gandhi. He told them how Jesus was a nonviolent resister, and active pacifism was not akin to cowardice.

Still, there were those who echoed the sentiments of one parishioner, who suggested they "kill a few whites" to show that the blacks were serious.

Nixon, who drove off a group of would-be bombers with his Winchester, told King, "I'm not about to let some white man hit me and get away with it." So he agreed not to march with King, but offered the services of his weapons if they were needed.

At two-thirty in the morning, Obie Scott arrived to take Coretta and Yoki home to Marion for their safety until things cooled off. "I'm sorry, Dad," Coretta said. "But I belong here with Martin."

He drove home alone.

February brought the resistance out of the closet.

Dynamite was thrown on Nixon's lawn. The draft status of twenty-five-year-old Fred Gray, the MIA's black attorney, was suddenly changed from exempt to 1-A. Reverend Graetz's home was bombed.

On February 3, 1956, Autherine Lucy became the first black student at the University of Alabama. That triggered two weeks of rioting, led by the KKK and the White Citizens Council. Attorney General Patterson said the school had the right to do what it wanted: it suspended her "for her own safety." Her attorney accused the university of conspiring against her. The officials said that statement was tantamount to insubordination, and Lucy was expelled permanently. The notoriety brought forty thousand new members to the Alabama White Citizens Council.

Four black women filed a suit in the U.S. District Court challenging the legality of the state's transportation laws. A hearing was set for May 11 before Fifth Circuit Court Judges Frank M. Johnson and Richard Rives of Montgomery and Seybourn H. Lynne of Birmingham. The fifth circuit was headed by Judge Elbert Tuttle, the grandson of a Union soldier whose health had been destroyed

In February 1956 a Montgomery County grand jury indicted King, Abernathy, and 117 other blacks for boycotting the buses. Far from being intimidated, the MIA viewed it as a cause for celebration (AP/WIDE WORLD).

King and his MIA associates were convicted in March for their illegal bus "conspiracy": Coretta congratulated her husband on becoming a felon (AP/WIDE WORLD).

at Andersonville, the Confederate prison camp. He was appointed by President Dwight Eisenhower in 1954, one of many Republican judges who owed nothing to the Dixiecrats.

A Montgomery County grand jury indicted 119 blacks for violating a seldom-used 1921 state statute prohibiting boycotts unless there was "just cause or legal excuse." The maximum penalty was six months in jail and a thousand-dollar fine. Rosa Parks, E. D. Nixon, and Reverend Abernathy were among those arrested.

The grand jury issued a presentment along with the indictments, stating that "violence is inevitable if we continue on our present course of race relations." The jury blamed the NAACP for fomenting the trouble.

King had been speaking at Fisk University in Nashville, Tennessee, when the indictments were handed down. He flew to Atlanta to pick up Coretta and Yoki before going back to Montgomery. A family crisis arose.

Daddy King did not want Martin to return. He assembled at his home a group of people whom Martin respected: Morehouse president Benjamin E. Mays, insurance executive T. M. Alexander, Sr., Atlanta University president Rufus Clement, and C. A. Scott, publisher of the Atlanta *Daily World*, a black newspaper. They pleaded with King to quit, to stay in Atlanta and avoid the danger of Alabama.

"I must go back to Montgomery," said Martin. "My friends and associates are being arrested. It would be the height of cowardice for me to stay away. I have begun the struggle, and I can't turn back. I have reached the point of no return."

Daddy King burst into tears. There was no more to say.

In the morning, Daddy King drove Martin, Coretta, and Yoki to Montgomery, where they rendezvoused with Abernathy. Together, King and Abernathy went to the police station to be booked and fingerprinted.

What had been meant as an intimidating gesture backfired. There was almost a holiday atmosphere at the jail, and hundreds of blacks had called up to find out if they were on the list of those indicted and expressed disappointment if they weren't.

The trial was set for March 19 for eighty-nine defendants, and the defense centered on the premise that blacks had just cause to boycott. Twenty-eight blacks testified about abuse on the buses. One woman's husband was shot and killed when he refused to leave the bus unless his fare was returned. After three days of testimony, Judge Eugene Carter pronounced King guilty and imposed a five-hundred-dollar fine or a year and a day in county jail. The other cases were all stayed pending the results of King's appeal.

The walking continued.

Though Montgomery was not the first to have a bus boycott, it had become a symbol of the fight against segregation. Donations poured into the MIA from around the world. Support groups, such as In Friendship in New York

After five months of walking and car pooling, spirits had not flagged. King and Abernathy were cheered as they announced the boycott would continue until the city caved in (AP/WIDE WORLD).

City, an amalgam of the liberal labor establishment and Jewish groups, formed to provide a variety of aid to the boycott leaders. In addition to money, In Friendship sent people like Bayard Rustin, Stanley Levison of the American Jewish Congress, Ella Baker of the New York NAACP, and A. Philip Randolph to Montgomery to discuss organizational strategies with King and his associates.

On their own, In Friendship did something that had not been contemplated in Montgomery: they began planning for the future; the need to develop a mass organization throughout the South instead of having unrelated and unsupported demonstrations in scattered locations.

The Montgomery protest was having an effect on other Alabama cities. Reverend Lowery's Alabama Civic Affairs Association threatened to boycott the buses in Mobile if they were not desegregated, and the city capitulated. They then gave the city two months to hire black bus drivers, and the city again gave in. They simply did not want to have the tension that existed in Montgomery.

"It was good in that they desegregated," said Lowery. "But it was bad in that we were never able to build up the kind of mass movement that they had in Montgomery, where they had different kinds of resistance. Within four years, all facilities in the city were desegregated."

Lowery, Rev. Fred Shuttlesworth of Birmingham, and C. G. Gomillion, who organized demonstrations in Tuskeegee, met monthly now with King and Abernathy to discuss their respective movements and share ideas and strategies for combating racism in Alabama. Gomillion eventually dropped out, but other ministers who were leading civil rights movements were brought into the ad hoc discussion group, and the idea of a coordinated, Southern antisegregation organization gradually gelled.

The boycott was back in the courts in May and June. The beleaguered bus company dropped its segregated seating policy in an effort to end the boycott, but a state circuit court ordered it reinstated. On May 11, the suit brought by four black women was heard by a three-judge panel in federal court.

The city maintained that desegregation would trigger violence in the city and therefore segregation should be maintained. King was gratified to hear an incredulous Judge Rives ask, "Is it fair to command one man to surrender his constitutional rights . . . in order to prevent another man from committing a crime?"

It seemed clear to King that the federal court would declare segregation unconstitutional, which it did on June 4 in a two-to-one decision, with Judges Rives and Johnson in favor of desegregation and Judge Lynne dissenting. The two judges had decided that the Supreme Court's 1954 decision barring segregation in education implied that segregation in any public area was wrong, and they ruled accordingly.

The case was now sent to the U.S. Supreme Court.

On June 1, Attorney General Patterson struck. "One of the things we came up with to slow down civil rights litigation," he said, "was to get rid of the NAACP."

Patterson obtained an injunction against the NAACP branch in the state, run by Ruby Hurley, charging that it was a foreign corporation, based in New York, and did not comply with state corporation laws. In addition, the court demanded a list of the NAACP's membership roles and imposed fines that would mount daily until the roles were turned over.

Instead of complying, Hurley closed up shop, and it was to be eight years before the NAACP could return to Alabama. That was a tactical error by Patterson, though he didn't know it at the time. In those days, the NAACP was opposed to the direct-action approach to racial injustice: it favored the slow legal method, which would have actually fit Patterson's delaying plans very well.

But with the NAACP gone, activists took the leading role and formed new organizations committed to direct action.

During the summer, public attention was on the sinking of the luxury liner *Andrea Doria* off the Nantucket coast. In Alabama, quiet pressure was put on the insurance industry not to handle the rolling churches—the station wagons —being used by the boycotting churches. Their coverage was canceled four times in four months, but in September, T. M. Alexander, the Atlanta insurance executive, placed coverage with Lloyds of London, and the car pools continued.

On October 30 the city struck at the car pools again, and Judge Carter was asked to enjoin the car pool as a public nuisance and a violation of the city's franchise law. The city also wanted fifteen thousand dollars in punitive damages. Judge Carter set a hearing on the motion for November 13.

At the mass meeting on November 12, King was despondent. He feared that they would lose in court the next day and did not know if the boycott could continue without their car pools.

"For the first time in our long struggle together," he said, "I almost shrank from appearing before them."

He told the mass meeting, "This may well be the darkest hour just before dawn. We have moved all of these months with the daring faith that God was with us in our struggle. We must go out with the same faith, the same conviction."

King and Abernathy were in court the next morning when suddenly a messenger came into the room and began whispering to Judge Carter. The judge began conferring with the city's attorneys and then called a recess. The two men were puzzled. Associated Press reporter Rex Thomas handed them a note saying, "Here is the decision you have been waiting for."

They read the startling, brief announcement: "The United States Supreme Court today affirmed a decision of a special three-judge U.S. District Court in declaring Alabama's state and local laws requiring segregation on buses unconstitutional."

"Thank you, Jesus!" exclaimed one black woman in the courtroom. "The Lord has spoken from Washington."

King called it a "glorious daybreak at the end of a long night of segregation." He cheerfully went back into the courtroom after the recess and watched Judge Carter dutifully issue an injunction against the car pool. It was a charade, he thought, for the local court to rule against the car pool on the same day that the U.S. Supreme Court had removed the obstacles that made the car pool necessary.

The Klan rode that night. Forty carloads of robed and hooded whites rode through the city's black community. Their demonstration had been announced on the radio, which normally prompted blacks to lock their doors and get out of sight.

But not tonight. "Negroes acted as if they were watching a circus parade," said King. They opened their doors, dressed up, came out on their porches, and watched and waved at the angry white men. The Klansmen, baffled by this lack of fear, left after driving only a few blocks.

There were two joyous mass meetings the following night because no one church was large enough to hold the crowd. They were long affairs, punctuated by singing, shouting, laughing, and crying. As King entered the Holt Street Baptist Church, where the first mass meeting had been held almost a year before, the four thousand people gathered rose en masse, chanted his name, and applauded.

Rev. S. S. Seay had started the emotional evening by bursting into tears as he described the unsuccessful Klan march the night before and declared, "Whenever the Klan may march, no matter what the White Citizens Councils may want to do, we are not afraid because God is on our side."

Next it was King's turn. He told them the bad news: they had lost in the lower court and "the transportation system is no longer operating."

Then he told them the good news: they had won. They thunderously voted to end the boycott. Procedurally, without the car pool, they would have to walk for the next three weeks, until a certified copy of the U.S. Supreme Court

edict was received in the district court and imposed on the city and the bus company.

He talked about the love and nonviolence that had sustained the movement for nearly a year. "We must take this not as a victory over the white man, but with dignity. Don't go back to the buses and push people around. We are just going to sit where there's a seat. We must not take this as a victory over the white man, but as a victory for justice and democracy.

"I wish I could say that when we go back to the buses on an integrated basis that no white person will insult you or that violence will not break out. If someone pushes you, don't push him back. We must have the courage to refuse to hit back."

Whites were angry. King received mail threatening that "if you allow the niggers to go back on the buses and sit in the front seats we're going to burn down fifty houses in one night, including yours."

They threatened to hang King and Hugo Black from the same tree.

During the first week in December, the anniversary of the start of the boycott, King and Abernathy led a weeklong "Institute on Nonviolence and Social Change," in which they discussed nonviolent resistance and tried to prepare black Montgomery for hostile receptions when the buses were integrated.

The White Citizens Council threatened that "any attempt to enforce this decision will lead to riot and bloodshed." The local government issued a statement December 18 declaring, "The city Commission, and we know our people are with us in this determination, will not yield one inch, but will do all in its power to oppose the integration of the Negro race with the white race in Montgomery, and will forever stand like a rock against social mixing of the races under God's creation and plan."

King warned the city that they needed to be more temperate, to prepare the whites for integration if they wanted to have a smooth transition. They stood by their statement. King appealed to the white ministers to address their congregations. They were silent. That left it to the MIA to continue to prepare blacks for a rocky road to integration through role playing and social dramas in which they practiced nonviolent responses to insults and attacks by whites.

At the December 20 mass meeting, the last one under the segregated bus system, King told an overflowing crowd in the St. John A.M.E. Church that they should be proud that "we came to see that, in the long run, it is more honorable to walk in dignity than ride in humiliation. So in a quiet dignified manner, we decided to substitute tired feet for tired souls, and walk the streets of Montgomery until the sagging walls of injustice had been crushed."

He urged the blacks to return to the buses with "calm dignity and wise restraint." They should remember the nonviolence that had kept them going for more than a year and continue trying to turn an enemy into a friend. "Violence must not come from any of us," King warned, "for if we become victimized with violent intents, we will have walked in vain and our twelve months of glorious dignity will be transformed into an eve of gloomy catastrophe.

"With this dedication, we will be able to emerge from the bleak and desolate midnight of man's inhumanity to man to the bright and glittering daybreak of freedom and justice."

For the second time in little more than a year, King anxiously waited for the 6 A.M. bus to pass his house. He had company this time. Abernathy, Nixon, and Rev. Glenn Smiley, a white minister, approached the bus together.

The door opened. The bus driver smiled and said, "I believe you are Reverend King, aren't you?"

"Yes, I am," the boycott leader answered.

"We are glad to have you this morning," the bus driver said.

Integration had come to Montgomery.

4
REFLECTION

BUT WHERE WAS IT GOING, AND WHY WAS THE FOCUS ON Montgomery?

There were other movements in the South. Reverend Shuttlesworth was shaking up Birmingham with a series of boycotts and demonstrations. Hosea Williams was leading youngsters on marches throughout the streets of Savannah, Georgia. Rev. C. K. Steele was leading demonstrations in Tallahassee, Florida. Blacks were on the move all across the Confederacy. But all eyes were on Montgomery and the spokesman for its movement, Rev. Martin Luther King, Jr.

In Montgomery, King had been thrust into the role of leader. The collective leadership decided before their first meeting with city officials that there would be only one spokesman after Rev. S. S. Seay noted, "We have not had a nationally recognized spokesman since Booker T. Washington.

"From now on, in public, King should be the one to speak for us. We cannot afford to be divided behind different leaders."

The advice was sound: it gave the MIA a set identity and unity that the white opposition could not pierce. King did not organize Montgomery; the city was already "organized" as such behind several small and relatively weak, independent factions. For the first time, however, King mobilized those factions and got them to work as a cohesive unit.

"He was the right man at the right time," said Reverend Shuttlesworth. "He was an incredible speaker: you simply rallied around him."

King didn't "just preach to you," said Jo Ann Robinson. "He made you see what was right. He made you feel what was right. When he spoke of Christian love and nonviolence, it was *the* thing you wanted to do."

King would have stood in a rarified rank of ministers simply because of his electrifying manner of speaking, the product of the naturally beautiful, resonant voice and the patient practice under the tutelage of Reverend Barbour and Daddy King. But there was more.

The philosophy of the social gospel worked out by King in his student days, the theory of the activist religion, the picture he painted of Jesus not as a pacifist but as the aggressive, nonviolent slayer of evil was a fresh vision to the black community.

The man of peace was heartbroken by the wave of white violence that followed bus integration in Montgomery. After six shootings and six church bombings, King collapsed at a rally after saying, "If anyone should be killed, let it be me" (AP/WIDE WORLD).

Theirs had been the religion of pie in the sky: suffer under the whites now —patiently—and you will reap the rewards accorded the meek later. This had been accepted, though blacks yearned for the freedom they saw in other segments of society. King offered a vision of dignity now. King offered a vision of freedom now. King offered a revitalized religion to people who had counted religion as the only possession they had. King offered a potential for salvation through suffering now, because this suffering was for the cause of justice, not the capricious whims of the Southern way of life.

King offered something that people who were organized to act could mobilize behind. So how could he best be used? The South rapidly needed a coordinating body to work with the burgeoning protest, and the subject was constantly being debated by Ella Baker, Bayard Rustin, and others in the In Friendship group in New York.

Baker preferred the development of what she termed a "group-centered leadership" rather than a "leader-centered movement." But the latter was what existed, and is what eventually spread.

It had its dangers, however, and King was aware of them. On more than one occasion he would tell Coretta, "I am really disturbed about how fast all this has happened to me. People will expect me to perform miracles for the rest of my life.

"I don't want to be the kind of man who hits his peak at twenty-seven, with the rest of his life an anticlimax. Neither do I want to disappoint people by not being able to pull rabbits out of a hat."

Rustin was spending a lot of time in Montgomery doing support work with the MIA and during talks at Christmas suggested the formation of a single group. The idea had already surfaced during the monthly meetings King and Abernathy held with Shuttlesworth and Lowery. Now that the boycott was over, King had time to really think about it. A meeting of about a hundred black leaders from around the South, most of them ministers, was scheduled for the weekend of January 12 in Atlanta to discuss the formation of a new regional organization.

Integration was not going to come easily. There had been scattered unpleasant incidents on the buses after they were officially desegregated on December 21. One black woman reported being slapped by a white man and later said, "I could have broken that little fellow's neck all by myself, but I left the mass meeting last night determined to do what Reverend King asked."

The Montgomery *Advertiser* reported that "the calm but cautious acceptance of this significant change in Montgomery's way of life came without any major disturbance."

Shuttlesworth had announced that blacks in Birmingham would no longer observe segregated seating after Christmas and asked the city to officially remove the now unconstitutional segregation ordinance.

"We thought there would be a lot of pressure on Montgomery, and the Klan would be down there," he explained, "and we wanted to take some of the pressure off."

That wasn't possible: hatred was everywhere. In Montgomery, city buses were fired on. A teenage black girl was brutally beaten up by four white men. A pregnant black woman was shot in the leg. The Klansmen began parading openly through Montgomery. The city cut service on the buses in black areas after 5 P.M., a move designed to bring more hardship on blacks and break their spirit.

Christmas morning brought sixteen sticks of dynamite to Reverend Shuttlesworth's home, blowing out his bedroom walls but miraculously leaving him lying on his mattress without a scratch.

The leaders of the white business sector and religious community followed the lead of city hall—they remained silent while the violence escalated.

On January 9, 1957, Abernathy and the Kings went to Atlanta to prepare for the upcoming leadership conference, to put the final touches on an agenda worked out with Reverends Lowery and Shuttlesworth. At 2 A.M., Abernathy was awakened by Alberta King, who said his wife was calling from Montgomery.

"What has happened?" he asked, fearing the worst. "Has my home been bombed?"

Alberta King handed him the telephone, and Juanita Abernathy, who was pregnant with their second child, confirmed his fears. "But the baby's apparently all right," she said of two-year-old Juandalynn, "because I hear her singing."

The telephone worked, but there were no lights, some of the walls were down, the floor supports seemed weak, there was a smell of gas, and Juanita was trapped. The Montgomery police, who were on the scene surprisingly fast, cordoned off the house and would not let anyone in or out.

A policeman leveled his gun at one neighbor who attempted to enter the home. She finally said, "Go on and shoot. There is a pregnant woman and a baby inside that house, and I'm going inside."

At that, the police relented, and Juanita called her husband back an hour later to tell him that neighbors had propped up the walls and had gotten a string of lights working. Then, in the middle of the conversation, she shouted, "Oh! There's another one! They have bombed our church!"

Abernathy collapsed onto a chair, stunned. King sat down beside him, but could think of nothing to say to a friend who had nearly lost his family.

"I looked at Ralph as he sat beside me," recalled King. "Both his home and his church bombed in one night, and I knew of no words to comfort him."

They knelt in the early morning darkness and prayed.

The terrorists didn't stop with Abernathy. They bombed four churches that night—First Baptist, Hudson Street Baptist, Bell Street Baptist, and Mount Olive Baptist—and two parsonages, Abernathy's and Reverend Graetz's.

Virginia Durr called Mrs. Graetz and suggested she bring the children and stay in the Durrs' house.

"It's late," Mrs. Graetz said. "I think we'd rather sleep in this bombed-out mess than pack up at this hour and trek across town."

Total damage was estimated at seventy thousand dollars. King's church was never bombed. Many felt that it was spared only because it was on the grounds of the capitol, and an explosion would have damaged that historic Southern edifice.

Hundreds of people were congregated around Abernathy's home when he and King arrived the next morning, and their mood was ugly. The two men worried that the rash of bombings might trigger reactive violence from the black community.

Abernathy was jubilant, however, on seeing Juanita, an island of strength and calm in the midst of a destroyed home. His fear was for his church. He walked the block to the site of First Baptist; then the reaction set in.

CONDEMNED was the word stenciled on the sign in front of what had been the proud, prestigious face of the First Baptist Church, which at one time had held the South's largest black congregation.

CONDEMNED across the broken stained glass windows that had been shipped from Italy in 1908 to the struggling black congregation whose members contributed a brick a week for a decade so blacks would have a proper place to worship.

CONDEMNED was across the carved motto above the door proclaiming that this church was "Towering Over the Wrecks of Time."

CONDEMNED was the word for the house of the Lord.

He and King walked past the police barricade and entered the church. He walked through the church, surveying the mangled pews, the workmen already trying to shore up the walls and roof, surveying the destroyed organ, surveying the broken altar and the shards of lead crystal glass that had filtered the sun's rays for half a century.

He was encased in a lonely corner of silence: no one spoke to the anguished minister on that bleak Friday morning. As the day wore on Abernathy became depressed. He did not know how his congregation would react to this outrage. He did not know if they would want him to continue the activist ways that had brought about this catastrophe.

There was some good news that day: for the first time, responsible elements of the white community spoke out for law and order. Montgomery *Advertiser* editor Grover Hall was still a segregationist, but he deplored the attacks on the churches. So did several white ministers, who said the attacks were unChristian and uncivilized. The leaders of the white business community also joined the condemnation.

Martin had to go back to Atlanta Friday night to continue with the discussions leading to the formation of a Southern Conference on Transportation and Nonviolent Integration. They decided to meet again in New Orleans on February 14 and finalize their plans. They sent two telegrams. The first went to U.S. Attorney General Herbert Brownell, asking him to take steps to curb the antiblack violence. The second asked President Eisenhower to come to the South and see what conditions were for black Americans. There was no response.

Abernathy was alone, wondering how well he really knew his congregation.

Sunday, January 12, he delivered his sermon in the basement of First Baptist Church, in the midst of its boarded-up windows and visible support braces. When he was done, eighty-year-old Suzie Beasley stood up and said, "I have discovered this morning that my pastor is troubled, and no leader can lead if he is troubled.

"Pastor, you have to hold your head up high. This is the First Baptist Church."

She told a story of the building of the church. She recalled how the parishioners at the turn of the century took turns working on what had been a pond, hauling away mud and buckets of water in a slow dredging process. She talked about the years of buying or scavenging for bricks. She talked about the running joke in the black community: "When future generations ask the question, 'What is the meaning of this hole?' they will be told it is where the First Baptist Church was supposed to have been built.

"But we built this church under the leadership of Pastor A. J. Stokes, and we will rebuild it under you," Suzie Beasley said. "They have bombed the church, and we will rebuild it. And they may bomb it again, and we will rebuild it again, for this church will always stand. So hold your head high, Reverend Abernathy."

She made a motion that the congregation give their embattled, lonely, twenty-nine-year-old minister a vote of confidence, but the vote was never taken. The choir director struck the chord for the "Hallelujah Chorus" from Handel's *The Messiah*, and the choir and congregation rose en masse and began singing, "And He shall reign for ever and ever."

And Abernathy burst into tears at the pulpit and never again doubted his own commitment to the struggle, nor the commitment of the black community he tried to serve.

King returned to Montgomery in time for the mass meeting on Tuesday, January 14. The bombings preyed heavily on his mind. The city commission had canceled the buses in the black area, ostensibly to curtail the violence. The blacks saw this as an erosion of their hard-won gains.

He was discouraged and began to blame himself for the black community's troubles. He was, after all, the lightning rod of the movement, and he wondered if the violence could have been avoided if he had handled something differently. It was with this guilt pressing on his heart that he addressed the Tuesday rally, an address he did not finish.

In the midst of the prayer, he said blacks had been the "victims of the most startling and appalling expression of man's inhumanity to man. To have bombed the homes was unpardonable, but to have attacked a House of God was tragic barbarity, devoid of moral sensitivity.

"Lord, I hope no one will have to die as a result of our struggle for freedom in Montgomery. Certainly, I don't want to die. But if anyone has to die, let it be me."

He broke down, could not continue, and had to be helped to his seat. The emotional outburst caused pandemonium in the church. Shouts of "No! No!" came from all sides and some people wept. It was a cathartic session for all, and they left with a renewed sense of purpose.

The city commission resumed bus service a few days later, but there was another rash of bombings January 28. Twelve sticks of unexploded dynamite were found smoldering on King's porch the next morning, and bombs did go off at a black service station and the home of a sixty-year-old black hospital worker. A group of white men drove up to E. D. Nixon's house, but left when he pointed his Winchester at them.

King again called for calm. "We must not return violence under any condition," he said to a crowd of blacks gathered in front of his home. "I know this is difficult advice to follow, especially since we have been the victims of no less than ten bombings. But this is the way of Christ."

This latest outrage brought a surprise: seven white men were arrested January 31 and charged with the bombings. A county grand jury indicted five of the men and released two. When the trial was held for the first two accused men, they were acquitted by an all-white jury—despite two signed confessions. The remainder were set free in an amnesty that also saw charges dropped against the eighty-eight blacks indicted with King for violating the boycott law.

King decided to pay his five-hundred-dollar fine and move on.

There was a lot to do. King and other black leaders from around the South met in New Orleans in February and formed the Southern Christian Leadership Conference, with the man from Montgomery named president by acclamation. Reverend Steele from Tallahassee was named vice president; Reverend Shuttlesworth, secretary; and Abernathy, treasurer.

The formation of SCLC established King and his nonviolent philosophy as the dominant institution in the South. SCLC's initial manifesto charged blacks to "accept Christian love in full knowledge of its power to defy evil. We call upon them to understand that nonviolence is not a symbol of weakness or

This photograph of Ella Baker was taken in 1979. She was the first executive director of the Southern Christian Leadership Conference (SCLC) (JOAN GRANT COLLECTION/ SOUTHERN PATRIOT).

cowardice, but as Jesus demonstrated, nonviolent resistance transforms weakness into strength and breeds courage in the face of danger."

These days, King was in demand. *Time* magazine wrote a lengthy cover story on him in its February 18, 1957, edition, titled "Attack on Conscience." The article termed King "the scholarly Negro Baptist minister who in little more than a year has risen from nowhere to become one of the nation's remarkable leaders of men."

Lee Griggs, of *Time*'s Atlanta bureau, added, "Martin Luther King, Jr., is, in fact, what many a Negro—and, were it not for his color, many a white— would like to be".

In March, the King family took time out for some travel. Kwame Nkrumah, president of Ghana, invited the Kings to attend Independence Day ceremonies in the capital city of Accra. King, who had never been abroad, often compared European colonialism to the oppression of blacks in America, and he looked forward to seeing the rise of a new black nation.

The Kings were guests of an English professor, and their every whim was catered to by black servants who, they later learned, were paid only 28 cents per day. Their servile attitude and cringing manner disturbed King greatly. It reminded him too much of a blues song he'd heard often in Atlanta: "Been down so long that down don't bother me."

During his stay he had a chance to dine with Nkrumah and received an invitation from Vice President Richard Nixon, who was representing America at the ceremonies, to visit him at the White House.

The most stirring episode came on the night of March 5, 1957. At midnight, fifty thousand Ghanians, many of them in tribal dress, crammed into the center of Accra and saw Nkrumah raise his hand and proclaim, "At long last, the battle has ended. Ghana, our beloved country, is free forever."

The Union Jack slowly sank down the flagpole, to be replaced by the green, yellow, and red flag of a new nation that rose in its place. There was one minute of silent prayer, and then fifty thousand blacks shouted, "Freedom!" in their various tribal languages.

King concluded that, in the end, "both segregation in America and colonialism in Africa were based on the same thing—white supremacy and contempt for life."

They took a circuitous route home, stopping in Lagos and Kano, Nigeria, where they were appalled at the poverty. King talked angrily about the exploitation of Africans by the British and was glad that blacks were throwing off the yoke of colonialism.

There was still much to do at home to throw off the yoke of racism. There were plans for a massive Prayer Pilgrimage in Washington on May 17 to commemorate the third anniversary of the Supreme Court's decision outlawing segregation in education and to petition the government to support new civil rights legislation drafted by the Justice Department. The legislation was intended to protect rights in housing, education, and voting.

The Prayer Pilgrimage to Washington, D.C., on May 17, 1957, to protest the slow pace of school integration was the first march on Washington Reverend King participated in. He emerged from this march as the undisputed leader of black Americans (PAUL SCHUTZER/ LIFE MAGAZINE).

King met in New York on March 25 with A. Philip Randolph and Roy Wilkins. Randolph admired the young minister, and there was an immediate bond between them. It was different with Wilkins, the head of the NAACP. Wilkins had had a distinguished career and was an incisive writer. But he was no orator and could not command the type of following King's personal magnetism generated. He was envious of the young man and worried that his new organization would take funds and support from the NAACP.

They were hoping to draw seventy-five thousand marchers to the Lincoln Memorial in the capital and were somewhat disappointed to attract but half that number. The crowd listened attentively to Congressman Adam Clayton Powell, Randolph, Wilkins, and others. But they came to their feet when Randolph introduced King, who was clearly the man they came to hear.

King tailored his address to take up where President Lincoln's last address ended April 11, 1865. At that time, Lincoln endorsed giving the newly freed Negroes the right to vote in the South. King said, "As long as I do not firmly and irrevocably possess the right to vote, I do not possess myself."

There is no freedom as long as "the Negro in Mississippi cannot vote and the Negro in New York believes he has nothing for which to vote."

By then, King's oratory was in full swing. The marchers were on their feet, hanging on his every word. It was a religious revival. He launched into the cry, "Give us the ballot."

When he was done, the *Amsterdam News* wrote that King emerged from Washington as "the number one leader of 16 million Negroes in the United States. . . . The people will follow him anywhere."

That column in the *Amsterdam News*, the largest and most influential of the black newspapers, was the first of a series of articles in the media examining the distinctions between the "established" black leadership and the methods of King. For despite King's protestations of loyalty to the NAACP and its ideals, there was growing discontent with the staid program of the Urban League, a social organization, and the NAACP, which sought justice in the courts, not in the streets.

An ad hoc committee of the heads of various Urban League chapters formed to examine their programs and fight for a more activist posture. Edwin Berry, executive secretary of the League's Chicago chapter and head of the ad hoc group, told the league it had "played it so safe that we are well behind the safety zone."

Blacks, he said, "are no longer willing to be half-slave and half-free. They are at war with the status quo, and will no longer accept the leadership of any agency or organization that does not know this and will not act on it forthrightly."

The NAACP was having its internal troubles as well. Several Southern states had followed Alabama's example, and the organization was in the midst of a series of tough legal fights to maintain its Southern existence. Ruby Hurley, who had been forced out of Alabama, established a Southern regional office in Atlanta, and she had investigated many of the atrocities against blacks.

The mood in black America was for action, and the NAACP and its approach appeared useless in the face of growing Southern resistance and lawlessness. By 1958, the *Amsterdam News* was saying that Wilkins was a "captive" of

Coretta Scott King
(MATT HERRON/BLACK STAR).

King with Ralph David Abernathy
(FRED WARD/BLACK STAR).

(left to right) *Roy Wilkins, Rosa Parks, and Christine King Ferris* (BOB ADELMAN/MAGNUM).

King with Marion Barry at Shaw University in Raleigh, North Carolina, 1960, at the formation of SNCC (HOWARD SOCHUREK/LIFE MAGAZINE).

At the Lincoln Memorial, August 28, 1963, the key organizers of the March on Washington. Standing (left to right): Matthew Ahamann, Rabbi Joachim Prinz, John Lewis, Rev. Eugene Carson Blake, Floyd McKissick, and Walter Reuther; Seated (left to right): Whitney Young, Cleveland Robinson, A. Philip Randolph, Martin Luther King, Jr., and Roy Wilkins (FRANCIS MILLER/LIFE MAGAZINE).

King at the memorial for Unitarian minister James Reeb, March 1965. Walter Reuther is to King's right (CHARLES MOORE/ LIFE MAGAZINE).

the many prominent whites on the NAACP's board, and Wilkins was not a "true" leader. Jackie Robinson, the most prestigious black on the board, did not endorse that opinion, but he added fuel to the growing internal fire by stating that the NAACP was not "aggressive" enough, and was not helping the "little man."

(The schism reflected growing pains that, a few years later, would spring up again when a new generation of activists would decide that SCLC was too slow and form its own organization, the Student Nonviolent Coordinating Committee.)

Early in 1958, Lowery, Abernathy, and King went to New York to meet with Wilkins and try to patch things up. "We were troubled," Lowery said. "The NAACP fought us so. They just never believed in sit-ins."

The meeting was a failure. Gloster Current, Wilkins's right hand, derided the MIA and SCLC.

"Martin tried to be very statesmanlike," said Lowery. "But we were stunned when Gloster said that the only victory to come out of Montgomery was the court decision that outlawed desegregation on the buses. We were astounded."

"How can you sit there and say that?" said King. "For the first time in our history, fifty thousand Negroes had come together in a self-determinant movement and refused to ride the buses, had walked and organized car pools for over a year. It was the most magnificent thing you have ever seen yet you say the only victory was in the bus decision?!"

But the NAACP brass wasn't finished. They insisted that after the NAACP won its legal fight with John Patterson and the organization was again allowed in Alabama, the MIA and SCLC should disband and all of its members should join the NAACP and support its efforts.

"We represented more direct action," said Lowery. "We were more radical, more activist than the NAACP. We couldn't go back."

This breach was never to heal. At times, NAACP officials would not sit on the same stage with SCLC officials, and Wilkins would refuse to address movements if King had addressed an earlier demonstration.

But SCLC was moving. After the Prayer Vigil in Washington, King took the Vice President up on the offer extended in Ghana, and he and Abernathy met with the politician on June 13, 1957. It was a fruitless meeting, with Nixon asserting he was sincerely interested in the problem, but doing nothing.

There was a pleasant meeting that summer with an eighteen-year-old college student named John Lewis, who wanted to transfer from the Baptist seminary he was attending in Nashville to the segregated Troy State College in his hometown, about fifty miles south of Montgomery.

King invited Lewis to come to Montgomery and talk about his hopes of cracking the white wall at Troy, and Abernathy sent the youngster bus fare for the trip. King joked that he "just wanted to see what fool would have the nerve to try to enter Troy State College."

He promised to give all the help he could, and the MIA's attorney, Fred Gray, offered free legal assistance. But Lewis was under age, and his parents refused to sign a lawsuit because of threats of economic reprisal. Disappointed,

he returned to Nashville, but it was the beginning of a long friendship between the young farmboy and the civil rights leaders.

On Capitol Hill, Senator Lyndon Baines Johnson of Texas shepherded a civil rights bill through the upper house. It was the first major civil rights legislation since Reconstruction days, but it was a weak bill and disappointing to most blacks. It created an advisory panel called the Civil Rights Commission to investigate conditions in the South, but it did not give the Justice Department injunctive power to enforce school desegregation or other rights.

The bill passed September 9 and created the Civil Rights Division of the Department of Justice and the investigative Civil Rights Commission. It was a weak beginning, but a beginning nonetheless.

Eisenhower was forced to act, however, that fall. Nine black Arkansas youngsters were enrolled in Little Rock High School under court order. Governor Orval Faubus sent the Arkansas National Guard to Little Rock to keep the children out. Mob rule became so outrageous that Eisenhower had to nationalize the state National Guard and send a thousand army paratroopers to Little Rock to patrol the halls and escort the children to and from school.

Eisenhower became the first president since Reconstruction to send soldiers to enforce the rights of blacks in Dixie.

There was good news in the fall: Martin Luther King III was born October 23, and the grown-up Martin Luthers were both ecstatic.

This was also election time in Alabama, and Attorney General Patterson was the easy front-runner. He had the endorsement of the KKK and the White

In the first of many trips to the White House, King conferred with Vice President Richard Nixon in June 1957 about the need for civil rights legislation. King came away empty-handed. Left to right: Senator Ives (R-NY), King, Nixon, and Labor Secretary Mitchell (AP/WIDE WORLD).

Before 1957 ended, King would write 208 speeches, travel 780,000 miles, and finish his first book, Stride Toward Freedom (HENRI CARTIER-BRESSON/ MAGNUM).

Citizens Councils, a reward for his leadership in the legal fight to delay integration. He easily won the November election. George Wallace simply couldn't match his appeal to the segregationists, which Wallace vowed would never happen again.

King, meanwhile, continued to crisscross the country, speaking out for concerted nonviolent action and against the daily injustices heaped upon black Americans. He was rapidly solidifying his hold on the position as the most sought-after black leader, making 208 speeches and traveling 780,000 miles before 1957 ended. He finished the first draft of his book *Stride Toward Freedom: The Montgomery Story,* which was to be published the following September by Harper & Row.

The new year marked the beginning of coordinated action by the SCLC. King was constantly being asked, "What are you going to do next?" He didn't know. Neither did the other leaders of and advisers to the young organization, other than that they would keep in touch and provide whatever support they could to each others' civil rights movements. SCLC in 1958 was more of a federation: it had not progressed to the point where it, as an organization, called the shots.

A series of all-night discussions with the SCLC leadership and Rustin and Levison led to the decision to launch a regional voter rights drive on February 12

—Lincoln's Birthday. It was to be kicked off with mass meetings in twenty-one cities.

Ella Baker was drafted to coordinate the effort. She became the de facto executive director of SCLC, which was supposed to have new offices in Atlanta and a $250,000 budget. Baker was an independent-minded woman who began labor and civil rights organizing in the 1930s with W. E. B. Du Bois.

She went to Atlanta on January 9, 1958, and found that no work on the coordinated mass meetings had been done, and "there was no office, there was no anything."

She was staying at the nearby Savoy Hotel, and "worked out of my vest pocket and whatever access I could have to a telephone at Ebenezer Baptist church." Her second week in Atlanta, offices had been secured and so had secretarial help.

The coordinated mass meetings came off without a hitch. King, in Montgomery, set their tone, declaring, "Let us make our intentions crystal clear. We must and will be free. We want freedom—now. We do not want freedom fed to us in teaspoons over another hundred and fifty years."

Baker, who had initially planned to return to New York after the rallies, stayed as executive director "because there was no one to take over at the time." But she was always to be an outsider on the inside, partly because she was a woman in a man's club and partly because she frequently clashed with King over SCLC's development as a leader-centered group, rather than a group-centered leadership. Baker felt they should organize the black community, rather than have America's millions of blacks all looking toward one man.

King said he was going to lead because "the people" wanted him to. More importantly, King and the other movement leaders at the time were Christian ministers who acted because they deeply believed they were "called" by the Lord to do so.

On June 23, King, Randolph, Wilkins, and Lester Granger, head of the Urban League, met at the White House with President Eisenhower. With Randolph as spokesman, they presented the President with a nine-point proposal designed to get the power of the Oval Office behind integration efforts in the South. They wanted the Justice Department's Civil Rights Division to have enforcement power, protection for blacks seeking voting rights, and the withdrawal of federal funds from segregated school systems, hospitals, and the like.

The President listened attentively, said little, and did nothing. A disappointed King wrote that "President Eisenhower could not be committed to anything which involved a structural change in the architecture of American society.

"His conservatism was fixed and rigid, and any evil defacing the nation had to be extracted bit by bit with a tweezer because the surgeon's knife was an instrument too radical to touch this best of all possible societies."

On September 3, the Kings went to recorders court in Montgomery to accompany Abernathy, who was involved in a civil case. As they waited outside the courtroom door, a policeman told King to "get the hell out of here."

King stood his ground, and the officer said, "Boy, you done done it now."

Coretta watched as King was manhandled by Montgomery policemen and arrested in September 1958 for loitering. He was found guilty, but the police commissioner paid his fine rather than let such a famous person spend time in jail (CHARLES MOORE/ BLACK STAR).

He and another policeman manhandled King down to city jail, where he was kicked and roughed up and thrown into a cell. He was initially charged with loitering, but a few minutes after being thrown into jail the policemen—in an extremely deferential mood—politely escorted him out of the jail and released him on his own recognizance. They had apparently learned exactly who this particular uppity nigger was and decided not to hold him. The charge was also changed to refusing to obey an officer.

The experience changed King. That night, he told Coretta that he knew he would be found guilty and that "I've had enough of this thing."

There was more. He said this was not the life he had anticipated when the two of them came to Montgomery just three short years ago. "But gradually," he told Coretta, "you take some responsibility, then a little more, until finally you are not in control anymore. You have to give yourself entirely.

"Then, once you make up your mind that you are giving yourself, then you are prepared to do anything that serves the cause and advances the movement. I have reached that point. I have given myself fully."

A crime in the name of civil rights was not a crime, was nothing to be ashamed of. He would not pay a fine, but would serve the time. Word of the arrest spread around Montgomery's black community and, through the media, around the nation—accompanied by photographs of two policemen twisting King's arms behind him.

On Friday, September 5, King appeared in a packed courtroom before Judge Eugene Loe, who quickly found him guilty and fined him ten dollars or fourteen days in jail. King surprised the judge by asking permission to make a statement.

It was granted. King declared his innocence and described his treatment by the arresting officers. He said he was not hostile to them, for they "are the victims of an environment blighted with more than three hundred years of man's inhumanity to man as expressed in slavery and segregation."

His conscience, he said, would not allow him to "pay a fine for an act that I did not commit and above all for brutal treatment that I did not deserve."

But King did not go to jail. Police Commissioner Sellers, aware that Montgomery officials would again bear the condemnation of the country if King went to jail, paid the fine.

Two weeks later, King's book *Stride Toward Freedom* was published, and King flew north for a round of publicity appearances. The book had been critically acclaimed, and King had been received by huge audiences in Chicago and Detroit. On September 20, he was signing autographs in Blumstein's Department Store on 125th Street in Harlem when a deranged woman, Izola Curry, stabbed him in the chest with a letter opener.

The letter opener was removed in a three-hour operation at Harlem Hospital, in which they had to cut away part of a rib. The letter opener had pierced

King was nearly killed on September 20, 1958, when a deranged woman stabbed him while he was signing autographs in a Harlem department store (NEW YORK DAILY NEWS).

the outer wall of the aorta, the body's major artery. Dr. Emil Naclerio, one of King's three surgeons, said later, "Had he sneezed or coughed, the weapon would have penetrated the aorta" and killed him.

Shortly after coming out of sedation, King inquired about his assailant. "This person needs help," he said. "Don't do anything to her; don't prosecute her. Get her healed." Izola Curry, who had never met King, was eventually committed to the Matteawan State Hospital for the Criminally Insane.

Meanwhile, thousands of cards and letters began arriving at the hospital, and Coretta, who had immediately flown to New York, spent much of her time greeting the long series of VIPs who came to pay their respects.

King said to Coretta, "I don't understand why there is so much business around my getting sick." The answer was simple: he had become a major force in American life.

Pneumonia slowed King's recovery. He was released from the hospital October 3 and spent the next three weeks recovering at the home of a New York friend before returning to Montgomery. The near-assassination brought a halt to his frenetic schedule, and the Kings made plans to accept an invitation from Prime Minister Jawaharlal Nehru to visit India, accompanied by Professor Lawrence D. Reddick, who had just completed a biography of King.

This was to be a special trip. As King said, "To other countries I may go as a tourist, but to India I come as a pilgrim."

They spent February and early March exploring India, its beautiful cities and the abject poverty of its slums and outlying areas—poverty on a scale the Kings had never seen before. King was heartened by his meeting with Nehru, one of Gandhi's chief associates during India's long struggle for independence. Nehru told him about India's caste system, particularly the eons of abuse heaped on the Untouchables, the caste at the bottom.

Nehru wanted a national day of atonement for all the centuries of indignities the Untouchables had endured. To Nehru, it wasn't enough just to say the caste system should be eliminated: the majority needed to share the Untouchables' pain, if for but a day of remembrance.

King was struck by the difference between Nehru and his willingness for all to suffer so that those on the bottom of society could be freed, and Eisenhower, who turned a deaf ear on the needs of those on the bottom of American society.

He returned from India March 10, with his faith in nonviolent action and the Gandhian concept of "soul-force" reinvigorated. He spent more and more time commuting between SCLC offices in Atlanta and Montgomery. The growing demands on his time were leaving him less and less time to meet his normal demands as a pastor. The Dexter Avenue Baptist Church congregation never complained: they loved the pastor who, in their view, was leading them to freedom. They appreciated the time he had to give them when he was in town. And they knew he was always in touch.

King was restless. There had come a point where he was either to be a full-time pastor to his congregation or a full-time fighter for civil rights. In addition, the SCLC was operating in the red and its regional programs were foundering.

On November 29, Dexter was packed. The rumor had spread that Reverend King might leave. King asked Rev. T. E. Brooks to deliver the sermon, and then he went to the pulpit and began his final address to the congregation with which he had gone through so much.

He talked about the difficult duties he had, and how "for almost four years now I have been trying to do as one man what five or six people ought to be doing. . . . After long and prayerful meditation, I have come to the conclusion that I can't stop now. History has thrust upon me a responsibility from which I cannot turn away. I have no choice but to free you now."

With that, he resigned as pastor, effective at the end of January 1960. The congregation rose and sang, "Blest Be the Tie that Binds," and Reverend King wept at the pulpit.

Two days later, King announced that with the new decade, "the time has come for a broad, bold advance" against injustice in the South, and the SCLC was preparing a "full-scale assault" against all forms of discrimination and segregation.

It was time for a change. In his six years in Montgomery, King had seen the beginnings of major change in the structure of American society.

"I think the greatest victory of this period," he said, "was something internal. The real victory was what this period did to the psyche of the black man. The greatness of this period was that we armed ourselves with dignity and self-respect. The greatness of this period was that we straightened our backs up.

"And a man can't ride your back unless it's bent."

King then prepared to move with his family to Atlanta and commit the rest of his life to the struggle for freedom.

5
GIRDING FOR BATTLE

KING WAS RIGHT.

1960 was to be the year of change. This was the year the converging forces in America came together to begin the tumultuous process of reordering society.

Some events were public and open. On the national scene, Sen. John F. Kennedy, a Roman Catholic from Massachusetts, was running for the presidency. His youthful appeal stood in marked contrast to the staid elder-statesman image of the outgoing President Eisenhower. That was an asset. His religion, however, worked against him.

The word was that Kennedy would be a "captive" of the Pope. He was outwardly opposed by many Protestants, and quietly opposed by a few others, like Daddy King.

Governor John Patterson of Alabama said his own minister gave him a hard time about it, but he had made up his mind to work hard for the senator from the Northeast.

"President Kennedy had never promised me anything as far as the race issue down here was concerned," he said. "We all knew that nobody could be elected President of the United States on the segregation ticket. But I did think he was sensitive to us. And I personally liked him."

In the first half of 1960, Governor Patterson was to pull out all the stops to make sure he led a pro-Kennedy delegation to the Democratic National Convention in Los Angeles. In doing so, he had to turn his back on the KKK and other old-line Dixiecrats who had helped put him into the statehouse, but he thought he had time to patch that up. Soon the state would move against Rev. Martin Luther King, Jr.

Some events at the time were quite secret. There had been a lot of violence in the South in resistance to desegregation efforts, and there promised to be more. Roger Everett Little, a captain of detectives in the Atlanta Police Department, went to Police Chief Herbert Jenkins and said the violence was likely to strike the metropolitan area sooner or later, and the department had no way to cope with it.

Chief Jenkins authorized Little to set up a special antiterrorist squad with

It was relaxing in Atlanta. Martin Luther King, Sr. and Jr., enjoyed pastoring Ebenezer Baptist Church together (ROLAND MITCHELL).

King now had more time to be with his growing family (ROLAND/MITCHELL).

("LEVITON-ATLANTA"/BLACK STAR).

(ROLAND MITCHELL).

detective Clyde Hanby to find out who the radicals were and keep an eye on them.

Little learned about a special group of segregationists based in Atlanta but willing to work throughout the South, anywhere their services were needed.

"They were a very radical group of segregationists," said Little, "and we thought they were responsible for a lot of the bombings. They were a splinter group, and most of them, at one time or another, had been members of the Klan. But they were kicked out because they were a little too radical for the Klan."

Translation: this group liked to kill.

That may not sound radical for Klansmen, but pause. It is easy to go along with the crowd—for twenty guys to beat up one lone demonstrator. But only one in the crowd is a killer. Only one in the crowd will use the club in such a way as to smash the demonstrator's skull rather than break his legs. Only one in the crowd can look at an unarmed, defenseless person and point a gun at him and blow his brains out. While the whole group may be glad the upstarts are gone, they are not happy having in their midst someone they feel is capable of cold-blooded murder, especially if he enjoys it.

Detective Little discovered a group of outcasts in Atlanta who met in restaurants and bars and in private homes and went under the name of Nacirema.

"It was taken from American spelt backwards," says Chief Jenkins, "which is what they were."

They had access to two large private farms in the Atlanta metropolitan area, said Little, and they would train regularly. They learned how to set fires. They learned how to handle explosives. They learned how to set fuses and timers. They learned how to properly handle Molotov cocktails and blew up several cars at one of their training sessions.

Sometimes, said Little, they worked with local Klan or other hate groups to blow up things, like the synagogue in Atlanta. Frequently, said Little, the members of Nacirema were in touch with a veteran radical Klansman from Birmingham named Robert E. Chambliss.

In some ways, it was all like a deadly game. There was, apparently, surreptitious eavesdropping on some of the ringleaders of Nacirema and their hangouts. Detective Little and his group tried to head off the worst of their rampages, when they had a chance.

But this was a time of training: the police trying to learn as much as they could and the twelve to fifteen members of the primarily gay Nacirema learning how best to kill large numbers of blacks.

The Federal Bureau of Investigation was also interested in the activities of the Klan, and in 1960 its Birmingham, Alabama, office began paying a young man named Gary Thomas Rowe for information about Klan activities. They paid all his Klan fees and added funds ranging from twenty to three hundred dollars per month, depending on how active he was.

And they encouraged him to be active, because only if he was an insider could he tell them what was going on. During this period he befriended a middle-aged Klansman named Chambliss.

CITY CAFE
COLORED ENTRANCE

The movement moved indoors (DANNY LYON/ MAGNUM).

The FBI also began taking a closer look at the growing efforts of the SCLC, but that interest was confined to determining if there was any Communist influence over the civil rights movement.

There would come a time when they would record Chambliss paying Rowe one of the highest of Klan compliments: "You can trust Rowe to kill a nigger and never talk." But the death of a nigger here or there was not the overall concern of the agency as it watched the spreading civil rights movement, so the comment was simply filed.

There was another strong current running through the country. Black college youths were in their early teens when the MIA was formed, and they followed its activities avidly. Here, for the first time in their young lives, was a black man standing up for all of them—and leading them in a fight for freedom. Montgomery showed them that concerted action could overcome the entrenched, racist forces of the South. They were eager for more.

Some students actively worked toward it. In Nashville, Rev. James Lawson, a Methodist minister and Southern regional secretary for the Fellowship of Reconciliation, had kept in close contact with the young Dr. King. Nonviolence was a way of life to Lawson, and he used to travel around the South giving workshops and sermons on the nonviolent way to fledgling SCLC chapters.

By 1960 he was director of nonviolent education for SCLC—and his favorite pupil was King. It was Lawson who showed King the Old Testament roots of nonviolent action, taken from Isaiah, the suffering servant who rejects violence as a way to lift up the oppressed. Here was the genesis of Jesus's manifesto, and King took it as a revelation that melded the Old and New Testaments for him.

In the beginning of 1959, Lawson and Rev. Kelly Miller Smith of the First Baptist Church formed an SCLC affiliate, the Nashville Leadership Council, and began holding a series of Tuesday workshops on nonviolence. The workshops started small, primarily with students from the American Baptist Theological Seminary like John Lewis and C. T. Vivian. They drew others from Fisk, like Marion Barry, Diane Nash, and James Bevel, who were attracted to Lawson's activist style.

Lawson appealed to the youngsters, for he was less interested in biracial committees and changing the hearts and minds of whites than he was in changing the power structure regardless of the moral posture of the whites holding it.

The NAACP was embroiled in a legal fight in Nashville at that time to desegregate the school system, and white resistance had included bombings of an elementary school and a synagogue.

In the fall, Nash said the group should attack segregation in the downtown stores. Black women in Nashville got tired going shopping and had no place to rest or get a cup of coffee, and black mothers had no place to change their children. In November and December 1959, they had a series of sit-ins in downtown restaurants, sending in small groups of students led by Lewis or Bevel, who, of course, would be refused service.

"At that time, we wanted to see what the pattern was and who actually made the decisions controlling the stores and restaurants," Lawson explained. "Then, after the Christmas holidays, we were going to go back en masse."

The sit-ins drew little opposition: there was no violence, and no service. As a result, there was also no publicity, and aside from the ripple of news passing through the black community, the event passed unnoticed.

At that point, history got ahead of them. On February 1, four students from all-black North Carolina Agricultural and Technical State College in Greensboro—Franklin McCain, Ezell Blair, Jr., David Richmond, and Joseph McNeil—walked up to a lunch counter in Woolworth's and refused to move unless they were served. The closing of the store for the day came first, and when they returned to campus, they found that news of their action had spread all over.

On February 2, twenty other students joined their protest, and within two weeks, there were major sit-ins in a half dozen North Carolina cities.

Lawson received a phone call from Douglas Moore, a student adviser at A & T, asking what the students in Nashville could do to support the sit-in efforts. On February 13, Moore had an answer. Five hundred Nashville blacks took part that day in the largest sit-in demonstration the South had ever seen, singing "We Shall Overcome" and trying to adhere to Lewis's admonition to "remember the teachings of Jesus, Thoreau, Gandhi, and Martin Luther King." Their massive sit-in tied up all of downtown Nashville.

It was peaceful, at first. But on February 27, a white minister warned the group at their predemonstration prayer meeting that the police and downtown businessmen had agreed to "let white hoodlums come into the stores and beat us up," said Lewis. "Then, they would come in and arrest us.

"There were about one hundred of us sitting at the upstairs balcony lunch counter at Woolworth's, when these white thugs came in and started just beating up people and spitting on them and putting lighted cigarettes down people's backs. We had been sitting there quietly, doing our homework, reading our books. It was a contrast that really galvanized the community."

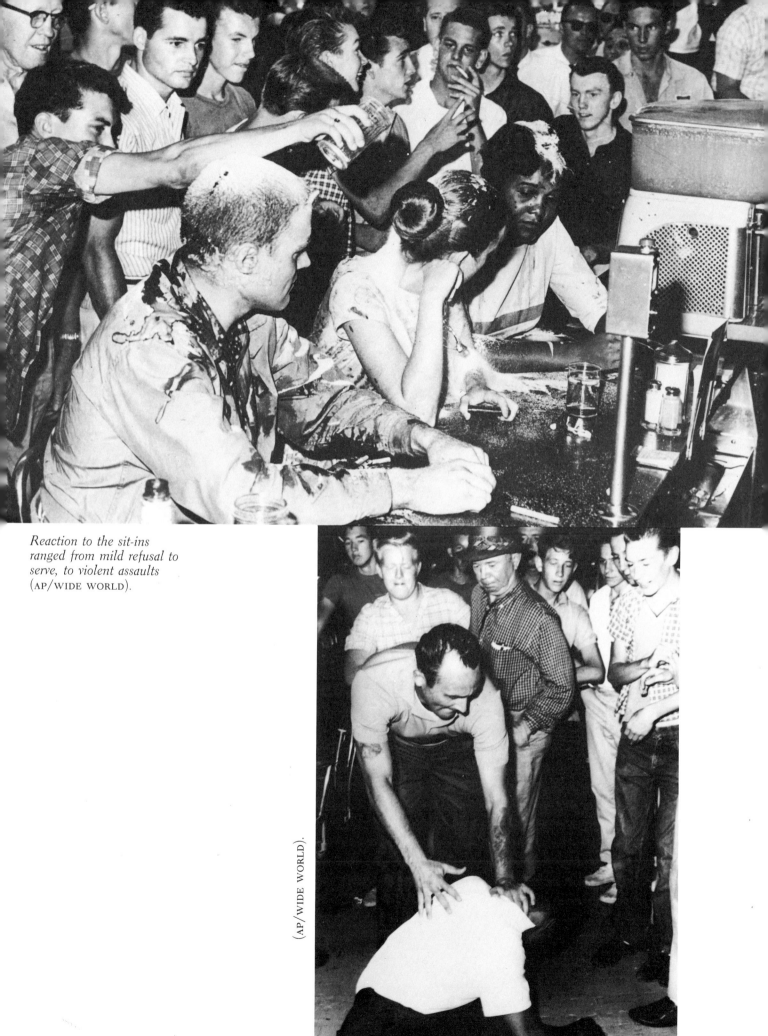

*Reaction to the sit-ins
ranged from mild refusal to
serve, to violent assaults*
(AP/WIDE WORLD).

(AP/WIDE WORLD).

Establishments that tried to integrate found themselves challenged by the KKK (DANNY LYON/MAGNUM).

King was busy interpreting the movement to the rest of America. He made it clear that this was a student action, not one directed by the elders, and that it was the inevitable result of continued delay in removing the shackles already declared unconstitutional by the U.S. Supreme Court.

He started Ella Baker working on a plan to bring the student leaders together, either as a youthful wing of SCLC or as an affiliate. King was not threatened by the fact that the students, of their own volition, were spontaneously tackling SCLC's unimplemented goal of the 1960s, to desegregate facilities all across the South.

King's personal attention was diverted by Patterson's Alabama. On February 17 a Montgomery grand jury indicted King for allegedly falsifying his state income tax returns for 1956 and 1958. The state said King reported his 1956 income as $9,150 when it should have been $16,162, and his 1958 income as $25,248 when it should have been $45,421.

King was crushed. He had no money, and he and the state of Alabama knew it. SCLC paid him one dollar a year, and Ebenezer, where he was copastor with his father, paid him six thousand. Sure, royalties from his book and honoraria for his speeches came to more than two hundred thousand dollars at one point, but all of his money went straight to the MIA and, later, to the SCLC.

He had been scheduled to fly to Chicago to address a rally when the indictments were announced: he immediately canceled the trip.

"Many people will think I am guilty," he said to Coretta. "You know my enemies have previously done everything against me but attack my character and integrity. I am not perfect, but if I have any virtues, the one of which I am most proud is my honesty where money is concerned."

King assumed he would be convicted: he did not have the personal funds to fight such a charge, and he did not expect justice in the Alabama courts. He was depressed, and he repaired to his study to think and pray. He decided that he had to hold his head high, no matter what, and he rescheduled his flight to Chicago. But he wondered, "Who will believe me?"

It didn't take long to find out. Support came in from all sides. Harry Belafonte, Rustin, and Levison in New York set up an emergency fund and promised to raise two hundred thousand dollars to cover any legal expenses. He had the services of not one but five attorneys. It became clear that many echoed the words of Dr. Ralph Bunche: "It's the word of the state of Alabama against the word of Martin Luther King. There is no question in my mind which the country will accept."

In March, demonstrations began in Atlanta and Montgomery, at Alabama State College. The Alabama police responded by storming the campus with shotguns and tear gas and threatening to arrest the entire student body. King, who was appearing before as many student groups as he could, despite his pending trial, went to Alabama State and deplored the "gestapo" tactics of the police.

King took pains to point out that he was not the leader of the student movement: he was not trying to take over their individual programs. But he saw the need to come together, so while the demonstrations continued, plans were made for a conference with the student leaders to be held at Shaw University in Raleigh, North Carolina, on April 1. Ella Baker, who was on the way out at SCLC, was the primary organizer of the conference and ensured that the resulting organization had the political thrust she wanted. It was initially called the Temporary Student Nonviolent Coordinating Committee, with Marion Barry of the Nashville group elected president.

The Nashville group was perhaps the most organized of all the student movements, the result of nearly a year of nonviolent training by Reverend Lawson. Throughout the spring, the students from Fisk, Meharry, Tennessee State, and the Seminary had been filling up the city's jails and tying up downtown—taking the thirty days instead of paying the thirty-dollar fine.

On April 18, the home of Alexander Luby, the students' attorney, was destroyed by a bomb. Furious, Diane Nash and C. T. Vivian led five thousand students to city hall. A beleaguered Mayor Ben West came out to talk to them—he wasn't about to order the police to try and disperse that many.

"The students were mad," said Lewis, "and Diane was a contrast on the city hall steps with her calm, cool manner. And she asked the mayor point blank, 'Do you favor the desegregation of the lunch counters and restaurants?'

"And the mayor looked at the crowd and said, 'Yes, young lady. I favor the integration of the lunch counters and restaurants.'"

He had publicly capitulated, and resistance crumbled. Within two weeks, downtown Nashville was integrated; the first major victory for the student movement.

Still, King was the acknowledged spiritual leader of the 145 students gathered at Shaw University. Many had carried picket signs saying, "Remember the teachings of Gandhi and Martin Luther King." He urged them to continue their nonviolent protests and pledged SCLC funds to help their organization until it was able to stand on its own, even if they chose not to affiliate with SCLC.

King brought the student leaders together to form their own organization: the Student Nonviolent Coordinating Committee. Among them (top row, left to right) are Bernard Lee, Alabama; Dave Forbes, North Carolina; Henry Thomas, Washington; Lonnie King, Georgia; Rev. James Lawson, Tennessee; (second row, left to right) Virginius B. Thornton, Virginia; Rev. Wyatt Tee Walker; Rev. M. L. King, Jr.; Michael Penn, Tennessee; (bottom row, left to right) Clarence Mitchell, Maryland; Marion Barry, Tennessee (HOWARD SOCHUREK/LIFE MAGAZINE).

The "Temporary" was dropped that October, when SNCC was formally organized with headquarters in Atlanta, a compromise that gave the Atlanta student movement control of the headquarters and the Nashville group the chairmanship. SNCC was to organize sit-ins across the country. But its major thrust was to mobilize the grass roots to get involved in the political process, particularly in the Black Belt—the rich cotton lands that had the highest percentage of blacks and the most recalcitrant whites.

They started early. Charles Sherrod, who came out of the Richmond movement, and Cordell Reagan from Nashville moved to Albany, Georgia, to try and organize the black community there. They concentrated, first, on the students at Albany State College, clashing with the NAACP, which felt they were tampering with and radicalizing its youth chapter. There was a fledgling movement there headed by Dr. William Anderson. Anderson's wife, Norma, had grown up across the street from Martin, and referred to his mother as Mama King. Anderson knew Abernathy from Morehouse, and King's right-hand man was his daughter's godfather.

Also that summer, a teacher in the Horace Mann School in New York named Bob Moses came to Atlanta to volunteer to work for SCLC. They didn't really need him at the time, but SNCC, which had a desk in Baker's office, needed someone to travel around Mississippi, Louisiana, and Alabama to see what organizational structures existed and find students who would be willing to attend SNCC's fall conference. Moses went recruiting.

Moses spent most of his time in Mississippi, traveling with an independent-minded black man named Amzie Moore. Moore was head of the Cleveland chapter of the NAACP, and one of the few black leaders left in the Mississippi

Delta. Others, like Gus Courts, Bill Zonie, and George Lee were murdered.

Moses invited Moore to address the students at SNCC's fall meeting: there, Moore invited SNCC to return to Mississippi and help him organize in earnest. Moore wasn't interested in sit-ins, however. He wanted SNCC to run a voter registration program. In Mississippi, that meant talking a lot of poor farmers and sharecroppers into risking economic retaliation, and a lot of SNCC personnel risking beatings and death.

The students agreed, and the Mississippi Project had begun.

In May, King went to trial for tax fraud. He was glad that the state of Alabama had not hurt his reputation for integrity among blacks, but he was still depressed by what he was sure would be his early conviction. His hope, he felt, lay in his appeal.

It began Monday, May 23, and was quickly exposed as a frame-up. On Thursday, defense attorney Robert Ming of Chicago forced the state's star witness, tax agent Lloyd Hale, to admit that there was "no evidence of fraud" and that King, in fact, had overpaid the state, though Alabama had not cashed the check pending the outcome of the trial. It was shown that the state had added to King's income the money spent on expenses for his civil rights activities.

On Saturday, May 28, twelve white men spent less than four hours in the jury deliberating room before surprising everyone with the verdict: not guilty.

A rejuvenated King went back on the hustings, speaking at rallies and demonstrations throughout the South. The campaign for the presidency was in high gear at the time, and Vice President Richard Nixon seemed to be ahead. Daddy King had indicated he would find it difficult to vote for a Catholic, and he liked Nixon.

In Atlanta, Lonnie King and Julian Bond, Morehouse College students and organizers of the student movement in Atlanta, had stepped up the pace. After organizing all summer, they decided to shift their attacks from public places to private ones and started with the biggest, Rich's Department Store.

"At the time," said Bond, "there was a real legal question about whether or not you could force a private business to accept customers if they didn't want to. There was no question about public places."

They wanted King to come with them and be arrested. Wyatt Tee Walker was opposed to it because King had been arrested that spring in DeKalb County for driving without a license. He had forgotten to get a Georgia driver's license, and his Alabama license had expired. He was fined twenty-five dollars in September and placed on a year's probation. An arrest now might be construed as a violation.

King also didn't want to get involved because this was home, and he had avoided any activity that might appear to be wresting the mantle of leadership from the black Atlanta leaders he had grown up with—especially his father.

The sit-in at Rich's was set for Wednesday morning, October 19. King had refused to go, but the night before, Lonnie King called him and said, "You've got to go to jail. You are the spiritual leader of the movement, and you were born in Atlanta, Georgia, and I think it might add tremendous impetus if you would go."

It was an argument King couldn't refuse; he agreed to meet the marchers outside Rich's at ten the following morning. Seventy-five students were sitting in

Martin Luther King, Jr., and student leader Lonnie King went to jail for demonstrating at Rich's Department Store in Atlanta in October 1960. They were released after a settlement was reached (AP/WIDE WORLD).

at lunch counters in several downtown department stores, and King joined Lonnie King at Rich's. Dick Rich, the owner, wept when he saw King with the demonstrators, knowing the national attention and pressure it was bound to bring on his establishment. King refused to pay a five-hundred-dollar bond and vowed to stay in jail "ten years if necessary."

King shared a cell with Bond and Lonnie King, Ben and Amos Brown, and Bernard Lee, whom he had met during the Montgomery bus boycott and who was now studying at Morris Brown College at Atlanta University. Lee had been stationed at the Air Force base there and was one of several blacks who defied military orders and spent their spare time in town helping out with the protest movement.

They were all in high spirits, said Lee, "and it was like a week away from home, a pajama party with the boys behind bars."

They organized regular nonviolent workshops and morning prayer sessions led by King and followed by hymns and movement songs.

That Saturday, October 22, Mayor William Hartsfield announced that on the recommendation of Senator Kennedy, he had worked out an agreement in which the charges against the demonstrators would be dropped, there would be a temporary truce in the sit-ins, and he would lead negotiations with the downtown merchants on integration.

All the demonstrators were released that evening, except King. He was ordered held by Judge Oscar Mitchell, the traffic court judge from neighboring DeKalb County. On Tuesday, October 23, Judge Mitchell said King had violated his probation by getting arrested for the sit-in, and he sentenced him to four months at hard labor in the state prison in Reidsville.

Dr. King was rearrested and sent to the state prison at Reidsville for violating probation on a traffic charge (DON UHRBROCK/ LIFE MAGAZINE).

It shocked everyone. Reidsville was a name whispered among blacks in Georgia. It was not uncommon for blacks to go to Reidsville on minor charges and just disappear. It was Klan country, and the guards were notoriously brutal.

Coretta, who was five months pregnant with their third child, burst into tears, losing her control in public for the first time. So did his sister, Christine. Daddy King asked for a stay pending a real hearing on the case. Judge Mitchell laughed at him and said, "I don't have time. I'm going fishing."

Coretta cried uncontrollably again at the jail, when she and Daddy King went to visit Martin.

"Corrie, dear," said Martin. "You have to be strong. You have to be strong for me." They had to accept the fact that he would probably have to serve hard time in the penitentiary.

Attorney Donald Hollowell went off to prepare an immediate appeal, but DeKalb County didn't wait that long. In the middle of the night, with no notice to the family or Hollowell, DeKalb County sheriff's deputies picked up King from the Fulton County jail in Atlanta and took him in chains to Reidsville, three hundred miles to the south.

As King languished in isolation, word of the treatment was circulating around the world. At the White House, Eisenhower and the man who hoped to succeed him, Nixon, decided to say nothing. The Kennedys were different.

The senator halted his campaign to call Coretta King and express his concern for the treatment and safety of her husband. "If there is anything I can do to help," Kennedy said, "please feel free to call on me."

And there was another phone call: Robert Kennedy called Judge Mitchell to ask why bail wasn't granted in such a minor case. He asked if King didn't have a "constitutional right to bail."

Mitchell suddenly decided King did have such a right and granted it the following day. Hollowell chartered a plane to bring King back home from Reidsville, landing at a suburban airport in DeKalb County. As the car crossed the Fulton County line, King saw more than one hundred of the student demonstrators waiting in the darkness for his return.

He got out and together they sang "We Shall Overcome." Then the triumphal motorcade continued to a packed Thanksgiving prayer service at Ebenezer. Word of the Kennedys' intervention had circulated, and they were receiving credit for Judge Mitchell's change of heart.

King did not make an endorsement of Kennedy, but he did tell reporters, "I am deeply indebted to Senator Kennedy, who served as a great force in making my release possible. For him to be that courageous shows that he is really acting upon principle and not expediency. . . .

"I never intend to reject a man running for President of the United States just because he is a Catholic."

On the pulpit, Daddy King, the Nixon fan, the Baptist minister who had opposed Kennedy largely on religious grounds, went even further. Daddy King said he was impressed with the Kennedys. "John and Robert had acted with moral courage, and stood up to be counted for what they, and all people of good will, knew was right.

"If I had a suitcase full of votes, I'd hand them over to John Kennedy, hoping he could use them in the upcoming election."

This was less than two weeks before a presidential election the pollsters said was too close to call. The Kennedys made the most of it, circulating in black communities two million copies of a leaflet about the episode entitled "No Comment Nixon versus a Candidate with a Heart, Senator Kennedy: The Case of Martin Luther King."

Kennedy won the election by a razor-thin majority of 34,227,096 votes to Nixon's 34,108,546: a margin of 118,550 votes out of more than 68 million cast. Kennedy captured more than 75 percent of the black vote in that election; Eisenhower would later say that "a couple of phone calls" gave Kennedy the White House.

The Atlanta boycotts that triggered this episode, however, ended on a sour note. Hartsfield kept his word in working out a deal with the downtown

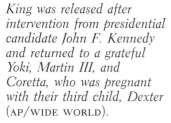

King was released after intervention from presidential candidate John F. Kennedy and returned to a grateful Yoki, Martin III, and Coretta, who was pregnant with their third child, Dexter (AP/WIDE WORLD).

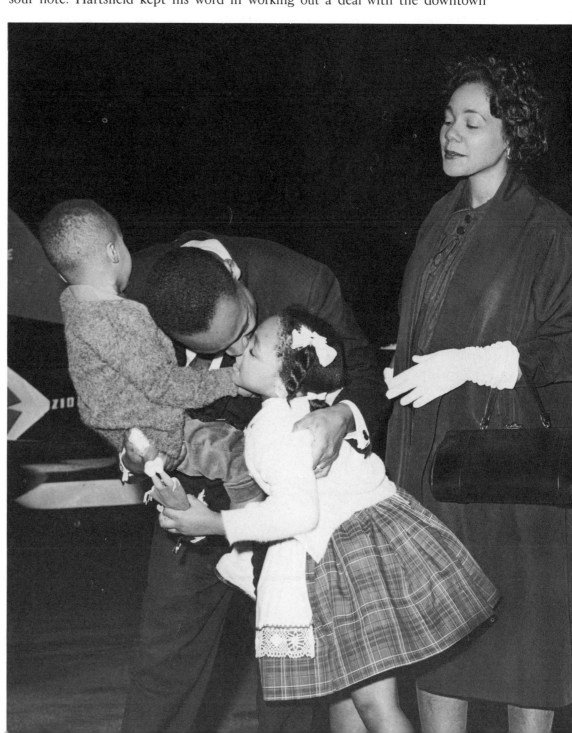

business community, but he made the deal between the downtown whites and the elder statesmen of the black community. This was not meant as a put-down: Daddy King and Rev. William Holmes Borders had been in the forefront of change for decades in Atlanta and had recently concluded a successful effort to desegregate the Atlanta bus system.

The agreement called for an end to the boycott, and downtown would integrate with the new school year, in September 1961. The student leaders were opposed to more delay and considered the deal a sellout. They were browbeaten by their elders, however, who saw nothing wrong with waiting ten months for integration after having already waited a lifetime.

"They did a good job," said Lee, "but they were not as impatient as the students were. We wanted all of our freedom now. We wanted it as of nine o'clock this morning, not tomorrow morning, not even this afternoon. But that was not the reality of the moment.

"The black leaders knew that a transition had to be made. But the students wanted it all right now."

They could not, however, browbeat the students in the Atlanta movement, and they were roundly booed and hissed when they tried to get a mass rally meeting in the Warren Memorial Church to agree to call off the demonstrations. The two thousand students at the meeting had read of the deal in the afternoon Atlanta *Journal*, which emphasized the fact that segregation would remain for nearly a year.

Lonnie King said later that only Martin was able to calm the crowd. "His daddy got up to make a speech and said that he had been working in this town for thirty years, and somebody jumped up and said, 'That's what's wrong.'

"It crushed that man."

Martin took the floor and, at times in tears, preached to the young protes tors about the need for unity, the need for togetherness, the need to avoid the "cancerous disease of disunity." He spoke of the need to respect the contributions the elders had made in bringing the movement this far; in building a bridge —of whatever construction—to carry this new generation of freedom fighters forward. He spoke of their need to cross that bridge without rancor and continue the struggle in their own way.

It was a painful experience for all: the students, who were disillusioned with the elders they had grown up under; the elders, who realized they had not passed on the torch of leadership but dropped it, and the students had picked it up and gone; and Martin Luther King, Jr., who was the only one with the power to gracefully preside over the fall of his father and his generation.

SCLC was also changing in 1960. In July, Rev. Wyatt Tee Walker took over from Ella Baker as director of the struggling organization, whose staff, at that point, consisted primarily of Baker and a secretary. Despite her organizational skills, SCLC was run by old-line Southern chauvinists, who never seriously considered a woman as executive director. Then, too, her constant clashes with King over the direction of the organization estranged her from the group.

Yet she accomplished what she set out to do—keep SCLC going—and got what she wanted. SCLC didn't change, but it didn't have to. It had its niche, once it got going. Now there was SNCC, which she constantly encouraged to go its own way and not be held back by the older generation in SCLC.

SCLC had grown under its new director, Rev. Wyatt Tee Walker. There were regular staff meetings . . . (ROLAND MITCHELL)

She had created the Young Turks, who viewed SCLC as too slow—as SCLC viewed the NAACP—and would go out and organize. The NAACP was always there to provide legal help and pursue its cases through the courts. SCLC, when it got going, could mobilize the growing numbers of organized blacks and put those energies to use in reshaping American policies. The three tiers—organization, mobilization, and litigation—were in place, and it was time for Ella Baker to move on.

Walker was a lanky, mustachioed six-footer who had spent the preceding eight years leading integration efforts in Petersburg, Virginia. He was blunt and cocky, in many ways the antithesis of the ministers who had sought harmony in SCLC operations. He said he was a "nuts-and-bolts man" and would, in time, refer to himself on occasion as King's "chief of staff" or "attorney general."

The first thing he did was lay down rules. During his first interview for the post, with King, Levison, and Rustin, he was adamant: King spoke freely, everyone else was to contact the executive director before saying anything to the media.

"We had had this problem," Walker said, "with Bayard saying one thing up in New York and the people in Atlanta not knowing anything about it. I did not want two voices speaking."

He wanted their backing as he attempted to "take advantage of King's high profile and translate it into an organizational image. It was not King's fault," he said, "that the press always called his name instead of his organization.

"Until SCLC took on some sinew and bone, nobody could notice it."

He had another meeting in Atlanta with King, Abernathy, and Shuttlesworth before taking the job, and found he had to begin almost at the beginning.

. . . and there was
occasionally time to relax
(SCLC).

SCLC had a fifty-seven-thousand-dollar budget and a staff of five, including Walker and the two people he brought with him, Jim Wood and Dorothy Cotton.

SCLC, said Walker, had never really gotten past the theory stage. "When I got there, SCLC was, for the most part, an idea in Dr. King's briefcase. It had just never developed. They needed a hard-nose, a nuts-and-bolts man."

Walker ruffled a lot of feathers in the process—many in SNCC wouldn't talk to him—but in four years SCLC had a budget of over a million dollars and a staff of one hundred across the South. In that time, it developed an economic arm called Operation Breadbasket, headed by Abernathy in Atlanta, and a Voter Education Project, on which a young man named Andrew Young came to work in 1961 and was soon moved up to executive vice president.

Walker had Levison set up a fund-raising office in New York, which used a direct-mail solicitation effort to help keep the funds rolling in consistently. And he marketed Martin Luther King, Jr.

"Martin would go to Houston, do a speech, and come back with eleven hundred dollars," Walker stated. "That was a waste."

He developed a twenty-one-page brochure, "How to Promote a Visit from Martin Luther King, Jr.," for use by local groups seeking a visit by the leader of SCLC. Walker or one of his staff would go to the city up to eight weeks before King's scheduled appearance and talk to the ministers and organizers about the visit. The black churches would begin *then* taking up collections for SCLC's efforts and continue through the day of King's appearance. Walker's staff provided sample press releases and explained the need for timed media exposure. As it developed, King's trips became highly choreographed, serving several disparate groups at each stop.

"By the time he finished speaking," said Walker, "I'd be back on the platform with a slip saying how much we had raised. Most of our money in those first two years came from black church groups, and we raised five hundred thousand dollars across the South."

He built a lean organization, which, by the end of 1961, would be ready to act. That was what King wanted. He had a heavy schedule of speaking engagements throughout most of the year and was trying to write a book of sermons, to be called *Strength to Love*, explaining the nonviolent philosophy and its applicability to the American experience.

But he wanted to do more than speak and write. He wanted to get back into the thick of the action, and that seemed to loom closer as SCLC under Walker began taking shape.

The coming year, with the end of the Eisenhower era and the advent of the Kennedys, the momentum of the student movement, and the reinvigoration of SCLC, was one to look forward to.

The period of reflection after Montgomery was drawing to a close.

6
THE SCENT OF VICTORY
The Sting of Defeat

1961 STARTED OFF PLEASANTLY ENOUGH—CORETTA GAVE birth to another healthy boy, Dexter.

And there was a new administration in Washington that showed promise.

"We liked the Kennedys," said Abernathy. "The President had the ability to articulate the longings, hopes, and dreams and aspirations of oppressed people. He talked about one fifth of our population who are isolated on a lonely island in the midst of our ocean of plenty—and that sounded good to us."

That love affair didn't last long, however. King began putting pressure on the Kennedy administration to abolish segregation through an executive order similar to Lincoln's Emancipation Proclamation and Truman's directive desegregating the military. He called for the President to push for a strong civil rights bill. "The intolerably slow pace of civil rights," he said, "is due at least as much to the limits which the federal government has imposed on its own actions as it is to the actions of the segregationist opposition."

The movement entered a new phase in May. James Farmer's CORE had pretty much disappeared over the years, but the new sit-ins revived its image and membership. Now Farmer decided on a bold new move. He was going to challenge the Southern intimidation that made interstate travel for blacks a nightmare. He sent out a call for black student volunteers to come to Washington and participate in a Freedom Ride from Washington through Virginia, North and South Carolina, Georgia, Alabama, Mississippi, and Louisiana.

The U.S. Supreme Court had outlawed segregation on interstate transportation in 1946 and in interstate bus and train terminals in 1960, but this was ignored below the Mason-Dixon Line.

Farmer had called King to explain his plans and solicit his support. King agreed to have SCLC pay for the tickets taking the students through Georgia and Alabama and had the SCLC chapters in Birmingham and Montgomery standing by to give any assistance needed.

He decided not to accompany them because he felt it was CORE's move and they should get all the credit.

On May 3, Lewis, Farmer, and eleven other Freedom Riders gathered in a Chinese restaurant in the capital for dinner. Farmer told them to eat hearty, because "this may be similar to the Last Supper."

In a way, it was. They were to quietly launch an assault on the Old South the day before Alan Shepard, Jr., was to be launched from Cape Canaveral into the new frontier of space.

The following morning, seven blacks and six whites split into two groups, boarded a Greyhound and a Trailways bus, and headed south.

Lewis, the leader of the Nashville group, was a quiet, sensitive man who had always wanted to be a preacher. He grew up on a chicken farm and had a special cemetery where he buried the dead chickens. He didn't just put them in a hole in the ground: he gathered his younger brothers and sisters around and held a full-fledged funeral service, praying over the departed bird. Throughout the civil rights period, no one recalls him ever raising his voice.

He got off the bus at Rock Hill, South Carolina, and headed toward the whites only rest room. He didn't get far. One white man punched him in the mouth and knocked him to the floor. Others began pummeling him and kicking him. He was saved by his seatmate, Albert Bigelow, a tall, white, ex-Navy man who stepped between the whites and Lewis. They finally succeeded in beating him to the ground, too, before the police decided to break up the activity.

The two men returned to the bus without pressing charges and continued on their way. Lewis left the ride after that to fly to Philadelphia and take care of some personal business, and Farmer had to leave from Atlanta after learning that his father had died in Freedman's Hospital in Washington.

(BRUCE DAVIDSON/MAGNUM).

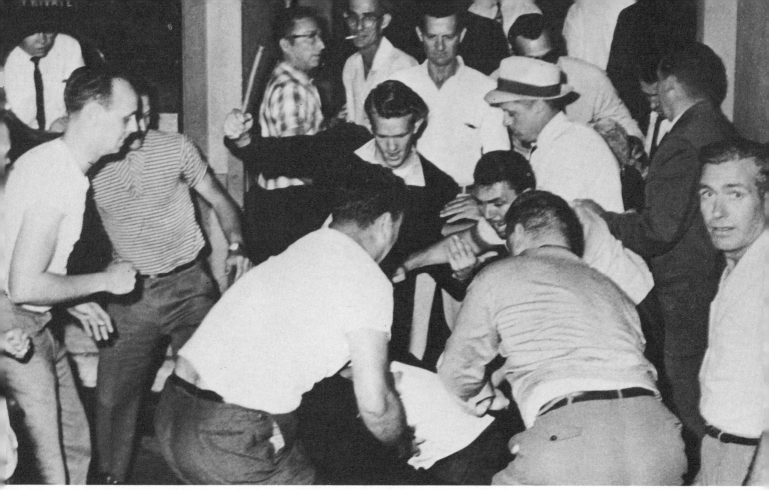

The remaining riders went to Alabama—and trouble. The Klan was waiting for them in Anniston. The tires were shot out from under one bus, and it was forced to stop.

Screaming Klansmen with sticks, brass knuckles, and lead pipes surrounded the bus, set it afire, and, at first, refused to let the Freedom Riders out.

Floyd Mann, then the Alabama public safety director, and Governor Patterson take credit for saving the riders' lives at that time.

According to Mann, officials knew there would be "serious trouble" in Anniston, and "we sent a state investigator named E. L. Cowling to board the bus in Atlanta. When the bus pulled into Anniston, they would not let the people off the bus after setting it on fire. Our man had to pull his gun and badge to get those people off the bus, or they would all have burned."

When they did get off the burning bus, however, they were beaten senseless. They were transported to a hospital in Anniston, which treated a white Rider, Genevieve Hughes, who had a split lip. They refused to treat the remainder.

Meanwhile, a huge mob had gathered in front of the hospital and was demanding the Freedom Riders. The hospital ordered them to leave, but they refused without police protection. There was none.

Then they heard an announcement on the radio that Reverend Shuttlesworth said he was going to Anniston "to get my people." Sure enough, the nonviolent minister led a fifteen-car caravan—with shotguns sticking out of the windows—through the Klansmen, rescued the beaten riders, and took them to his home in Birmingham.

It was open season on Freedom Riders in Birmingham, Alabama, on Mother's Day, 1961. Police Commissioner Bull Connor had given his policemen fifteen minutes off to "visit their mothers"—leaving the students to the Klan. The students, said the governor, were picking fights (THE BIRMINGHAM NEWS).

The second bus made it to Birmingham that Mother's Day: there was a bigger reception waiting for them. No plainclothes police were on this bus.

As far as Governor Patterson was concerned, the protection of the Freedom Riders was not a moral issue. "When the bus got to Birmingham," said Patterson, "it became a matter of law enforcement for the city of Birmingham. And Mr. [Bull] Connor had his own ways of dealing with it.

"And as long as he wanted to do it himself, we were content to let Birmingham handle its own affairs."

Police Commissioner Eugene "Bull" Connor did have a way of handling it. He watched from the window of his office in city hall as Klansmen and sympathizers gathered with clubs and other weapons around the Birmingham Trailways station. He watched as the city policemen disappeared—he had given them unwritten permission to "visit their mothers" for fifteen minutes since it was, after all, Mother's Day.

For fifteen minutes, there would be no one to greet the Freedom Riders to Birmingham but the KKK. The Freedom Riders were beaten to a pulp. James Peck needed fifty stitches to close the wound on his head, which had been split with an iron pipe.

Freedom Rider James Peck survived a clubbing with a lead pipe (THE BIRMINGHAM NEWS).

These, too, were taken to Shuttlesworth's home, though one rider, Hank Thomas, was flown to a hospital in New Orleans.

As far as the governor was concerned, the Freedom Riders got what they deserved. "They were not really bona fide interstate passengers traveling through Alabama," he said defensively. "These passengers would buy tickets from town to town. They came to create disturbances.

"They would get off the bus and they'd go to the nearest place where they figured they could start a fight. You can walk into anyplace in the world and you start bumping up against somebody in a lunch counter and you're gonna start a fight. This is what they were doing and they were doing it deliberately to bring attention to themselves."

He said he didn't blame them for trying, however.

With this rationale, the chief executive of the state of Alabama saw no reason to afford these troublesome passengers any special form of protection. They were causing trouble, as opposed to receiving it.

Lewis had flown to Birmingham to rejoin the Freedom Riders for the rest of their trip, but it was too late. Farmer said that CORE had proved its point and he was calling off the Freedom Rides before anyone else was hurt. Besides, the bus companies refused to carry the riders through to Montgomery.

It didn't end there. Lewis flew back to Nashville for an emergency meeting at the First Baptist Church with the leaders of the Nashville group. In Washington, Bobby Kennedy had said there should be a cooling-off period, and the Freedom Rides should stop for now. Many whites suggested that cooler heads would prevail if the waters were allowed to settle.

The SNCC chapter in Nashville wouldn't hear of it. Diane Nash was insistent that violence could not be allowed to triumph over nonviolence, and they had an obligation to continue the rides—with or without CORE.

James Farmer, Walker (standing), Abernathy, King, and John Lewis announced that the Freedom Rides would continue and called for federal protection from the lawlessness in Alabama (BRUCE DAVIDSON/MAGNUM).

The students prayed before continuing on into Mississippi (PAUL SCHUTZER/LIFE MAGAZINE).

The decision wasn't made immediately. Said Vivian, "We broke for a half hour to let the students think about it. There were students who broke down and cried thinking that they had to go to Mississippi. You didn't talk that easily about going to Mississippi to do anything. Everybody knew we could be killed. If buses were burned and people were beaten in Alabama, think what could happen in Mississippi."

Their final decision, however, was that "more people were dying and being destroyed through a passive acquiescence of violence than would ever be destroyed as a result of nonviolence."

Nash called Shuttlesworth to inform him of the new group of riders; he was shocked. "Do you know what you're doing?" he asked her. "Don't you know that you can get killed? Birmingham is a hell of a place, and these people mean business." Lewis and nine other students returned to Birmingham on May 17, but were stopped outside city limits by Bull Connor, who commandeered the bus and took them to jail.

At four in the morning, Bull Connor had the group placed in two station wagons, and he and other policemen drove them to the Alabama-Tennessee state line and left them. An elderly black couple let them call Nashville, and Nash sent a car to take them back to Birmingham. She also told Lewis that eleven others had gone to Birmingham to join the ride.

Shuttlesworth escorted all of them to the Greyhound bus station Friday evening, but they couldn't get a driver to take them further.

"I have only one life to give," the driver said, "and I'm not giving it to CORE or the NAACP."

Bobby Kennedy got on the telephone with Alabama state officials and bus company executives, finally insisting that either they get a driver to take the riders to Montgomery or he would fly in black drivers from Washington, D.C. He had also dispatched John Seigenthaler, a presidential assistant, to confer with Alabama officials.

That didn't work out. Patterson was furious at Robert Kennedy for what he perceived to be meddling. "There's nobody in the whole country that's got the spine to stand up to that nigger except me," he ranted to Seigenthaler.

The buses moved Saturday morning, with a police escort, a state trooper stationed every fifteen miles along the highway, and a plane flying overhead to make sure there were no ambushes planned.

But outside of Montgomery, there was nothing in sight. Governor Patterson had a hands-off policy with regard to the state capital, too, because the Montgomery police department assured him that all was well. Still, he ordered Floyd Mann to take an officer and "keep an eye on it."

What they saw was no Montgomery policemen and a lot of armed Klansmen waiting at the bus station.

"We stepped from the bus," said Lewis, "and hundreds of people came running towards the bus with every conceivable weapon: chains, baseball bats, whips. They started beating the media people first, then they turned on us."

There were four women in the group, two white and two black. They saw a black taxi nearby and ran after it. The cabbie allowed the black women inside but would not defy state law and permit the white women to go as well. They therefore had to run for it. The crowd chased them and would have caught them but for a sacrificial lamb: John Seigenthaler, who had come to Montgomery without informing Patterson.

Seigenthaler walked between the crowd and the two white women, giving them a chance to get away. The crowd left him unconscious, with a concussion, in the middle of the street.

"They caught most of us in the middle of the street," said Lewis, "and just beat us. I was hit in the head with a wooden soda bottle crate and left lying there. Floyd Mann saved the day. After the beating went on for a while—especially when it looked like they were beating William Barbee to death—Mann fired a shot and said, 'There will be no killing here today.' And that dispersed the mob."

They were left lying there in the street; as they came to, the Alabama attorney general handed them injunctions prohibiting interracial groups from using public transportation in Alabama.

King was livid when he heard the news and watched the carnage on television. He and Abernathy had been in Chicago and said they were flying immediately to Montgomery. Robert Kennedy called from Washington to ask him not to go because there was no way to guarantee their safety. But King insisted, for they were to address the students and a mass rally the following night, May 21, in Abernathy's First Baptist Church.

The battered Riders were cheered by the news of King's coming. "He brought a certain amount of protection, a certain amount of attention and visibility to the Freedom Ride," explained Lewis. "That was the first time he had identified with us, and we were very happy with it."

Kennedy began burning up the telephone lines to Patterson, telling him off about the lawlessness in the Alabama state capital. Patterson said it wasn't what it seemed, and the President should send an observer.

Kennedy told him he had already sent one, and Seigenthaler had been left lying in the middle of the street with his head split open by the cream of the Confederacy. What kind of law and order was that?

Patterson, proud and temperamental, the man who had delivered votes to the elder brother, John F. Kennedy, wasn't ready to take that from the younger brother, even if he was the Attorney General of the United States. "He was hard-headed, unreasonable, opinionated, and arrogant," ranted Patterson. "He was not like his brother at all. I don't believe Robert ever read the Constitution of the United States."

Patterson wanted Kennedy to put the blame on the Freedom Riders. "All you have to do," he insisted to Kennedy, "is publicly say people ought to obey the law, and take your grievances to the courts. If you do that and tell everybody to go home and behave themselves, this thing would be over."

But Kennedy wouldn't budge from his position that the blacks had a right to travel and it was Alabama that was recalcitrant. Patterson insisted that he had the manpower to keep everything under control, but Kennedy didn't believe him, and dispatched five hundred federal marshals to Montgomery.

At that point, the Cradle of the Confederacy was simmering. The Klan came to town en masse. George Rockwell brought his Nazis. "It seemed like every nut in the United States was coming here," said the governor.

Patterson activated the National Guard and brought them to the city limits for use if needed, then waited to see what the federal marshals could do.

The marshals escorted King and Abernathy to the church, passing through a screaming mob of whites that stretched for three blocks around. They got angrier as time passed and burned the car of a white woman journalist who tried to go to the church.

Shuttlesworth drove to town with James Farmer of CORE and parked outside the range of the mob. Shuttlesworth was a legend in the civil rights movement for his absence of fear. Ever since the Christmas bombing of his home in 1957, he had assumed God would protect him and anyone with him. So he grabbed Farmer and walked through the Klansmen, telling them to get out of his way so he could go to church. They parted like the Red Sea.

Inside, an emotional King said, "The ultimate responsibility for this hideous action in Alabama must be placed at the doorstep of the governor of the state.

"We heard the familiar cry that morals cannot be legislated. This may be true, but behavior can be regulated. The law may not be able to make a man love me, but it can keep him from lynching me."

That is what the ten thousand whites outside wanted to do. They began to storm the church, easily overrunning the marshals. King called Kennedy and said they needed protection, that the whites were about to invade the church.

Kennedy got on the phone immediately with Patterson and there ensued a heated conversation in which the two officials cursed each other out.

Patterson declared martial law and had the national guard move in and protect the church. That meant dispersing the rioters with hand-to-hand fighting —all to protect a group of blacks.

Patterson told Kennedy that it wasn't their fault: there was no way the Guard could protect one man, namely Martin Luther King, Jr.

Kennedy, equally livid, demanded that Patterson put Major General Henry Graham, head of the National Guard units, on the telephone. "I want to hear a general of the U.S. Army say he can't protect Martin Luther King, Jr."

Patterson backed down, bitterly. "This was uncalled for," he said. "Here were people getting off the bus and going down the streets looking for fights. Now how can you protect people from being injured who are doing that? You could not assign bodyguards to travel with these people when they were engaged in trying to violate the law.

"I was sore about it. I finally told Kennedy to quit calling me."

The riot wasn't over until the wee hours of the morning, and the people attending the meeting had to each be escorted to their homes.

Robert Kennedy then tried to get King to call off the Freedom Rides, something he didn't have the authority to do. Kennedy complained that the rides and the violence were embarrassing the President, who was then holding summit talks with Nikita Khrushchev.

"Doesn't he know we've been embarrassed all our lives?" retorted Abernathy. Farmer sniffed at the idea of a cooling-off period, saying, "We've been cooling off for one hundred years. If we got any cooler we'd be in the deep freeze."

King asserted, "This is no time to engage in the luxury of cooling off or to take the tranquilizing drug of gradualism. Now is the time to make real the promises of democracy."

Besides, the students had no intention of stopping. They announced Monday that they were going on to Mississippi, and they were disappointed to learn that King would not be going with them. King said he couldn't go because he was under probation in Georgia, and if he went with them his probation would be revoked.

Many of the SNCC people didn't believe him: they thought he was just scared. Farmer didn't want to go either, but since it was all his idea in the first place, he couldn't refuse a direct request from the students to go with them to Mississippi.

The Freedom Riders went on to Jackson under a National Guard escort, where they were thrown into jail for forty days. During the summer, hundreds of black and white students followed their example: more than four hundred would be arrested throughout the South.

King spent his time furiously raising funds for bail and legal fees for the students and explaining time and again why these students were willing "to fill the jails as if they were honors classes."

In Mississippi, Bob Moses and SNCC associates were expanding their organizational base. They now had representatives in Jackson, Macomb, Cleveland, and Liberty, all coordinated by Moses.

The buses were integrated— with white federal troops escorting the Freedom Riders into Mississippi (BRUCE DAVIDSON/MAGNUM).

In Mississippi, Bob Moses began organizing a massive voter rights effort; slowly recruiting volunteers, getting beaten, and recruiting some more. Some of them were murdered (HENRY KIRKSEY/ BOB MOSES).

SNCC was a patient organization. Its field-workers were driven around by well-known locals, like Amzie Moore, and they would sit and talk to farm workers about voter registration. They didn't interrupt workers. They didn't preach to them, either.

If the worker was shucking corn, they sat down and shucked with them. If they were cutting watermelon, the SNCC staffers would do likewise. There was no rush. In time, the conversation would get around to what the young feller was doing there, and the right to vote would be discussed.

Moses's group began holding classes in voter registration, showing interested blacks what a registration form looked like and how to fill one out. Whites didn't like that, and there were economic reprisals against farmers who were known to have attended these meetings.

Moses was staying with E. W. Steptoe in Amite County that summer, a county that had had a strong NAACP chapter until the sheriff got hold of the NAACP membership list. Moses led his first voter registration effort in Liberty, the county seat, and was beaten up by the cousin of a state legislator.

"I was practicing nonviolence at the time," said Moses, "and just went into a crouch to protect my head as best as I could. But he opened it up with a knife handle, and I had to have eight stitches."

John Handy was staying in Walthall County, and at his first registration effort the county registrar pistol-whipped him out of the building. There were no mass marches in those days. "The people were kind of paralyzed," explained Moses. "But we did get a few who would try to register, fail, and we'd get them to try again."

At first, there was no violence directed at the "locals": whites seemed to think they could scare the outsiders into going back where they came from. But that didn't work.

So they shot Herbert Lee. Lee was a farmer who had lived near Steptoe, known him for years, and began attending the voter registration classes Moses was conducting. The white state senator, a cousin of the man who beat up Moses and a neighbor of Steptoe's, shot Lee dead in front of a cotton gin.

It happened in the middle of the morning, right out in the open. The state senator said it was self-defense, that Lee attacked him with a tire iron. Moses knew better and began scouring the landscape for someone who knew something else.

He found a witness, a black man named Lewis Allen. "Allen wasn't involved in the voter education movement at all," said Moses. "He lived nearby and minded his own business. He was not looking for trouble."

He told Moses that he had been at the cotton gin, and the state senator shot and killed an unarmed man. He said he told the grand jury that Lee had been armed with a tire iron because whites had threatened his life. Moses, seeking justice, told the head of the local FBI office and asked him to quietly investigate.

"Allen suffered for that," said Moses. The FBI told the local police about the black lumberjack who was changing his story, and "the sheriff picked Lewis Allen up, took him to jail, and he got beaten something terrible."

Allen didn't get involved with SNCC after that episode, either. "He thought he could just live his life and the whites would leave him alone. He was wrong."

Nacirema was busy too. They had had practice: they were suspected of participating in some of the fifty unsolved bombings in the area of Birmingham that became known as Dynamite Hill. Now they had a more ambitious target. They would teach these student agitators a lesson.

They had stolen a vanload of dynamite from Virginia, said Captain Little, "and they had somehow obtained a map of the sewer system under the Atlanta University area. They planned to go in and place large dynamite charges in various places and blow the whole complex up.

"They were going to place not just sticks of dynamite, but cases of dynamite and set them off in a series."

The detectives would have preferred to catch the group in the act, but that was too risky. There were simply too many people who could have been killed if their timing was off. So they used another tactic.

"We had them under continuous surveillance," said Little. "Whenever they would show up, we'd show up. They eventually called it off."

In September, the Interstate Commerce Commission issued an order, effective November 1, 1961, outlawing segregation in interstate bus facilities.

King thought the Freedom Rides were a resounding success, but they also provided him with a valuable lesson. The pressures brought on the ICC, the Kennedy administration, and Governor Patterson were the result of intensive media exposure of the violence, lawlessness, and brutality of Southern resistance. It became clear to King that confrontation was necessary to produce results—and it had to be witnessed.

The Freedom Rides also showed him that time was passing him by. The students had taken the initiative, fought the battles, and won the victory. Yes, he was out front. That wouldn't last forever, though, if nothing else changed. And he relished leading a movement rather than just interpreting someone else's.

Wyatt Tee Walker had brought SCLC to the point where it had the making of a strong, regional organization. Abernathy had left the First Baptist Church in Montgomery and taken the helm of the West Hunter Street Baptist Church in Atlanta, a post that allowed him to resume his place as King's right hand and alter ego.

It was time for SCLC to make its move.

Being overeager usually leads to mistakes, however, and Albany, Georgia, was no exception.

There was a movement in Albany waiting to be led. Albany was an agricultural town of some fifty-six thousand, nearly half of them blacks, whose commerce centered around corn, pecans, and peanuts. Before the Civil War, it had been the slave-trading center for the cotton plantations in southwestern Georgia and southeastern Alabama.

Albany had a five-man FBI office, and four of its members were Northerners. What counted, however, was the fifth agent—Marion Cheeks, who was the dominant agent in the field office. Cheeks was described by Arthur Murtagh, an agent in the Atlanta regional office, as "a nice guy but a racist. He had very strong feelings and he made them known to everybody around him."

That included giving instructions to the four subordinate agents that they disregard the complaints local blacks made about police misconduct whenever they investigated civil rights cases. Cheeks also had the responsibility of forwarding all investigative reports to the FBI headquarters in Washington, and he deleted or seriously watered down anything that reflected poorly on the way the local law enforcement agencies handled civil rights. The result was that the Justice Department's weak and young Civil Rights Division always had a skewed view of the situation in that part of the world when making decisions as to where to investigate.

Albany also had something almost nonexistent in the South—a police chief named Laurie Pritchett. There were other police chiefs, and the name wasn't that unusual. But Pritchett believed in honor. Pritchett believed in kindness and decency. Pritchett believed in keeping his word. And Pritchett believed in law and order for all.

It was here that SNCC had sent its first workers—Charles Sherrod and later Cordell Reagan and Charles Jones—to organize. SNCC had made the rounds of Albany, educating the black community about the need for voting and launching a series of voter education and registration drives. SNCC field-workers always earned the respect in Black Belt communities because of their casual dress and seeming fearlessness of the potentially dangerous power structure. Moreover,

Albany, Georgia, Police Chief Laurie Pritchett (left) was a gentleman. He bowed his head as seventy protesting clergymen prayed—and then politely arrested them. The absence of violent confrontation made it difficult for SCLC to sustain the Albany Movement (AP/WIDE WORLD).

they didn't just encourage people to vote, they were in the front of the march, between the residents and the police.

There was an active NAACP chapter in Albany, though demonstrating was not part of its style, and Sherrod had no difficulty converting the entire chapter to be supporters of SNCC. There were also several civic groups that had formed around one issue or another.

In early 1961, Dr. William G. Anderson, an osteopath, called a meeting of the leaders of several of the disparate groups and persuaded them to form a loose coalition called, simply, the Albany Movement.

The Albany Movement got under way in September, when Freedom Riders led by Farmer were arrested at the Albany train station. That sparked a number of mass demonstrations by students organized by Sherrod at the all-black Albany State College. Anderson lead a mass protest of the coalition the following day to protest the arrest of the students, and there was a series of arrests by a polite but firm police department.

"There were twelve hundred arrested in the first week," said Anderson. "That was the time when the Albany Movement was well organized and we were holding rallies every night, filling two or three churches every night."

But there were two problems: they couldn't fill the jails, and there was no major media attention. Without that external pressure, white intransigence seemed destined to break the movement.

(DANNY LYON/MAGNUM).

"That's why I invited King to come in," said Anderson. "He had the expertise. He had the recognition."

He also invited the NAACP, but they refused because they had not been consulted before the marches began. SNCC was already there and was furious that the more renowned group, which it referred to as SLICK, was coming in to steal the spotlight.

Anderson called King on December 14 and asked him to come and address a mass rally of the foundering Albany Movement. It was an invitation King couldn't refuse. Anderson was family. He and King had organized the youth chapter of the NAACP on the Morehouse campus in 1948. He was in undergraduate school with Abernathy at Alabama State and became godfather to the Andersons' first child, Laurita. His wife, Norma, grew up across the street from the young Mike King, and they considered each other cousins.

Anderson wanted King to come to Albany as soon as possible. Pritchett's police were ignoring the ICC order and arresting Freedom Riders at the train and bus stations even after they were "officially" desegregated on November 1.

King didn't have any background on Albany's problems, and he didn't want to get involved with their ongoing fight. He did agree to speak for one night. He was in New Orleans when the call came, and he agreed to fly to Albany with Walker and Abernathy the next day and then return to Atlanta. It became a long one-night stand.

Anderson picked them up at the airport. They spoke of home and old times, and then Anderson told them about the new time, the hard times, the struggle that seemed to be failing. He told them about the mass rallies, the continuous demonstrations that did not seem to move the city council at all. He told about the jail overcrowding: at one point fifty-four young women were crammed into a stone cell built to hold only six.

He took them to the Shiloh Baptist Church, the main gathering place for the demonstrators, and King and Abernathy received a thunderous ovation when they walked into the nave. The residents in what W. E. B. Du Bois had called the "cornerstone of the Cotton Kingdom" were chanting "Freedom!" and "Hallelujah!" at the sight of the living monuments from the movement in Montgomery.

Abernathy did not have King's gift for oratory, but he was renowned for his uncanny ability to read the mood of a room and rouse an audience to fever pitch. He had the throng on its feet when King took over, and King had them weeping and swaying and pledging allegiance to nonviolence and a willingness to suffer for the cause of freedom.

When there was a pause after singing all the verses of "We Shall Overcome," Dr. Anderson stood up and said, "Be back in the morning at nine o'clock and bring your marching shoes, and Dr. King is going to march with us."

Then, turning to his guest, "You will lead us, won't you, Dr. King?"

How does one who is a symbol of a movement say no at a time like that? King couldn't refuse, and SCLC was thus committed to its first crusade.

That didn't frighten Laurie Pritchett at all. To Pritchett, King was no bogeyman, no evil person bent on tearing down the cherished "Southern way of life." To Pritchett, King was no miracle worker with a pipeline to power.

No. To Pritchett, King was a very good tactician who could be defeated by another tactician. Pritchett considered himself a very good tactician indeed.

He took the time to do something no other Southern policeman had bothered to do—he studied King and his movements and his speeches. He saw that King often quoted Gandhi, so he studied Gandhi and his philosophy and his major campaigns as well. He knew about the Great Salt March, which broke the back of British colonialism in India, and he knew it wasn't the salt that killed colonialism, but the brutal response by the British authorities and the Indians' willingness to overflow the jails.

He knew of the power of the national press, and how it had bowled over Governor Patterson a few months before. He decided he knew how to beat Reverend King at his own game.

He would keep the jails open, "and at no time would any [demonstrators] be housed in our facilities in Albany or Dougherty County."

He drew circles around the city—ten miles, twenty miles, thirty miles . . . up to one hundred miles from downtown Albany—and located the jail facilities in each of these spheres. Then he commandeered a fleet of buses, and after demonstrators were booked, they were bused to the farthest available jail.

"We sent personnel along to see that they were not mistreated," Pritchett added. "We stayed with them in the jails to see that nobody in the other counties mistreated or mishandled them." That didn't mean there was never any abuse. Nor did it mean that prison conditions weren't, in general, deplorable. But going to jail under Pritchett's Law was nothing like going to jail anywhere else.

He would do his best to see that nothing happened to King and his associates. He placed a police car at King's disposal, to chauffeur him from meeting to meeting for his protection. He stationed guards at rallies and around the clock at the headquarters hotel. Some whites protested this "waste" of public money. Pritchett successfully argued that Albany could never withstand the pressure if King were assassinated there.

That was Pritchett's other plan, gleaned from his study of Gandhi and King. He would fight nonviolent action with nonviolent police work.

He earned a reputation for decency. At one point, in the midst of a month of steady protests, a meeting in Pritchett's office was interrupted by the arrival of a telegram, which seemed to upset the police chief. King asked about it, and was informed it was from Mrs. Pritchett, wishing her husband a happy anniversary.

King then found out that Pritchett had not been home for three weeks and was about to miss his twelfth wedding anniversary. King said, "Well, Chief Pritchett, you go home tonight. No, right now. You celebrate your anniversary.

"I give you my word that nothing will happen in Albany, Georgia, till tomorrow and you can go take your wife out to dinner. Tomorrow, at ten o'clock, we'll resume our efforts."

So Pritchett went home and celebrated, and the next morning the struggle resumed.

All that was still to come, however, and King didn't know about Pritchett's tactics as he prepared to march with the Albany Movement, a movement that he was roped into leading. Anderson had given the city until noon, December 16, to open formal negotiations, or the Albany Movement would increase its demonstrations.

King accompanied Anderson to city hall, but officials refused to talk. They returned to Shiloh, where King told the waiting crowd, "Hundreds of our brothers and sisters, sons and daughters, are in jail.

"We will not rest until they are released. I can't afford to stand idly by while hundreds of Negroes are being falsely arrested simply because they want to be free."

He then led 237 blacks from the church toward downtown, where they had their first confrontation with Chief Pritchett.

The police were waiting for the marchers with a line of paddy wagons. Pritchett asked the marchers to disperse or be arrested. King, Abernathy, and Anderson instead led the group in prayer. Pritchett, a Catholic, politely bowed his head until they were finished and then had them all carefully arrested on charges of parading without a permit, disturbing the peace, and obstructing the sidewalk.

King said that if convicted, he would not pay the fine. "I expect to spend Christmas in jail, and I hope thousands will join me."

That wasn't to be, for there was more than official intransigence to deal with. There was jealousy and factionalism among the black groups.

"They clashed over everything," said James Bevel, whom Walker brought to Albany to try and work things out with SNCC. "They clashed over who would be in a news conference. They clashed over who would sign off on the latest statement. They clashed over who would be on the front page."

Too much energy, said Bevel, was spent trying to get people to align themselves with one group or another, rather than getting them to work together for a common purpose.

In addition, there was the generation gap. Said Abernathy, "SNCC was a little more militant than we, an organization headed by Christian ministers. SNCC had its own leaders, and they were trying to project their leaders and get credit for achievements."

The infighting went public. SCLC would call mass meetings, and SNCC would call counter mass meetings at another location.

During his first arrest, King thought he heard good news from the outside. The city had met with an interracial group and had agreed to desegregate the bus and train terminals immediately and to seriously negotiate the rest of the black community's grievances beginning January 23, when a new city administration took office. The city promised to drop all charges against those arrested for demonstrating and would allow the more than four hundred then in jail to go free on their own recognizance, rather than pay a cash bail. In return, the demonstrations were to stop and the invitations to students and clergymen from all over the country to come and fill the Albany jails for Christmas were canceled.

King thought this was a quick victory and allowed bail to be paid. He and Abernathy got out of jail. Then they discovered the truth. They had gotten nothing. The "settlement" was a nonbinding verbal agreement—quickly reneged on—that was worked out by rival factions hoping to steal the limelight from King and SCLC.

"At the end of mass demonstrations," said Anderson, "we walked away empty-handed except for a verbal commitment on the part of the town officials. And they broke every one of those commitments. It was a mistake for us to agree to come out of jail without more binding commitments."

For the man from Montgomery, it was an embarrassment and a setback. The New York *Herald Tribune* called it "one of the most stunning defeats of his career."

During the hiatus between the prison releases and January 23, 1962, selective boycotts were begun of downtown businesses and the city's major newspaper, the segregationist Albany *Herald*. The blacks in Albany also began a boycott of the city bus line, whose patronage was 90 percent black.

The bus company knew it was in danger and offered to immediately end segregated seating and hire one black bus driver. King, however, insisted that the company state its new policy in writing before any boycott was called off.

"We should have accepted that," says Anderson. "We wanted to put pressure on downtown and thought it was best to keep the people away from downtown—and one of the best ways to do that was to boycott the buses.

"People need victories along the way; people are encouraged to endure longer if they have a victory now and then. We did not accept an agreement with the bus company, and that would have been a victory. That was a mistake we made. Then the bus company went bankrupt, and the blacks suffered that loss the most."

Part of the problem was that the leadership was leading by trial and error. King was made vice president of the Albany Movement, and the leadership committee would meet daily and plan the next day's strategy.

"We might decide tomorrow we will send fifty people downtown to picket a street," explained Anderson. "We could not come up with a strategy we could predictably stick with from day to day. We modified our approach on an hourly basis."

They were also learning. Going to jail, for example, sounds noble. But it is hard. It is debilitating. It is confining. It is dirty and the food is often inedible. They found that most people couldn't take more than three or four days of that kind of dehumanizing experience and be willing to risk doing it again.

"After that," said Anderson, "people became extremely restless and gave second thoughts to their motivation—that is, is it worth this?"

They didn't have organized time charts of who was arrested and when they should be bailed out; who could stay in four days, who could last a week, who could go the distance. Pritchett, with his insistence on cash bonds of two hundred dollars each—and only cash—was tying up thousands of dollars of SCLC funds.

On January 12, 1962, the city began arresting SNCC workers and leaders Sherrod and Jones for "loitering" in a white Trailways dining room. Eleven days later, the city council voted to renounce the earlier agreement to consider the black community's demands.

There were continued demonstrations, though not approaching the size and intensity of the demonstrations of late 1961. And Pritchett's police killed a black man—reportedly in self-defense.

King was shuttling between Atlanta and Albany during this period, wondering what to do. He had gotten roped into leading a factionalized movement he hadn't bargained for and was being blamed for its demise.

On February 20, 1962, the nation gave itself a collective pat on the back after John Glenn became the first American to orbit the earth. One week later, King and Abernathy were back in Albany to be convicted of the charges stemming from their December march, but the sentences were held in abeyance.

King decided to embark on a fund-raising tour to help mobilize support and raise money for the more than seven hundred blacks in jail as a result of the scattered boycotts and the decision of the city council to renege on its amnesty agreement. Harry Belafonte held a fund-raising concert in Atlanta in June, which was marred by the refusal of a downtown restaurant to serve lunch to the black singer and his entourage.

On July 10, King and Abernathy were sentenced to forty-five days in jail for leading the previous December's demonstrations in Albany, but three days later, they were evicted from jail over King's bitter objections.

"I've been thrown out of a lot of places in my day," Abernathy said at a mass meeting that night, "but never before have I been thrown out of a jail."

This was the result of Pritchett's homework. There had been a meeting of Albany segregationists and a few conservative blacks, which Pritchett attended, where it was decided to emulate Chief Sellers of Montgomery and bail King out of jail. Pritchett agreed with them that bailing King out of jail would nullify his publicity impact and cause some dissension within the Albany Movement itself.

Pritchett left before the meeting adjourned, however, because he did not want to know if they actually decided to go through with the plan, nor did he want to know who was going to post bond.

King was in demand as a preacher, and spent three quarters of the year on the road (JOHN TWEEDLE).

(BOB ADELMAN).

(ROLAND MITCHELL).

On July 13, three days after going to jail, King was bailed out by one of the blacks at that clandestine meeting. When summoned to Pritchett's office and informed he had been bailed out, King said, "I don't want to leave."

"Well," said Pritchett, "I can't keep you."

In the divided ranks of the Albany Movement, there were whispers that King had had himself bailed out, or his friends in the Justice Department had arranged his release.

King didn't know what had happened. But he knew that now he had to commit himself fully to Albany. He announced on July 16 that he was staying in Albany and was going to lead a massive nonviolent movement until the city commission gave in.

But four days later, U.S. District Court Judge J. Robert Elliot, a recent Kennedy appointee, issued a federal injunction barring King, Abernathy, and Walker of the SCLC, Ruby Hurley of the NAACP, and Charles Jones and Marion Page of SNCC from further illegal activity through July 30, when there would be a hearing for a permanent injunction.

King denounced the injunction by the avowed segregationist judge and filed an appeal. But they decided to obey the injunction for now and encourage others to continue demonstrating.

The nonviolence, however, ended July 24.

As expected, Judge Tuttle threw out Judge Elliot's injunction, and King announced he would lead a demonstration the next morning. It was not to be. A sheriff's deputy savagely attacked Mrs. Slater King, the pregnant wife of a movement leader, when she tried to bring food to demonstrators in a jail thirty-five miles outside Albany. He beat her unconscious and kicked her until she miscarried.

That night, two thousand Albany blacks rioted, battling police with rocks and bottles. Pritchett had a field day with the media, asking them to observe "them nonviolent rocks." Gov. Ernest Vandiver offered to send twelve thousand National Guardsmen to help quell the riot.

King called off the July 25 march and declared a "day of penance" instead. He was appalled by the violence and toured the city, trying to spread the word to blacks not to allow themselves to be drawn into the same type of violent acts that whites committed.

In King's view, answering violence with violence was not only morally wrong, it was a tactical error. But the movement itself was in trouble. There was a war council in Slater King's back yard, and the SCLC contingent was flayed for three hours by the younger leaders of SNCC.

SNCC viewed the day of penance as demeaning in the wake of the savage assault on Mrs. Slater King. And they were fed up with the peremptory ways of Wyatt Tee Walker: where did SCLC get the right to come into this community and act as if it were in charge? SCLC was invited in, it hadn't been organizing in Albany for the past two years. SNCC felt King's group had no right to dominate the movement as they had. King conceded that he had made mistakes in Albany, and it was not their intention to "take over" the leadership. But the antagonism of the young ran deep.

Two days later, King, Abernathy, Anderson, and ten others were arrested at a prayer vigil in front of city hall—but at the mass meeting that night, no one else wanted to go to jail with them. There were mass demonstrations in the beginning of August, after another sheriff's deputy beat black attorney Chevene King, Slater King's brother. More than a thousand people went to jail.

But the cohesion was gone.

"We could not sustain a movement any more," said Anderson.

On August 10, the group came up for trial and they were convicted. Albany wanted King gone, however, so the group was given suspended rather than jail sentences. They were free, and King announced he was returning to Atlanta.

"There comes a time to leave," said Abernathy. "We had considered it for some time. Anderson informed us that he was going to be leaving soon and going to Detroit, and we decided that was as good a time as any to get out as well."

In Mississippi, SNCC was running into increasing opposition. By now, Moses had recruited more than a dozen Mississippi blacks to join his group of SNCC volunteers and help organize in Holly Springs, Clarksdale, Greenwood, Greenville, Cleveland, and Ruleville, in Sunflower County, the home county of segregationist U.S. Senator James Eastland. Eastland was the ranking Democrat in the Senate. He had a 5,400-acre plantation in Ruleville where blacks earned 30 cents an hour, though he got more than one hundred thousand dollars annually in agricultural subsidies from the government.

There was a registration effort in Greenwood, headed by Lawrence Guyot. It was the hub of Leflore County, which was 80 percent black and had one registered voter. One night, the police chief drove by their office accompanied by two carloads of armed whites. Guyot and other SNCC staffers escaped by climbing out a rear window onto the roof of a neighboring building and shinnying down a television antenna to safety.

This was the summer when whites began shooting into the homes of Mississippi residents who were known to be sheltering SNCC field-workers. This was the summer Allen Lewis received more beatings—at irregular times and places—to punish him for having dared to tell what he had seen at the cotton gin.

Moses was conducting workshops for a lot of high school students, "getting them ready for what was coming; freedom. We had a feeling we were going to stay in this thing until there were some basic changes in the state."

Jim Bevel came down from Nashville and was working with Amzie Moore in Cleveland before leaving to join SCLC in the fall. Annelle Ponder came over from SCLC's citizenship training program to help the expanding network of voter registration classes. On August 31, 1962, Fannie Lou Hamer, an uneducated sharecropper from Ruleville, joined seventeen others on a rickety bus to go to Indianola—home of the White Citizens Council—and try to register. Police took Bob Moses off the bus and arrested him. When Hamer got back to the plantation where she had lived and worked for eighteen years, she was told she had to withdraw her voter registration application or be thrown out.

"I didn't go down there to register for you," Hamer said. "I went down there to register for myself."

There were other reprisals in Mississippi that summer. Welfare was cut off to people involved or suspected of being involved in civil rights activities.

Credit was cut off. Bank loans were cut off. It was hard for rural blacks to eat. So Moses began a food program, soliciting free food and clothes from around the nation.

"We gave away food and clothing in return for people being willing to register to vote," says Moses. "We viewed it as a minimum effort on their part, it was what they could do to help themselves."

He had help. Comedian Dick Gregory in Chicago, one of several black entertainers who supported various parts of the civil rights effort, sent whole truckloads of food and clothing to SNCC food outlets in Mississippi.

"That just escalated the white response," said Moses. They knew there would be more trouble when SNCC resumed the offensive the following summer.

Meanwhile, Albany in the fall of 1962 was as segregated as ever, and Pritchett was a hero: the policeman who broke King. The KKK rejoiced in its fashion: four black churches around Albany were dynamited in a single week in September 1962.

It was disturbing for the SCLC brass to have to admit defeat. King returned to Albany several times during the remainder of 1962 to speak at various rallies. But there was no longer a movement.

In retrospect, none of the participants regretted Albany, because one learns more from losses than victories. They saw the absolute need for cohesion and never again tried to confront segregation in SNCC "territory."

They learned to look at the local organization critically, to see if the framework was there before they came in and mobilized. They watched for the influence of Uncle Toms, who, King said, were "Negroes who will never fight for freedom. There are Negroes who will seek profit for themselves from the struggle. There are even some Negroes who will cooperate with their oppressors."

They also took a more jaundiced view of the Justice Department, since the FBI did not bother to investigate abuses against blacks, but launched a full investigation of the boycott. That led to a protracted prosecution of Anderson and eight other Albany leaders for "obstruction of justice."

King publicly criticized the FBI for its one-sided activities, calling them "vaguely interested observers of injustice, who diffidently write down complaints and do no more. One of the great problems we face with the FBI in the South is that the agents are white Southerners who have been influenced by the mores of the community.

"To maintain their status, they have to be friendly with the local police and people who are promoting segregation. Every time I saw FBI men in Albany, they were with the local police force."

In Washington, J. Edgar Hoover was furious. There had been ongoing but periodic investigations into the civil rights movement, but these were primarily confined to the activities of Stanley Levison, who according to the F.B.I., had been a member of the hierarchy of the American Communist Party until his sudden resignation in 1955.

Hoover was a prim martinet who had carved a fiefdom for himself by spying on just about everyone in power. His home was a fortress, and he avoided people spying on him by having an electronic console by his bed, which activated a shield over the windows in his and the adjoining bedroom, usually occupied by

his chief aide and sole companion, Clyde Tolson. He was an enigma—a conserva- tive man, yet the walls of his dining room were a kaleidoscope of different colored arc lights, and his downstairs bar was covered from wall to wall with Vargas nudes clipped from *Playboy.*

He had a phobia about real and suspected Communists, and had had a wiretap on Levison's telephone for the past eight months. In Hoover's view, Levison never really left the Communist Party, but was a "secret member" who had resigned so he would be free to influence the civil rights movement, which Hoover felt was subversive.

He had been bombarding Robert Kennedy with reports of Levison's sup- posed Communist activities and, on November 23, had another tap placed on Levison's home phone—with Kennedy's permission. The Atlanta office began a full-scale investigation of SCLC and its potential Communist connections, but the agents there did not see any infiltration. Control of the investigation was then given to the New York office, which, in Hoover's view, had a better attitude.

Now Hoover set out to get King once and for all. What had been a probe merely to determine the possible extent of Communist infiltration of the civil rights movement shifted.

King didn't know that at the time. This was his period for reflection: he was not sure he wanted to continue in the civil rights movement. Maybe he was wrong. Maybe someone else should lead.

The news around the nation was just as depressing. In September, James Meredith tried to enroll at the University of Mississippi in Oxford. He got to go to school October 1 with an order for admittance from the U.S. Supreme Court and an escort of U.S. marshals.

From October 22 through November 2, the world held its breath while

Coretta and Martin at home (ROLAND MITCHELL).

(ROLAND MITCHELL).

President Kennedy ordered a blockade of Cuba and demanded the removal of Soviet missiles from the island nation, whose Communist leader, Fidel Castro, had seized control just three years earlier. Russian Premier Nikita Khrushchev backed down, ending the immediate threat of nuclear war.

Conventional warfare was growing, however. Kennedy was in the midst of a quiet buildup of American "advisers" to the corrupt regime of Ngo Dinh Diem in Vietnam, a buildup that would have fifteen thousand soldiers in Southeast Asia in another twelve months.

King was spending more time writing his second book, the philosophical *Strength to Love*, and was getting a chance to see his family.

For the past seven years, more than 75 percent of his time had been spent away from home, and he missed Coretta, who was pregnant again, and their children.

"We had quality time," said Yoki. "Whenever he was home it was as if we were the whole world."

Martin had a game he started with Yoki, which he played with each of the others as they grew. He'd say, "Let's go up," and Martin would put his little girl on top of the refrigerator. She would leap into his arms, knowing her daddy would never drop her. As time passed, the older children would leap from the stairs. Coretta worried that one day Martin would miss.

But he didn't. Home was his fortress of solitude, even though at any given time one or a dozen people might drop by. It was a sanctuary: a place of healing. In the aftermath of Albany, he needed it.

The SCLC staff had gelled, too. They had licked their wounds from Albany and knew what they needed to do if they took on another major project. There was occasionally time to relax with them, as well. There had been a tentative decision to support Shuttlesworth's Alabama Christian Movement in Birmingham during 1963, but that hadn't been finalized.

He got an offer from Sol Hurok Productions to be its principal lecturer around the world—for the amazing sum of one hundred thousand dollars per year—and he had to make a decision as to what he wanted to do with the rest of his life.

Hurok pressured King for a decision. He said no.

"I think if he hadn't had to directly turn that offer down," said Andrew Young, "he might have drifted awhile longer."

Once he was committed to the struggle, it was time to act. In 1963, SCLC would again take the offensive.

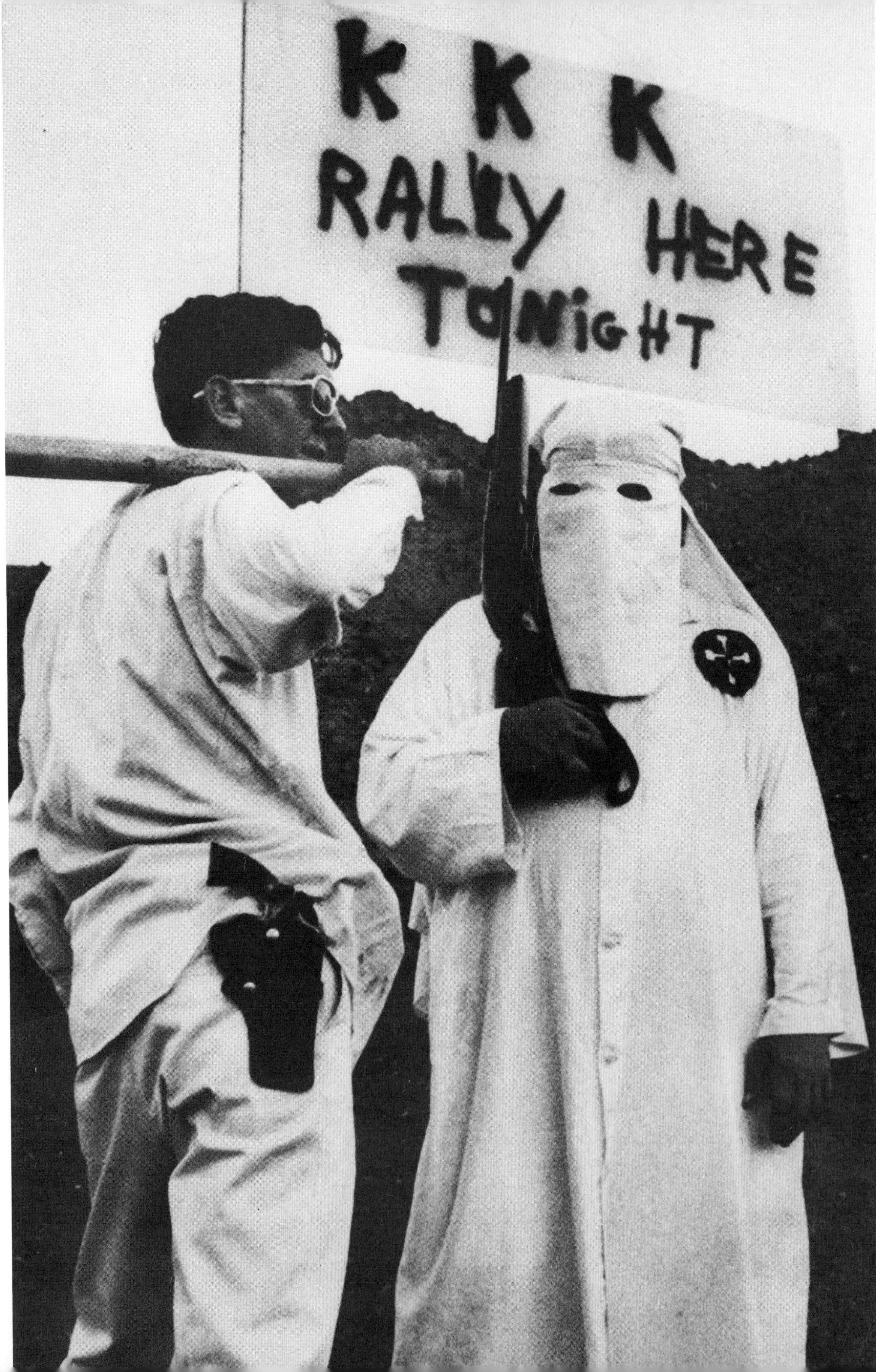
KKK
RALLY HERE
TONIGHT

7
1963: THE TURNING POINT

PART ONE: THE CHILDREN'S HOUR

JANUARY 1, 1963, WAS THE CENTENNIAL OF PRESIDENT Lincoln's Emancipation Proclamation, the stunning wartime edict that brought freedom to the millions of blacks in the Confederacy.

King asked President John F. Kennedy to "make its declaration of freedom real," one hundred years after the fact, by issuing a second Emancipation Proclamation putting the full weight of the government behind the elimination of the modern-day form of slavery—segregration. King had written a lengthy legal brief called "An Appeal to the President of the United States," which graphically laid out the injustices heaped upon black Americans in education, housing, transportation, and the courts.

Only the government, King argued, could counter people like Alabama's Governor Patterson, who said, "There is no such thing as token integration or planned desegregation. Once you let the bars down, it's all over!

"If the federal government continues its present course, the only solution will be to close the schools."

But President Kennedy was cautious; no declaration was forthcoming. Freedom would have to be won.

Freedom was not going to be won easily in Mississippi in 1963. The message was driven home early. A group of white men drove to the home of the beleaguered Lewis Allen and killed him with a shotgun blast as he stood on his lawn, in sight of his wife and children. He had never become active in any SNCC activities.

He was simply an object lesson.

On January 10, 1963, King, Abernathy, and the rest of the SCLC leadership met in Dorchester Center, Georgia, with Shuttlesworth to discuss Birmingham. They had tentatively agreed in September to help Shuttlesworth's movement this year; but if that were to happen, a lot of decisions would have to be made immediately.

First: should they, and could they, tackle Birmingham? That they should was never in doubt.

Birmingham, a city of 350,000 at that time, was reputed to be one of the most violently segregated in the South. It was an industrial town, and the South's

Birmingham, Alabama
(BIRMINGHAM POST HERALD).

center for iron and steel production. If Birmingham could be cracked, any place could.

But could they crack Birmingham? That was more difficult, for this intransigent city was a haven for the Klan and other violent elements, all backed by a city government that fought hard to preserve the status quo.

In Birmingham, Shuttlesworth had been beaten with brass knuckles and chains, and his wife stabbed for trying to enroll their children in a white school. In Birmingham, the city chose to close the parks, close the library, and close the pools rather than adhere to court decrees won by Shuttlesworth to end segregation.

"We had desegregation, legally, in Birmingham," said Shuttlesworth. "But ours were all Pyrrhic victories. We wanted a victory that could be felt."

The good whites in Birmingham banned the touring company of the Metropolitan Opera because it played to integrated crowds; banned the Southern Association baseball team because it featured integrated teams, and banned a children's book because it had the temerity to show black and white rabbits.

Birmingham also had Eugene "Bull" Connor, a small man with a booming voice who, as police commissioner, set the tone for the lawlessness and ruthlessness used to keep blacks in their place.

Levison pointed out at the meeting that Connor "had an ugly history with the labor movement, and had fought it for years to keep it out of Birmingham. The use of forced brutality and all kinds of devices were employed to defeat what was then a powerful movement.

"We were not as powerful as the labor movement had been in its organiz-

Above:
Sidney Poitier was not far behind, putting his movie Oscar to work for the movement (JOHN TWEEDLE).

Above, right:
Mahalia Jackson was King's favorite to close any rally (JOHN TWEEDLE).

ing days, and consequently we had to realize that we were facing a rough adversary with much less power than the earlier movements."

King's reply was sobering. "There are something like eight people here assessing the type of enemy we're going to face. I have to tell you that in my judgment, some of the people sitting here today will not come back alive from this campaign. And I want you to think about it."

They did. They thought they should limit their attack to specific targets, so they chose the downtown business community. This was a lesson learned from Albany, where they had tried to tackle all forms of segregation in the city and discovered the hard way that in tackling everything, it is easy to win nothing.

They discussed logistics. In the weeks ahead, Walker was to case downtown Birmingham. "I visited the stores we were to hit," said Walker, "and counted the seats [lunch counters] in the stores. I timed how long it would take a young person and an old person to walk downtown."

In the end, he had lists of who would be willing to go to jail, and for how long. They would not have people languishing in jail, their spirits sagging, as they had in Albany. This effort also required money, and they came up with a projected budget of $475,000 for the campaign.

The money would come from a whirlwind fund-raising tour by King and fund-raising efforts out of New York by Levison and Harry Belafonte. The black singer was to prove particularly valuable in this area: the rally he organized in Los Angeles with the Western Christian Leadership Conference raised seventy-five thousand dollars. And he brought seventy-five influential people to his New York apartment in February to hear from King and Shuttlesworth about the horrors of

Birmingham. The group, which included representatives of Governor Nelson Rockefeller and Mayor Robert Wagner, pledged its support and influence to back the coming campaign.

The planners had learned the lesson of divisiveness from Albany well, and decided that King, Abernathy, and Walker would visit sixteen Alabama cities, including Montgomery, Anniston, Talladega, and Gadsden, to drum up regional support for the coming campaign.

Shuttlesworth, through his seven-year-old movement, had already earned the support of many of the leaders in the city, but SCLC did not want to ruffle feathers. They arranged meetings with A. G. Gaston, a black millionaire who was to make his Gaston's Motel available to the SCLC leadership as their headquarters throughout their campaign.

James Bevel and James Orange would begin organizing in Birmingham—particularly among the young—to get their support behind SCLC. Said Bevel, "In Albany, there weren't enough people going to jail: they were sending the same people to jail over and over.

"They had to get people out of jail and send them back to jail the next day to give the appearance that there was a movement, and you can't fake a movement. So you have to get the schools involved and get the young people to come to the prayer meetings and fight for their future—and by that I meant the junior high, high school, and college." Dorothy Cotton, Andrew Young, and Shuttlesworth would make the rounds of the rest of the black community, paying attention to the black churchmen.

There was one other lesson learned in Albany: for the movement to grow, there has to be confrontation. Bull Connor was no Laurie Pritchett. So they designated "Project C," for confrontation, and decided to tie up Birmingham in a series of escalating protests until Bull Connor reacted as they knew he eventually would.

A few days after the retreat ended, there was a changing of the guard in Montgomery. George Corley Wallace, who had vowed he would never be "out-niggered again" after his 1958 loss to John Patterson, was sworn in as the new governor of Alabama. He took the oath of office in the same spot that Jefferson Davis had taken his a century before, and thundered, "I draw the line in the dust and toss the gauntlet before the feet of tyranny. And I say segregation now, segregation tomorrow, segregation forever!"

Among his first appointments was a man named Al Lingo, who was made public safety director, Alabama's highest-ranking law enforcement officer. Lingo preferred the title he gave himself—Colonel—and he had the state highway patrolmen referred to as state troopers. He was known for his familiarity with ranking, radical elements of the Klan and his insistence on putting their ilk in his troopers, although some of them were illiterate.

President Kennedy did not issue a second Emancipation Proclamation, but he went as far as he thought he could in February by introducing a new civil rights bill to Congress. It went nowhere, explained Robert Kennedy, because "there wasn't any interest in it. There was no public demand for it. There was no demand by the newspapers or radio or television. Nobody paid any attention."

The Birmingham campaign—dubbed B-Day—was to start March 6, the day after new city elections. King and his staff moved to Room 30 of the Gaston

The family of Police Commissioner Eugene "Bull" Connor, a small man with a large dose of hate (BIRMINGHAM POST HERALD).

Motel to make the final preparations for the campaign. They were beseeched by a number of local black leaders to wait. Connor was running for mayor against Albert Boutwell, a segregationist who wasn't as repugnant as Connor, and the blacks did not want any disturbances to occur that might shift public opinion in Connor's favor.

King and his staff were reluctant to change their timetable; Walker already had his first 250 demonstrators selected. But they had learned in Albany to do everything they could to secure the widest possible support, and B-Day was pushed back two weeks. As it turned out, neither Boutwell nor Connor could pull a majority, and a runoff election was scheduled for April 2. Rather than waste time, however, King and most of the SCLC staff left Birmingham, to return election night and begin the campaign April 3.

That was fine with King. He was able to be home March 28, when Coretta gave birth to their fourth child, a daughter named Bernice Albertine. Nationally, blacks cheered the selection of Sidney Poitier as best actor at the annual Oscar Awards Ceremony for his performance in *Lilies of the Field*.

The Birmingham election put the city into turmoil. Boutwell won easily and was to head the new mayor and council system. But Bull Connor and the other two members of the old commission system wouldn't leave. They challenged the legality of the new form of government in court, and while that legal wrangle was working its slow way through the halls of justice, Connor had a free hand to deal with outside agitators as he saw fit.

He had gotten some advice on the subject from Laurie Pritchett, who had flown up to Birmingham at Connor's request. He had already briefed the city's police chief, Jamie Moore, about the Albany method of handling the

Connor tried meeting the protests with professionalism (FRED SHUTTLESWORTH COLLECTION).

He tried to arrest A. D. King, Andy Young, and other demonstrators with a minimum of violence, while seeking help from the Southern courts (AP/WIDE WORLD).

King was troubled. Should he defy a court injunction and go to jail? He turned to prayer (MOREHOUSE COLLEGE).

He put on his jail uniform and led a Good Friday march in which he, Abernathy, and fifty others were arrested and . . . (AP/WIDE WORLD)

desegregation battle, and Moore wanted to follow the same procedures in Birmingham. For a while, it seemed the malevolent Connor would allow Moore to do just that. But only for a while.

King kicked off the campaign for the salvation of Birmingham with the "Birmingham Manifesto," at once a call to arms and a litany of the evils that had precipitated this nonviolent revolution. It demanded the desegregation of the downtown lunch counters, fountains, and rest rooms and the hiring of blacks in local businesses and the government.

The reaction from the white community to the Manifesto was, predictably, negative. Robert Kennedy said the assault was "ill-timed," and evangelist Billy Graham said there should be a cooling-off period until the new city administration could get involved.

But this was not a time for cooling off. Shuttlesworth led the first group of fifty-two demonstrators downtown to sit in at five stores. Twenty of them were arrested—politely for Birmingham—and taken to jail.

There were rumblings from within the black community, however, particularly from the middle class, which was not sure it wanted the city's racial boat rocked just yet. King told a large rally that first night that "we are heading for freedom land and nothing is going to stop us.

"We are going to make Birmingham the center of antidiscrimination activity in the nation."

Fearing another Albany, King spent the ensuing week making the rounds of meetings with black ministers and social leaders, trying to cajole and coerce them into going along with the plan to desegregate Birmingham now.

"To hear him speak and hear him articulate the facts was soothing," said Shuttlesworth.

Sometimes he spoke harshly. Toward the end of the first week, he said at

. . . thrown into the Birmingham jail. "You will never know the meaning of utter darkness until you have lain in such a dungeon," said King (CHARLES MOORE/ BLACK STAR).

a rally, "There are some preachers in Birmingham who are not with this movement. I'm tired of preachers riding around in big cars, living in fine homes, but not willing to take their part in the fight. . . . If you can't stand up with your own people, you are not fit to be a leader."

What private pleadings failed to do, the public scolding did. Dissension in Birmingham ceased for all practical purpose.

Meanwhile, Bevel and others on King's staff had been conducting daily workshops on nonviolence. These were massive combinations of prayer services, revivals, and school in which the philosophy of the nonviolent movement was added to the Christian orientation of the volunteers.

Bevel had drawn up a ten-point "commitment card" that pledged the volunteer to meditate daily on the teachings of Jesus and pray daily "that all men might be free."

One had to sign a commitment card before being allowed to participate in a demonstration. Through these meetings and through sociodramas, SCLC molded a core of volunteers for the assault on Birmingham.

For the first three days, the demonstrations were peaceful. "But we knew it was in the nature of Bull to be a bull," said Shuttlesworth. "Bull thought he was going to try Pritchett's strategy, but his own philosophy wouldn't allow him to do that. He couldn't just let us march—that was what we wanted to do."

On Saturday, April 6, forty-five blacks marched two abreast to city hall and were arrested. They were the first of an escalating number of marchers who were to head for the seat of power during the next thirty-four consecutive days.

On Palm Sunday, Connor's K-9 corps showed their dogs for the first time, snapping at demonstrators. By Wednesday, April 10, as the nuclear submarine *Thresher* was sinking to the bottom of the North Atlantic, some three hundred blacks had been jailed. Walker, who kept a running list of who was

Bull Connor's patience with the movement finally gave way to his natural feelings of hatred. "Get those little niggers!" he bellowed. "Let 'em have it!" (CHARLES MOORE/BLACK STAR).

The firemen "let 'em have it," hitting the kids with water from high-pressure hoses that could take the bark off a tree forty feet away (CHARLES MOORE/ BLACK STAR).

They let 'em have it with water that could knock out a grown man and easily wash younger boys and girls down the street (CHARLES MOORE/ BLACK STAR).

Right:
Bull Connor turned to the K-9 corps and said, "Let 'em have it!" and the killer dogs were set on black adults, black teenagers, and black children as the world watched in revulsion. President Kennedy said it made him sick (CHARLES MOORE/BLACK STAR).

The kids kept coming back for more, for this was the Children's Hour, and they were not to be denied (CHARLES MOORE/ BLACK STAR).

arrested when and where, had them bailed out as soon as possible from the limited Project C warchest.

Connor had blocked off the area around Kelly Ingram Park, opposite the Sixteenth Street Baptist Church, the site of most of the confrontations between the police and the marchers.

The police commissioner also tried an end run and secured an injunction from state court judge W. A. Jenkins, prohibiting King, Abernathy, Walker, Shuttlesworth, and other specified movement leaders from engaging in any form of protest against the city's segregation practices. The injunction was being used across the South as a weapon against the civil rights movement.

"Part of the agreement to come to Birmingham," said Shuttlesworth, "was that we would violate any court order. We had to march until we had gotten a victory. In Albany, they had marched and not gotten a clear-cut victory, and we could not have a repetition of that. In Birmingham, we had already demonstrated and won the legal victories, but they violated them."

King announced he would lead a demonstration on April 12, Good Friday, in defiance of the court order. But it was not to be that easy. On Thursday, Connor and Jenkins struck again, declaring that the reserves of the group's bonding company were no longer sufficient, and they would have to post cash bonds for anyone who was to be released. Project C, only a few weeks old, did not have that kind of cash in hand.

There followed an intense meeting Thursday night at the Gaston Motel. Several of the local ministers were uneasy about defying a court order and wanted to halt. Others felt that only King could raise the kind of cash that would be necessary to bail people out of jail, and he should therefore obey the court injunction and begin a series of speaking engagements. There were those who felt that without King raising money, the movement would be lost. King agreed with that gloomy assessment. He left the room to be alone with his God.

A half hour later he returned to Room 30, wearing overalls. "I have decided to take a leap of faith," he said. "I've decided to go to jail."

They joined hands and sang "We Shall Overcome" and then left to address a rally at the Zion Hill Church. King told the hundreds of blacks gathered there that "things were so bad in Birmingham that they could be changed only by the redemptive influence of suffering." He said he wanted to be a good servant of the Lord, who was crucified that same day, so many centuries before. He said he was going to jail.

It was a triumphal march to jail. The streets were lined with blacks who were singing and smiling and waving and urging King, Abernathy, and fifty others onward, proud that the Birmingham movement hadn't faltered. So far.

Things changed in jail. Connor had King put in isolation, and the marchers were not even allowed to use the telephone or call an attorney. King worried —which was all he could do in the darkness, on bare steel springs without a blanket—that the movement was foundering. It was. His brother, A.D., who was pastor of a church in Birmingham, led fifteen hundred blacks on a prayer march toward the jail after Easter Sunday services. They were stopped and arrested.

King's attorneys, Arthur Shores and Orzell Billingsly, were allowed to see him briefly on Sunday, and they said there was no money and little comment from the outside world—especially Washington—about his arrest.

But the picture slowly began to change. On Monday, word came that Belafonte had raised fifty thousand dollars over the weekend and could obtain more as it was needed. King was suddenly allowed by suspiciously solicitous guards to use the telephone to call home.

He soon learned why. President Kennedy had called Coretta, who was still recovering from childbirth. He told Coretta that Birmingham "is a very difficult place," but that he had ordered the FBI to investigate what was happening there. Kennedy had also telephoned Birmingham officials, and he informed Coretta that her husband would "soon be phoning home."

This explained why King suddenly obtained a mattress and blanket and was allowed to shower and change clothes. King told Coretta, using code names, to tell Walker what had happened so he could inform the media. This was done, and the resulting publicity gave a needed lift to Birmingham's black community.

Tuesday, April 16, as Gordon Cooper became the last Mercury astronaut to splash down in the ocean, King's attorneys brought him a copy of the Birmingham *News*, which had two interesting items: a statement from more than sixty local black leaders supporting the protest movement and a statement signed by eight white Christian and Jewish clergymen denouncing the protest.

At first this was depressing. King, first and foremost, was a man of God, and nothing bothered him more than the fact that Sunday at noon was the most segregated time of the week. This "Appeal for Law and Order and Common Sense" urged the black community to seek redress through the courts; while King was in jail they had actively tried to persuade Birmingham's black clergy to show restraint.

They had challenged the wrong person. On margins in the Birmingham *News*, on scraps of toilet paper, and on a notepad secreted to him by a black trusty, King set out to answer the questions raised by white men of God.

He wrote "Letter from a Birmingham Jail" not just to the "Dear Fellow Clergymen" to whom it was addressed, but to the world.

The clergymen had challenged King's right to be involved in the Birmingham dispute, since he was an outsider.

"I am here," he wrote, "along with several members of my staff because we were invited here. . . . Beyond this, I am in Birmingham because injustice is here. Just as the eighth-century prophets left their little villages and carried their 'thus saith the Lord' far beyond the boundaries of their hometowns; and just as the Apostle Paul left his little village of Tarsus and carried the gospel of Jesus Christ to practically every hamlet and city of the Graeco-Roman world, I, too, am compelled to carry the gospel of freedom beyond my particular hometown. Like Paul, I must constantly respond to the Macedonian call for aid."

The clergymen were upset that King was impatient and would not wait for the courts to decide what was right and wrong. King acknowledged that the courts had merit, but those gains had come only on the heels of concerted nonviolent pressure, because "privileged groups seldom give up their unjust posture."

History, he wrote, has shown that "freedom is never voluntarily given by the oppressor; it must be demanded by the oppressed. Frankly, I have never yet engaged in a direct action movement that was 'well-timed' according to the timetable of those who have not suffered unduly from the disease of segregation. For years now I have heard the word 'Wait.' It rings in the ear of every Negro with a piercing familiarity.

"This 'Wait' has always meant 'Never. We have waited for more than 340 years for our constitutional and God-given rights. . . . I guess it is easy for those who have never felt the stinging darts of segregation to say 'Wait.'

"But when you have seen vicious mobs lynch your mothers and fathers at will and drown your sisters and brothers at whim;

"When you have seen hate-filled policemen curse, kick, brutalize and even kill your black brothers and sisters;

"When you suddenly find your tongue twisted and your speech stammering as you seek to explain to your six-year-old daughter why she can't go to the public amusement park that has just been advertised on television, and see tears welling up in her little eyes when she is told that 'Funtown' is closed to colored children, and see the depressing clouds of inferiority begin to distort her little personality by unconsciously developing a bitterness toward white people;

"When you are forever fighting a degenerating sense of 'nobodyness'— then you will understand why we find it difficult to wait."

The clergymen had challenged SCLC's use of direct action, even though it had been nonviolent. They preferred negotiation as the more Christian course.

King was struck by the fact that they would deride the demonstrations but had been silent on the "ugly record of brutality," the bombings and killings and beatings that had made this campaign necessary.

Negotiation? Yes, said King, "you are quite right in calling for negotiation." This is the purpose of direct action, for it creates "such a crisis and establishes such a tension that a community which has constantly refused to negotiate is forced to confront the issue."

King was not, he wrote, "afraid" of tension. In fact, "there is a type of constructive nonviolent tension that is necessary for growth."

The philosopher Socrates, he said, created a form of tension in the medieval mind that forced men of his day to put aside the myths they had lived with and reach for truth and objectivity. In the same fashion, "we must see the need of having nonviolent gadflies to create the kind of tension in society that will . . . inevitably open the door to negotiation."

The ministers had said his nonviolent demonstrations must be condemned because they broke the law. That, King answered, is blaming the victim. It is blaming the robbed man for having money, or blaming Jesus because his piety precipitated his crucifixion.

King answered that charge of the clergymen by quoting from St. Augustine, who said that there are just laws and unjust laws, and "an unjust law is no law at all." A just law, King said, is one that "squares with the moral law or the law of God. An unjust law is a code that is out of harmony with the moral law. . . . Any law that uplifts human personality is just. Any law that degrades human personality is unjust.

How could these laws in Alabama be just, he asked, when blacks were excluded from voting for the legislators who enacted them? He noted that everything Hitler did in Germany was "legal," while everything the unsuccessful freedom fighters in Hungary did was "illegal" in the eyes of the Soviets who crushed them.

Then there was the charge that the desegregation campaign was extreme. He found this depressing and asked is extremism all that bad? "Wasn't Jesus an extremist for love—'love your enemies, bless them that curse you, pray for them that despitefully use you.' " The clergymen seemed to have forgotten that. In fact, the white clergy of the South had forgotten a lot. He was "disappointed" in their failure to speak out for what was right; to follow what they preach. Now, when he sees a beautiful church, he is compelled to wonder "what kind of people worship here? Who is their God? Where were their voices when the lips of Governor Barnett dripped with the words of interposition and nullification? Where were they when Governor Wallace gave a clarion call for defiance and hatred? . . .

"If the church does not recapture the sacrificial spirit of the early church, it will lose its authenticity, forfeit the loyalty of millions, and be dismissed as an irrelevant social club with no meaning for the twentieth century."

It was an unanswerable challenge to the white members of the clergy and to the segregationists who had looked to them for moral absolution.

There was more. King had to issue one more statement to the people he represented at the bottom.

"Before the Pilgrims landed at Plymouth, we were here. Before the pen of Jefferson etched across the pages of history the majestic words of the Declaration of Independence, we were here.

"For more than two centuries, our foreparents labored in this country without wages; they made cotton 'king,' and they built the homes of their masters in the midst of brutal injustice and shameful humiliation—and yet out of a bottomless vitality, they continued to thrive and develop.

"If the inexpressible cruelties of slavery could not stop us, the opposition we now face will surely fail. We will win our freedom because the sacred heritage of our nation and the eternal will of God are embodied in our echoing demands."

The letter was smuggled out of the jail cramped page by cramped page and eagerly typed up by movement leaders at the Gaston Motel. When they were done, Walker suggested calling it, simply, "Letter from a Birmingham Jail." The nine-thousand-word statement became a classic in protest literature. Millions of copies circulated around the nation.

The eight white Alabama clergymen, needless to say, never tried to respond.

On Saturday, April 20, 1963, King and Abernathy accepted bail and came out of jail. They had not capitulated: rather, they sensed that the movement was at a standstill and unless something happened—and soon—it could founder. There was still picketing and marching, but they had dwindled. An ad hoc group had begun some tentative negotiations with members of the business community, but they were sure to fail if the pressure was not maintained.

The movement's leaders went to court Monday, April 22, before Judge Jenkins on both civil and criminal contempt charges and remained in court all week. Judge Jenkins threw out the civil charge, because it meant the leaders had to stay in jail until they apologized, and he didn't want martyrs. The criminal charges carried a penalty of only fifty dollars and five days in jail. It was such a light penalty that the leaders considered it a victory, however small.

But the larger victory eluded them. In their strategy sessions that weekend, a decision was made that changed the course of the civil rights movement.

Bevel had been assiduously organizing the black students in Birmingham, and he had been urging the use of a children's march against Bull Connor's police.

"We wanted to get the nation involved in Birmingham," said Bevel, "and get a larger segment of Birmingham involved. We knew if the students were involved the parents would come out to find out what was going on."

It was risky. Hundreds of young people had been coming to regular workshops organized by Bevel and attending the mass rallies at night. Bull Connor had gotten vicious, and they could not count on him becoming nicer if his opposition were black children instead of adults. But they were in a bind.

"We needed the kids," said Shuttlesworth. "It would have been much longer and much more difficult to have won without the massive inpouring of students. And we knew we were morally right."

It was massive. D-Day was set for Thursday, May 2, 1963. Initially, scores of high school and college students were to be used in the demonstrations, but they all wanted to participate, and many showed up with their little brothers and sisters. There were six year olds and seven year olds who could not pronounce half the words in the movement songs but who insisted on the right to join the fight for freedom.

They went out in groups of from twenty to fifty, all heading downtown by various routes. They poured out of the Sixteenth Street Church and three other black churches at the same time, their movements coordinated by Bevel and older students with walkie-talkies.

Bull Connor was furious. "Get those little niggers!" he shouted to his police. They did. They arrested 959 young black people—ranging in age from six to sixteen—and hauled them off to jail.

The children's crusade stunned Birmingham, galvanized the black adult community, and sent shock waves through America's collective conscience. There was some criticism—expected—about King's "exploiting" children.

He silenced that criticism by asking why these people had kept quiet during the years in which black children were being brutalized. Bevel pointed out, "You get an education in jail too. You learn the price of freedom."

SCLC was ecstatic. King saw an encounter between a policeman and an eight-year-old girl. "An amused policeman," he told his associates, "leaned down to her and said with mock gruffness, 'What do you want?'

"The child looked into his eyes, unafraid, and gave her answer. 'F'eedom.' She could not even pronounce the word, but no Gabriel trumpet could have sounded a truer note."

The mass meeting that night showed that Bevel had been right: get the kids involved, and the recalcitrant parents would follow. "They were upset, and we had to have four churches for mass meetings. We told them they should join the kids. Segregation was incorrect and their children were used because they, the adults, had been irresponsible."

If he couldn't break their bodies, Connor wanted to break the kids' spirits. Hundreds were crammed into tight, makeshift quarters with little or no sanitary facilities (CHARLES MOORE/ BLACK STAR).

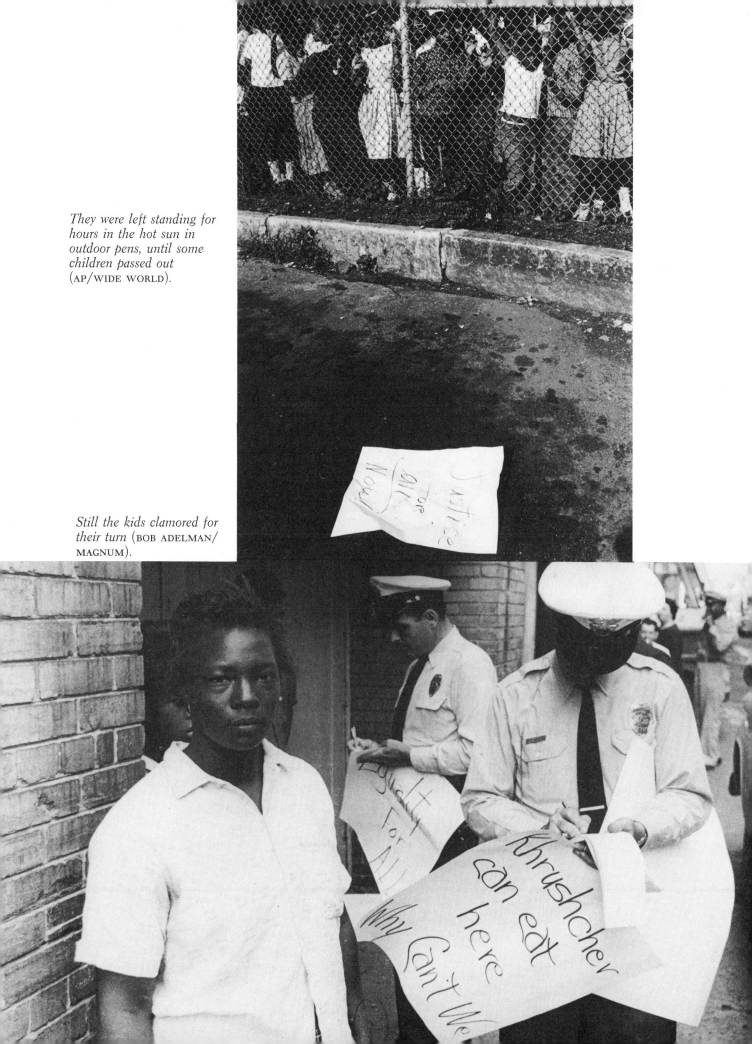

They were left standing for hours in the hot sun in outdoor pens, until some children passed out (AP/WIDE WORLD).

Still the kids clamored for their turn (BOB ADELMAN/ MAGNUM).

Justice for all Now!

Equality For All

Khrushchev can eat here Why Can't We

They waited patiently to be arrested . . .
(BOB ADELMAN/MAGNUM)

Friday, May 3, was Double D-Day. Again, hundreds of squads of young people fanned out throughout the town, running through police lines, challenging the police to catch them. It was fruitless: as fast as they could grab one set of youngsters, more would come running by.

Captain Glenn V. Evans recalls a fellow captain turning to him as they herded groups of arrested into buses and saying, "Evans, ten or fifteen years from now we will look back on this and we will say, 'How stupid can you be?'"

King, Abernathy, and Shuttlesworth left their command post at the Sixteenth Street Church and hit the streets. "The kids were in the street and we had the town," said Shuttlesworth. "The police couldn't hold them. It was almost a situation where the kids were taunting the police.

"I knew we had reached a critical point. I knew something had to give. The kids were going through the streets like wildfire. One policeman was trying to hem a kid in, and was going round and round on his motorcycle. I said 'Officer, don't hurt yourself.'

"And I said to Martin 'This is it. We got to have a victory.'"

Bull Connor escalated as well. As the television cameras rolled and the reporters recorded, he bellowed his defiance to change.

"Let 'em have it!" roared Connor as the K-9 corps sicced its hundred-pound attack dogs on the little black boys and little black girls.

"Let 'em have it!" roared Connor as the firemen turned their high-pressure hoses on thousands of young black people. These were the hoses that could take the bark off a tree. These were the hoses that took skin off a person's back. These were the hoses that knocked grown men down and swept children down the street, peeling their skin and breaking arms and ribs in the process.

"Let 'em have it!" roared Connor, as his policemen unleashed their pent-

. . . and join their schoolmates in jail as if they were going to an honors seminar (BRUCE DAVIDSON/ MAGNUM).

up frustration by wading into the swarms of black children and teenagers with fists and feet and curses and billy clubs.

Bull Connor "let 'em have it" as the world watched in revulsion. There were Senate denunciations that the attack on the children "would disgrace the Union of South Africa or Portugese Angola."

President Kennedy said on May 4, that the sights of the assault in Birmingham made him sick, and now he could "well understand why the Negroes of Birmingham are tired of being asked to be patient." He dispatched two emissaries, Assistant Attorneys General Burke Marshall and John Doar, to see if they could mediate the dispute and bring it to an end. He also summoned Sid Smyer, the city's leading businessman and a staunch segregationist, to a secret meeting in the White House. There, Smyer was told that if the business community couldn't end this nightmare, Kennedy would have to step in and take over.

Smyer assured the President that the business community could straighten out its own affairs and would.

The attacks also enraged Birmingham's black community, which was now solidly behind the movement. Andrew Marrisett, a black resident who had not been involved in the demonstrations, was passing by Kelly Ingram Park and was stunned to see a K-9 dog attack a six-year-old girl.

"I went and stood in front of the girl and grabbed her," Marrisett said, "and the dog jumped on me and I was arrested. That really was the spark. I had an interest all along, but that just took the cake—a big burly 285-pound cop siccing a trained police dog on that little black girl. Then I really got involved in the movement."

By Sunday, State Public Safety Director Lingo had brought eight hundred of his marshals to the outskirts of the city and wanted permission to join in quelling the disturbances. He was furious with the city for coddling the demonstrators. When informed that some plaster was thrown at a policeman, he said "I'd shoot them, that's what I'd do. You people just too easy on them people."

Sunday saw one of the largest demonstrations. Rev. Charles Billups and other ministers led three thousand youngsters on a mass demonstration, and Connor ordered them to turn back. Instead, they knelt in prayer. Connor continued ranting at the demonstrators until Reverend Billups had had enough. He walked over to Bull Connor and dared him. "Turn on the water!" he shouted. "Loose the dogs! We ain't going back. Forgive them, O Lord."

With that, the marching children rose and began walking toward the firemen and their hoses. Bull Connor yelled and the firemen aimed at the youngsters . . .

And nothing happened.

Suddenly there was no water pressure in the nearby hydrants. The children, convinced this was the hand of God, continued walking, singing, and praying in exultation. The firemen, stunned, fell back, confused, as the nonviolent crusade filed by and went to a prayer meeting in the park.

By May 7, Burke Marshall had started negotiating, shuttling back and forth between the downtown business leaders and the movement leaders. They started out poorly. The movement had four nonnegotiable demands that were to be met before the demonstrations ended: complete desegregation of all facilities in the downtown stores; the hiring of blacks in sales and clerical positions; the release of the arrested demonstrators, and the formation of a permanent biracial committee to work out a timetable to desegregate the rest of the city.

Marshall's meeting with the 125 white businessmen downtown seemed to be useless—until they broke for a recess. King had mounted the largest of the demonstrations that day, and the white men came out of their meeting and found downtown covered for several square blocks with a sea of black faces.

Back inside, Smyer broke into tears and said, "I'm a segregationist from bottom to top, but gentlemen, you see what's happening. I'm not a fool. Now, we can't win. We are going to have to stop and talk to these folks."

Meanwhile, the demonstrations had again turned ugly. There was some rock and bottle throwing by youngsters who were attacked by the K-9 corps, and the police retaliated furiously. Shuttlesworth was coming out of the Sixteenth Street Church when Connor spotted him and ordered the firemen to train their hoses on him.

The hose slammed Shuttlesworth's head into the stone wall and knocked him out. He was taken to the hospital for treatment.

The negotiations were going on in earnest while the demonstrations continued. On the evening of Wednesday, May 8, Shuttlesworth, who had been sent home to recuperate, was driven out to the home of attorney John Drew. There he found King and Abernathy and the Justice Department's Marshall and Doar.

He knew something was amiss when he entered and saw King looking out the big picture window.

"Fred," said King without turning around, "we've got to call the demonstrations off."

"Say that again, Martin."

King turned around, looked at Shuttlesworth, and repeated, "We've got to call the demonstrations off. They say they can't talk with all the demonstrations going on."

Shuttlesworth was furious. "No, Martin. We won't call the demonstrations off and if you call it off your name will be mud. You know what happened in Albany. The rumor gets around that you get people into trouble and run off and leave them.

"If you call it off, I am going to call them back on. This is not Albany. We will demonstrate till we get a victory this time."

At this, Marshall interjected that promises had been made to the business community, and there was supposed to be a joint announcement the following day in Washington by the President and in Birmingham by King that the demonstrations would temporarily cease. Doar was in the adjoining room, telling Kennedy that Shuttlesworth was holding up the agreement.

Marshall insisted that the merchants would accede to the movement's demands, but Shuttlesworth insisted that "when they sign, then it will be over."

Shuttlesworth threatened that if there was a public announcement that the demonstrations had been called off, he would announce a new series of demonstrations and get out of his sickbed to lead them. Then he left.

King turned to Marshall and said that the demonstrations therefore could not be called off, "because we have to have unity."

King had not forgotten the lessons of Albany. The difference between his position and Shuttlesworth's involved faith and pressure. It was Shuttlesworth who had initially organized Birmingham, beginning with a bus boycott in 1956, and Shuttlesworth was the acknowledged local leader.

Shuttlesworth had not been able to lead a movement, however, and that was King's ability and responsibility. On King was the pressure of winning and losing. On King was the agony of command: having to give the order to allow the children to march in the face of possible death by a vicious, racist law enforcement system. To King came the weeping and angry parents of children who had been mauled—in a just cause—but mauled nonetheless in the Children's Hour.

"I don't want to imply that King cracked," said Shuttlesworth. "He didn't. But he was under so much pressure from the White House that I don't think he had figured the consequences of not going through. He didn't consider that the merchants could always say we didn't agree to anything.

"He really thought that with the government throwing its weight behind us he could appease them and quiet down and we would still win. Besides, nobody defies the President of the United States."

Abernathy said they had felt that "we had achieved our goals. We had them in the bag. It was needless and useless energy to go to jail any longer."

The issue was unresolved that night. By midday Thursday, a tentative agreement had been reached and King announced a temporary end to the demonstrations. He warned that they would resume Friday morning if no agreement was signed before then.

It was. Friday morning King, Abernathy, and Shuttlesworth read a conciliatory statement at a press conference in front of the Gaston Motel saying, "Birmingham may well offer twentieth-century America an example of progressive racial relations; and for all mankind a dawn of a new day, a promise for all men, a day of opportunity and a new sense of freedom for all America."

The business community had agreed to virtually everything. During a ninety-day transition period, facilities in the downtown stores would be desegregated, and black personnel would be hired in the next sixty days. The more than three thousand arrested demonstrators in jail were to be released immediately on bail—amounting to $237,000—and the interracial committee was to be formed within two weeks. Most of the charges against the demonstrators would be dropped ten days later when the U.S. Supreme Court ruled that it was legal to hold sit-ins in cities enforcing segregation. That nullified the Southern segregation laws under which Birmingham's and other black demonstrators had been arrested in the past.

King was ecstatic, and he and Abernathy flew back to Atlanta to rest and celebrate SCLC's first major victory with their families. It was, in some ways, a flawed victory. Critics quickly pointed out that it ignored segregation in the school system, and they were dubious of its staying power, since it had not been negotiated with Birmingham's white political leaders.

But it was a victory. It was the first time that a protracted, active, nonviolent campaign brought a city to a standstill and forced leading white citizens to sit down and negotiate with blacks. SCLC's mobilization and King's personal magnetism and leadership ability had forged a successful movement that had forced public capitulation in a ferociously segregated Southern city. The Children's Hour had shown King to be not only a moral leader but a great tactician. The decision to allow the children to put their bodies into the movement forced white America to come to grips with its self-proclaimed morality.

Excuses can always be made for a clash between white policemen and black adults. But the country simply could not witness an assault by grown men and killer dogs on little boys and little girls, regardless of their color, and live with its conscience.

King had pondered in his "Letter from a Birmingham Jail" just what kind of God these people worshiped. How could they stay silent in the midst of atrocities? The answer, as King knew it would be, was that they all worshiped the same God.

It just took the Children's Hour to remind them.

Above, left:
Victories don't come easily. The home of Rev. A. D. King, Martin's brother, was blown up on May 11—along with the Gaston Motel—a day after the settlement was reached in Birmingham (BIRMINGHAM POST HERALD).

Above, right:
That triggered a night of rioting, in which at least two blacks were killed (BIRMINGHAM NEWS).

It did not come easily. In addition to the injuries sustained by hundreds during the demonstrations, the Klan struck May 11.

Two bombs went off at the home of King's brother, A. D. King, blowing off the entire front of the house. Connor pulled police away from the area of the Gaston Motel, and Room 30—SCLC's headquarters—was also blown up.

This touched off rioting in the city by blacks seeking retaliation, which is what the Klan and the segregationists wanted. Al Lingo's troopers began patrolling the streets with shotguns.

Klansman Gary Thomas Rowe said he called a contact at the local FBI office and reported shooting a black man. The agent told him to stay where he was, then called back to say a black man had been shot through the eye.

"This is not the one," said Rowe. "I'm an excellent shot, and I hit this nigger right in the chest."

The agent checked again, and said, "You're right. You killed him."

Since Rowe hadn't been recognized by anyone, the agent reportedly told him to "sit tight and don't say anything else about it."

Andy Young and other movement leaders were running through the streets, trying to persuade people to go back to their homes. Walker heard angry blacks cry, "Let the whole city burn!" There was rock throwing and fire setting throughout the night in white-owned shops in the black area.

Mother's Day, May 12, 1963, King went back to Birmingham to help cool the situation. President Kennedy sent federal troops to the area, but the violence died down, so they were not needed.

Kennedy publicly praised the pact and pledged that the federal government would guarantee its implementation. On May 22, the Alabama Supreme Court ended the overt dissension by ruling that Connor and his fellow commissioners were out, and Boutwell and the new city council were in. The white business community made Connor an offer: get out of city politics permanently, and they would see to it that he was elected to the state public service commission. Under the circumstances, he accepted.

The end of the Birmingham campaign firmly established King as *the* spokesman for the nation's blacks, and SCLC as an organization that could deliver.

It was time to move to the national stage.

But the conflict soon ended. Shuttlesworth, King, and Abernathy were convicted on May 16 of violating the ban on demonstrations in Birmingham, and four days later the U.S. Supreme Court held that the segregation ordinances were unconstitutional (AP/WIDE WORLD).

PART TWO: THE SUMMER

THESE WERE HEADY TIMES.

If the protracted Montgomery bus boycott had stirred black America, the successful Birmingham campaign had it up and running. Birmingham was more than an economic victory, like the war of attrition won in Montgomery. Birmingham was a head-to-head confrontation with some of the worst elements segregation had to offer—live and in color, yet.

King was more sought after than ever as a speaker. He embarked on an ambitious tour throughout the country, appearing before larger and larger throngs. There were 10,000 waiting to hear him in Chicago, 25,000 in Los Angeles, and 125,000 followed King on a Freedom Walk through Detroit.

There were stirrings in Washington, as well. Robert Kennedy had come of age. He had been sensitized to the problems of blacks in the South during his confrontations over the sit-ins and Freedom Rides. Birmingham had turned him into a desegregation loyalist.

He began to argue with his brother that it was time to answer King's long-ignored call for a second Emancipation Proclamation and push through Congress a major civil rights bill. Every member of Kennedy's cabinet argued against such a move, saying it was impossible to get such a bill through Congress, and to try would be political suicide.

Alabama was to provide a clinching argument. At the beginning of June, Robert Kennedy had to federalize the Alabama National Guard and dispatch Assistant Attorney General Nicholas Katzenbach to Tuscaloosa to enroll Vivian Malone and James Hood at the University of Alabama. Governor Wallace had fought efforts to integrate the school but had promised President Kennedy in a secret telephone conversation that he would not do anything to cause trouble if he could just make a statement.

Katzenbach, disgusted by the defiance, told the governor's intermediary to "tell him it can't be over two minutes long. I don't want a speech."

With that, Wallace took his infamous "stand in the schoolhouse door," vowing to fight for segregation forever. Katzenbach enrolled the two black students.

King described it as "a fatuous display of political pomposity," and it was all it took to get the President to move. On June 11, 1963, President Kennedy

The U. S. Attorney General had to send his assistant, Nicholas Katzenbach, and federal troops to Tuscaloosa, Alabama, in June to enroll two blacks at the University of Alabama over the objections of Gov. George Wallace (BIRMINGHAM POST HERALD).

told the nation in a televised address that "one hundred years of delay have passed since President Lincoln freed the slaves, yet their heirs, their grandsons, are not fully free.

"They are not yet freed from the bonds of injustice; they are not yet freed from social and economic oppression. And this nation, for all its hopes and its boasts, will not be fully free until all its citizens are free. . . .

"We preach freedom around the world. . . . But are we to say to the world—and much more importantly, to each other—that this is the land of the free, except for the Negroes; that we have no second-class citizens, except for the Negroes; that we have no class or caste system, no ghettos, no master race, except with respect to the Negroes?"

The President took the stand King had been urging for three years, declaring, "We face a moral crisis as a country and a people." He announced he would shortly give to Congress a sweeping civil rights bill.

The bill, delivered June 19, outlawed segregation in interstate public accommodations and let the Justice Department sue to force school integration and shut off money to federally funded programs that practiced discrimination.

The euphoria of that televised address was lessened the following morning. Medgar Evers, head of the Mississippi chapter of the NAACP, was shot in the back by a racist in front of his house in Jackson, Mississippi. Evers, unlike many NAACP officials in the South, challenged segregation head on and openly worked with SNCC and anyone else who would help crack Mississippi. He had even persuaded Roy Wilkins to join a voter registration march in Jackson—and become one of the seven hundred blacks arrested.

The killing of Evers was a sign of things to come in Mississippi. The segregationists decided to crack down, as if their past actions had been mild. Now the beatings would be more severe, changing from bloody noses and black eyes to broken skulls and ribs. Now the "chivalry" was gone and women would be as likely to be beaten as severely as men. Now the gloves were off, and instead of attacking just the organizers—Lewis Allen had been an exception—they would begin attacking *anyone* who was defiant enough to think about desegregation in Mississippi. They began a wave of bombings of churches and homes of suspected and known SNCC sympathizers. Nightriders began riddling the homes of blacks with shotgun and automatic rifle fire.

This was the summer Bob Moses and SNCC would make their preparations for the final push to crack the toughest state in the South. They decided to merge all Mississippi efforts—SCLC, NAACP, and CORE—with SNCC to form the Council of Federated Organizations (COFO), with Moses at the helm and CORE's Mississippi director, Dave Dennis, as the number-two man.

All the groups were stepping up their activities in the Delta, with predictable results. Moses, Jimmy Travis, and Randy Blackwell were traveling from Greenwood when their car was raked with machine-gun fire. Travis was hit in the back, but survived.

Moses responded by focusing on Greenwood and Greenville "to combat any feeling that we could be frightened off."

Mississippi, in 1963, disregarded *all* desegregation edicts. Fannie Lou Hamer, SCLC worker Annelle Ponder, and fourteen-year-old June Johnson were arrested June 11 when they made the mistake of trying to get served at a bus stop in Winona, in the center of the state.

Hamer remembers the screams coming from down the hall where the police had taken Ponder. "And I started hearing screaming like I had never heard. And I could hear the sounds of the licks. . . . And I hear somebody when they say, 'Can't you say yessir, nigger? Can't you say yessir, bitch?'

"And I could understand Miss Ponder's voice. She said, 'Yes, I can say yessir. I don't know you well enough.' I could hear when she would hit the floor, and then I acould hear them licks just sounding.

"She kept screaming and they kept beating on her, and finally she started praying for them, and she asked God to have mercy on them because they didn't know what they was doing.

"And after that, I heard some real keen screams." That turned out to be when they repeated the treatment on the teenager, June Johnson.

Then it was Hamer's turn. They had special treatment for a former sharecropper from Ruleville who had gotten too uppity to stay on the farm. They brought in two black male prisoners and had them take turns beating her with a blackjack until she, too, reached the screaming point.

Lawrence Guyot, an SCLC field-worker out of Greenwood, drove over to Winona after hearing of the arrests. Nine policemen stripped him and took turns beating him with fists, feet, and rifle butts for the next four hours.

They then sent him to other jails for brief periods, and brief beatings, while COFO tried to locate him and Andrew Young was dispatched to make bail for him. He was seen twice by white doctors, who were called by guards to see how much more he could take.

Young got the beaten man and the women out of jail on June 12, before going to Jackson for Evers's funeral.

On June 22, 1963, three days after submitting his civil rights bill to Congress, President Kennedy invited King, Lewis, now chairman of SNCC, Wilkins, Farmer, Randolph, and Whitney Young of the Urban League—the "Big Six" of civil rights—to a meeting at the White House. The President knew that there was a lot of opposition to his proposed civil rights bill, and he would need the active support of the group if there was to be any hope of passage. The President, brother Robert, and Vice President Lyndon Johnson wanted to discuss pending problems about civil rights in the South, particularly the possibility of more violence.

The President surprised them by remarking, "Our judgment of Bull Connor should not be too harsh. After all, in his way, he has done a good deal for civil rights legislation this year."

There was another agenda. Randolph was the primary spokesman at the meeting, and this civil rights veteran was again issuing a call for a march on Washington. He had threatened to bring a hundred thousand blacks to Washington in 1941 and 1947 to protest discrimination in the armed forces. In 1962 he had sent out a call to other black groups to participate in a march on Washington to protest the slow pace of desegregation. That call had gotten a mixed reaction: the NAACP said it would consider it, but did nothing; the Urban League rejected the idea; and SNCC, CORE, and SCLC said they would go along, but for Randolph to organize it. That was after Albany.

Now, however, in the wake of Birmingham and its galvanizing effect on the black community, they were eager to participate in a mass effort that they hoped would dwarf the thirty-five thousand who attended the 1957 prayer vigil at the capital.

The President, however, did not like the idea at all. There would be enough trouble getting this legislation through Congress without a march on Washington. Its potential for violence would turn off already reluctant lawmakers, and others would claim that they did not want to vote for a bill while under seige.

King argued that a march could dramatize the issue at hand and mobilize support from all parts of the country. Randolph said, "Mr. President, the masses are restless, and we will march. We will have a march on Washington."

Kennedy asked, "If you bring that many people here, how are you going to control them? If something happens, there would be no way we could get civil rights legislation passed. There would be a backlash."

They all insisted it would be a nonviolent march. As the meeting ended, the President asked King to walk with him in the Rose Garden for a private chat. There ensued a disturbing conversation.

FBI director Hoover had been steadily monitoring SCLC and bugging the telephones of Levison and Jack O'Dell, who worked with Levison in SCLC's New York fund-raising arm. O'Dell, who was black, had been a Communist Party organizer in New Orleans in the early 1950s. On June 17, Hoover had given Robert Kennedy a briefing about the "Communist influence" over King, whom the director viewed as a dupe of the Communist Party. Both Burke Marshall and Robert Kennedy had spoken to King earlier in the day, telling him he should sever all ties with O'Dell and Levison for the sake of appearances.

The President's request was stronger. He told King his friendship with

Levison could seriously hurt his civil rights efforts. "They are Communists," said the President flatly. "You've got to get rid of them." He said Southern opponents of the civil rights bill would use any means they could find to destroy it, and continuing to consort with Communists was playing with fire that could burn both the movement and the administration.

"If they shoot *you* down," the President warned, "they shoot *us* down too —so we're asking you to be careful."

King said he had no problem getting rid of O'Dell, but he simply wouldn't believe the tales about Levison without proof.

Kennedy couldn't give him that, for it would betray the identities of double agents within the American Communist Party. They were Jack and Morris Childs, brothers operated by the FBI under the code name Solo, who had been active in the American Communist Party since the 1920s. They became disenchanted with the party, however, and in 1952 began a twenty-five-year career as double agents. They had risen to the point where they were part of the system by which the Soviet Union channeled more than a million dollars annually to its American offshoots, with Jack Childs receiving the Soviet money in cash for disbursement. Solo provided the FBI with inside knowledge of everything that happened in the ACP, and Morris, through his annual trips to the Soviet Union, provided details of inside conversations with Soviet politburo leaders, such as Leonid Brezhnev, and other figures, such as Mao Tse-tung.

Jack Childs told the FBI that Levison had been a secret financier for the party from 1946 through 1955, when he withdrew. By 1957, however, the FBI had dropped Levison from its list of people to watch since Childs said he had no contact with the Communist Party hierarchy and ACP officials were disappointed that he had turned away from them.

As the civil rights movement expanded, Hoover came to believe that Levison's withdrawal, despite the lack of any evidence from its wiretaps or Solo, was a fake and set out to prove it. His memos to Robert and John Kennedy never mentioned the fact that Solo maintained Levison hadn't been involved with the ACP for several years.

There was more. The FBI maintained a special "enemies list," and King was placed in "Section A" of its reserve index. This consisted of individuals who were "in a position to influence others against the national interest." The Atlanta FBI office was notified to seize King as a dangerous individual in the event of a national emergency. This limited distinction had been ordered May 11, 1962, solely because King was a close friend of Levison.

King, of course, was not aware of this. His position on communism was well known. His college papers, if the FBI cared to look, were public record and they showed his abhorrence of that atheistic system.

Communism's atheistic premise and its "dreadful philosophy that the end justifies the means" were simply intolerable to any Christian. The "hard challenge" for Christians, wrote King, was to "make the world safe for democracy and secure for the people of Christ."

Hoover didn't care about that. As far as he was concerned, without Communist influence, there would be no SCLC. He made it quite clear in the FBI that he wanted King discredited: many of his Southern agents had already shown they were willing to overlook murder to comply.

King returned from his June 22 meeting in the White House East Room troubled. He joked with Andy Young that the President must have been worried about being bugged by Hoover himself, or they would not have had to walk in the Rose Garden. He did not sever ties, however, with O'Dell or Levison.

Hoover retaliated by leaking a story to the Birmingham *News*, which appeared June 30, that O'Dell, with known Communist affiliations, was active with SCLC. Three days later, King formally severed ties with O'Dell, but had problems severing relations with Levison.

Levison proposed his own solution. He quit speaking to King, and in the future they communicated through Clarence Jones, a black attorney who had worked on King's defense during his 1960 tax trial and had worked closely with SCLC and Levison's fund-raising activities ever since.

Hoover, however, pressured Robert Kennedy for permission to tap Jones, SCLC offices in Atlanta and New York, and King. Kennedy granted the first two with little hesitation and was to give in on King by October.

Eventually, however, King eliminated Jones as a middleman. He decided he had more reason to trust Levison—the man who helped him with his taxes, who produced his first book, who raised thousands of dollars for SCLC, and who gave consistently sound advice—than Hoover, whose organization was more comfortable working with Southern whites who killed blacks than with any blacks. He resumed his open friendship with Levison.

It was a busy summer for the civil rights movement. The Big Six met July 2, 1963, at the Commodore Hotel in New York to discuss the forthcoming march on Washington. There was an immediate hitch. Most of them were accompanied by their chief assistants—Abernathy and Shuttlesworth were with King; Bayard Rustin with A. Philip Randolph; John Marcell with Roy Wilkins. Wilkins insisted that only the leaders themselves should be present at this first, organizational meeting for the proposed march the following month and wanted the others to leave the room.

"We got into a serious argument about it," said Lewis, "but Wilkins was adamant, and we finally had to agree just to get the meeting started."

It turned out that Wilkins didn't want Rustin to have any part in organizing the march because of his past associations with leftist causes and his reputed homosexuality.

King insisted that "we are not concerned with Bayard or the past associations or affiliations of any participants. We are not going to conduct a witchhunt."

They compromised by letting Randolph chair the march, knowing his administrative assistant, Rustin, was going to be the de facto director of the entire undertaking. "Bayard had the time, the ability, the organization, and the skills to run it," Lewis said.

They decided to issue an immediate call to blacks and whites to come to Washington on August 28 "for Jobs and Freedom." They invited the heads of several major organizations to take an active role in the march, including the National Council of Churches, the American Jewish Council, the National Catholic Conference for International Justice, and the United Auto Workers. George Meany's AFL-CIO was conspicuously absent.

He wasn't needed. Rustin was a superb organizer, and SCLC's Walter

Walter Fauntroy spent the summer of 1963 in the nation's capital, coordinating The March on Washington for Jobs and Freedom (SCLC.)

Fauntroy was brought in to coordinate logistics in Washington. They had been hoping the call to arms would bring one hundred thousand people to Washington, but their estimates were way off.

There were more than 90,000 blacks and whites around the Lincoln Memorial before 10 A.M. on August 28, and another 150,000 were pouring into the city on foot, in cars, by plane, train, and bus.

There was friction. John Lewis was pressured into altering his speech at the last minute.

At that point, Lewis was a bit angrier than the other leaders of the march, for SNCC had been busy and Lewis, as chairman, was involved to some degree in all their major projects. There was, of course, Mississippi. Nashville was in turmoil as SNCC launched the last major effort to destroy the remaining vestiges of discrimination in the city. Lewis spent most of June and July working with Gloria Richardson, who was leading a series of desegregation battles against Mayor Calvin W. Mowbray and the city of Cambridge, Maryland. The violence here took on Deep South proportions.

Martial law was finally declared, and Robert Kennedy had to federalize the National Guard. Despite a truce, they were to remain in Cambridge for a year.

"Bobby Kennedy finally called a meeting of black leaders in the Cambridge Nonviolent Action Group," said Lewis, "as well as representatives of the governor and the generals of the National Guard on July 22 in his office. He kept interrupting the meeting to hear the heavyweight rematch between Sonny Liston and Floyd Patterson in Las Vegas. [Patterson was knocked out in the first round, again.]

"Bobby Kennedy had simply gotten on the phone and said, 'I want you people to come to my office and work out an agreement. We cannot have this growing tension and violence on the eastern shore of Maryland, this close to Washington.'

"He simply got all of us in a room and kept us there until we had an agreement. We would cease demonstrations if they would hire black police officers and desegregate all facilities. He insisted that they live up to the agreement —and they did."

Coming fresh from a confrontation in a city that was still under martial law, Lewis was not prepared to mince words. He had initially denounced the proposed civil rights bill because "there was nothing in this legislation to protect people involved in peaceful, nonviolent demonstrations in the South from being harassed, beaten, jailed, and killed."

In addition, the Kennedys suggested that anyone with a sixth-grade education should be able to vote, "and it was our position at SNCC that the only qualification to be able to register and vote in this country should be that of age and residence."

Lewis had the effrontery to declare that if a strong bill wasn't passed, the next march wouldn't be on Washington. Blacks would march all through the South "the same way Sherman did."

He toned down the rhetoric considerably, and even endorsed the Kennedy civil rights bill, though he said it didn't go far enough. Lewis's was one of the best-received speeches that day.

King was in a quandary. He was given but eight minutes to do the closing, and he wanted to adhere to the timetable so he wouldn't offend the sensitive Wilkins. He had worked feverishly in his hotel room the night before on an elaboration of the speech he had made in Detroit, when he first spoke of his dream of a better America. But he wasn't satisfied with his work. Coretta and his aides prevailed on him to use his speech as an outline, and let the Lord guide him.

In the end, it didn't matter what had gone on before. It didn't matter, really, what stars—white or black—put in an appearance before the estimated 190,000 black and 60,000 white *peaceful* people gathered in the great mall between Lincoln's final resting place and the Capitol rotunda.

It didn't matter, really, what the sensitivities of the planners were. For the largest protest crowd ever to descend on the nation's capital had really come to hear one man—the man who symbolized the hopes and dreams of blacks who wanted to be free and whites who wanted to feel good about their country.

They had come to hear Martin Luther King, Jr.

He started with his prepared text. He was standing in the shadow of the statue of Abraham Lincoln and recalled how "five score years ago, a great American . . . signed the Emancipation Proclamation. This momentous decree came as a great beacon light of hope to millions of Negro slaves who had been seared in the flames of withering injustice. It came as a joyous daybreak to end the long night of captivity.

"But one hundred years later, we must face the tragic fact that the Negro is still not free. One hundred years later, the life of the Negro is still sadly crippled by the manacles of segregation and the chains of discrimination. One hundred years later, the Negro lives on a lonely island of poverty in the midst of a vast ocean of material prosperity. One hundred years later, the Negro is still languishing in the corners of American society and finds himself an exile in his own land. . ."

The prepared text was there, but he didn't need it. This was classic King. This was the mature King; building a message on wave upon wave of studied, polished, emotion-laden phrases with logic that removed doubt and a cadence that demanded a following.

"In a sense," he said, as his rich baritone carried across the throng, "we have come to our nation's Capitol to cash a check. When the architects of our republic wrote the magnificent words of the Constitution and the Declaration of

More than 250,000 blacks and whites responded to the call, filling the area in front of the Lincoln Memorial and demanding passage of the civil rights bill proposed by President Kennedy and the attainment of rights supposedly granted with the Emancipation Proclamation in 1863 (LEONARD FREED/MAGNUM).

"But one hundred years later, we must face the tragic fact that the Negro is still not free. . . . Now is the time to make real the promises of Democracy . . . (BOB ADELMAN/MAGNUM).

". . . Now is the time to rise from the dark and desolate valley of segregation to the sunlit path of racial justice." (BRUCE DAVIDSON/MAGNUM).

Independence, they were signing a promissory note to which every American was to fall heir. This note was a promise that all men . . . would be guaranteed the unalienable rights of life, liberty, and the pursuit of happiness.

"It is obvious today that America has defaulted on this promissory note insofar as her citizens of color are concerned. Instead of honoring this sacred obligation, America has given the Negro people a bad check, a check which has come back marked 'insufficient funds.' But we refuse to believe that the bank of justice is bankrupt. We refuse to believe that there are insufficient funds in the great vaults of opportunity of this nation. So we have come to cash this check—a check that will give us upon demand the riches of freedom and the security of justice. We have also come to this hallowed spot to remind America of the fierce urgency of *now*. This is no time to engage in the luxury of cooling off or to take the tranquilizing drug of gradualism. *Now* is the time to make real the promises of Democracy. *Now* is the time to rise from the dark and desolate valley of segregation to the sunlit path of racial justice. *Now* is the time to lift our nation from the quicksand of racial injustice to the solid rock of brotherhood. *Now* is the time to open the doors of opportunity to all of God's children."

Now he had them. A quarter of a million people were hanging onto his words.

"This sweltering summer of the Negro's legitimate discontent will not pass until there is an invigorating autumn of freedom and equality. 1963 is not an end, but a beginning. Those who hope that the Negro needed to blow off steam and will now be content will have a rude awakening if the nation returns to business as usual. There will be neither rest nor tranquility in America until the Negro is granted his citizenship rights. The whirlwinds of revolt will continue to shake the foundations of our nation until the bright day of justice emerges.

"I have a dream that one day this nation will rise up and live out the true meaning of its creed; 'We hold these truths to be self-evident—that all men are created equal' " (BOB ADELMAN/MAGNUM).

"But there is something that I must say to my people who stand on the warm threshhold which leads into the palace of justice. In the process of gaining our rightful place, we must not be guilty of wrongful deeds. Let us not seek to satisfy our thirst for freedom by drinking from the cup of bitterness and hatred. We must forever conduct our struggle on the high plane of dignity and discipline. We must not allow our creative protest to degenerate into physical violence. Again and again we must rise to the majestic heights of meeting physical force with soul force."

King reflected on the campaign just concluded, thinking of the "Letter from a Birmingham Jail," and dealt with the question of patience.

"We can never be satisfied as long as the Negro is the victim of the unspeakable horrors of police brutality. We can never be satisfied [they repeated, 'Never be satisfied!'] as long as our bodies, heavy with the fatigue of travel, cannot gain lodging in the motels of the highways and the hotels of the cities. We cannot be satisfied ['Cannot be satisfied!'] as long as the Negro's basic mobility is from a smaller ghetto to a larger one. We can never be satisfied ['Never be satisfied!'] as long as a Negro in Mississippi cannot vote and a Negro in New York believes he has nothing for which to vote. No, no, We are not satisfied, and we will not be satisfied until justice rolls down like waters, and righteousness like a mighty stream."

And then he poured it out. He spoke from the anguish of his heart. He spoke with the anguish of a leader who has suffered for many. He spoke from the hope that had kept him going in the dark days of bombings and despair because he *knew* there were better days ahead. He wanted to share that knowledge, now.

"I say to you today, my friends, that in spite of the difficulties and frustrations of the moment I still have a dream. It is a dream deeply rooted in the American dream.

"I have a dream that one day this nation will rise up and live out the true meaning of its creed: 'We hold these truths to be self-evident; that all men are created equal.'

"I have a dream that one day on the red hills of Georgia the sons of former slaves and the sons of former slaveowners will be able to sit down together at the table of brotherhood.

"I have a dream that the state of Mississippi, a desert state sweltering with the heat of injustice and oppression, will be transformed into an oasis of freedom and justice.

"I have a dream that my four little children will one day live in a nation where they will not be judged by the color of their skin but by the content of their character.

"I have a dream today.

"I have a dream that the state of Alabama, whose governor's lips are presently dripping with the words of interposition and nullification, will be transformed into a situation where little black boys and black girls will be able to join hands with little white boys and white girls and walk together as sisters and brothers.

"I have a dream today.

"I have a dream that one day every valley shall be exalted, every hill and mountain shall be made low, the rough places will be made plain, and the crooked places will be made straight, and the glory of the Lord shall be revealed, and all flesh shall see it together.

"This is our hope. This is the faith with which I return to the South. With this faith we will be able to hue out of the mountain of despair a stone of hope. With this faith we will be able to transform the jangling discords of our nation into a beautiful symphony of brotherhood. With this faith, we will be able to work together, to pray together, to struggle together, to go to jail together, to stand up for freedom together knowing that we will be free one day.

"This will be the day when all of God's children will be able to sing with new meaning,

> My country, tis of thee
> Sweet land of liberty, Of thee I sing:
> Land where my fathers died,
> Land of the pilgrims' pride,
> From every mountainside
> Let freedom ring.

"And if America is to be a great nation this must become true. So let freedom ring from the prodigious hilltops of New Hampshire. Let freedom ring ['Let freedom ring!'] from the mighty mountains of New York. Let freedom ring ['Let freedom ring!'] from the heightening Alleghenies of Pennsylvania!

"Let freedom ring from the snowcapped Rockies of Colorado! Let freedom ring from the curvaceous peaks of California! But not only that; let freedom ring from Stone Mountain of Georgia! Let freedom ring from Lookout Mountain of Tennessee! Let freedom ring from every hill and molehill of Mississippi. From every mountainside, let freedom ring.

"When we let freedom ring, when we let it ring from every village and every hamlet, from every state and every city, we will be able to speed up that day when all of God's children, black men and white men, Jews and Gentiles, Protestants and Catholics, will be able to join hands and sing in the words of the old Negro spiritual, 'Free at last! free at last! thank God almighty, we are free at last!'"

It was a stunning, heart-wrenching tour de force. Thousands were shouting King's name, shouting for joy, weeping for happiness for themselves, their country, and their collective future. Shouting in exultation because in their faith in God and the persona of Martin Luther King, Jr., they thought they saw a way up.

King, though elated, would take several hours to realize that it had become *his* day, just as Lincoln had stolen the day at Gettysburg a century before. For King, this was the crowning achievement for A. Philip Randolph, and he hurried to congratulate a patriarch of the labor and civil rights movement on "finally" getting his March on Washington.

King and the other leaders of the march went to the White House afterward, where a jubilant President Kennedy ordered them lunch from the White House kitchen and discussed the tremendously successful day. It was after ten o'clock before King got back to his hotel suite and he and Coretta could celebrate privately.

For all involved in the advancement of civil rights, it had been a great day.

J. Edgar Hoover was not, however, in that category. For him it had been horrible. Just before the march, the FBI's domestic intelligence division had sent Hoover a sixty-eight-page report detailing the ACP's efforts to influence the civil rights movement in general and King in particular and concluding that the puny party's 4,453 members had had little luck.

Hoover rejected the report with the devastating reply that "this memo reminds me vividly of those I received when Castro took over Cuba. You contended then that Castro and his cohorts were not Communists. . . . Time alone proved you wrong."

Assistant FBI Director William C. Sullivan, head of the division, took the rebuke seriously, and made a U-turn. On August 30, 1963, he wrote another memo to Hoover, stating in part that "the Director is correct. We were completely wrong about believing the evidence was not sufficient to determine some years ago that Fidel Castro was not a Communist or under Communist influence. On investigating and writing about Communism and the American Negro, we had better remember this and profit by the lesson it should teach us."

Considering the impact of King's address to the hundreds of thousands at the Lincoln Memorial, Sullivan added that "we must mark King now, if we have not done so before, as the most dangerous Negro of the future in this nation from the standpoint of Communism, the Negro, and national security. . . ."

In that light, Sullivan continued, they should forgo niceties of the law and realize "it may be unrealistic to limit ourselves as we have been doing to legalistic proofs or definitely conclusive evidence that would stand up in testimony in court or before Congressional committees."

In other words, the FBI should declare open warfare on Rev. Martin Luther King, Jr., and the movement he headed.

That made Hoover happy. The war against King commenced.

Even Hoover's personal animosity could not detract from the fact that a high water mark had been reached—and King was responsible.

August concluded with a truce in Savannah, Georgia, following a summer of nonviolent demonstrations led by Hosea Williams, who had been ousted from NAACP for being too militant. The business community had agreed to desegregate after it had had enough of a new form of demonstration—the night march.

"The sight of thousands of young niggers marching through their neighborhoods at night scared them half to death," Williams laughed. It did not scare the police enough to get them to refrain from using tear gas, fire hoses, and billy clubs on the marchers.

In the end, the city caved in, and desegregation was to begin October 1.

Nonviolent protest had been elevated to the top status as a means of protest, and Reverend King was its leading exponent. Before the year drew to a close there would be some ten thousand nonviolent racial demonstrations across the country, and more than five thousand blacks would be arrested for choosing this method to be free.

Now it was time to go to school.

PART THREE: THE FALL

Throughout the south and border states, 9.2 percent of the black children were now going to integrated schools. There were protests in the North over discrimination in education, as well.

In Chicago, 220,000 black students, about half the total school population, stayed home to protest the de facto segregation policies of school superintendent Benjamin C. Willis. This was the start of a concerted effort by a coalition of black and white civic groups in that Midwestern city to tackle a broad range of discriminatory practices in the city founded by a black fur trader.

This was the beginning of a series of Northern battles over educational inequities, and it sparked a backlash in the form of Protect Neighborhood Schools organizations in Chicago, New York, Detroit, and Cleveland.

As their interests were threatened, white attitudes hardened as well. A Gallup Poll found that only 21 percent of whites thought demonstrations helped blacks, and that figure was to drop steadily during the next twelve months.

The real horror was just beginning. Nacirema, too, was busy. There had been a lot of contact recently with Robert Chambliss, better known around Birmingham KKK circles as "Dynamite Bob," a protégé of Bull Connor. He was very good with dynamite and delayed fuses.

At the end of the summer of 1963, Chambliss worked with the group to plan the bombing of a Birmingham church. It was a plan discovered by Detective Little's undercover group, though it was out of their jurisdiction.

He did, however, share their information with the Birmingham police, since "it wasn't our problem," and with the FBI. That agency should have known all along what was going on, since its paid informant, Rowe, was involved in the planning as well and the bureau had encouraged him to get involved in violent acts so they would have a better way of identifying who was involved in these kinds of things.

"The planning for Birmingham was for a very specific time," Little said. "But they went in a few weeks prior to that."

No one knows why. Perhaps it was just cunning to alter the target date at the last minute. Perhaps Nacirema suspected an informant. Sometime after mid-

On Sunday morning, September 15, 1963, Klansman Robert Chambliss placed a bomb next to the rear of the Sixteenth Street Baptist Church in Birmingham (BIRMINGHAM NEWS).

IN MEMORY OF

DENISE McNAIR   CYNTHIA WESLEY   ADDIE MAE COLLINS   CAROL ROBERTSON

THEIR LIVES WERE TAKEN BY UNKNOWN PARTIES ON SEPTEMBER 15, 1963 WHEN THE SIXTEENTH STREET BAPTIST CHURCH WAS BOMBED.

"MAY MEN LEARN TO REPLACE BITTERNESS AND VIOLENCE WITH LOVE AND UNDERSTANDING"

It blew in the rear wall of the church, killing four little girls who were putting on their choir robes (BIRMINGHAM NEWS).

It gutted the rear of the church, destroying the offices . . . (BIRMINGHAM NEWS)

. . . and blowing the face of
Jesus Christ off a stained
glass window near the altar
(AP/WIDE WORLD).

. . . destroying the pews and
windows . . .
(DECLAN HAUN/BLACK STAR)

The police had been warned
of the plot, but they arrived
much too late
(BIRMINGHAM NEWS).

night Sunday, September 15, someone—possibly the FBI's Rowe—drove Chambliss to the Sixteenth Street Baptist Church. He crept to the rear of the church and placed a bucket of water beside the house of worship.

There were two important things about that bucket: it contained several sticks of dynamite connected to a battery, and it was filled with water that slowly dripped through a hole in the bottom. As it drained, the connecting wires on a cork bobber moved closer to the detonator.

Early Sunday morning, Rowe called up his contact at the Birmingham FBI office, and their logs show he asked if anyone had heard a bomb go off around daylight. The answer was no, and he hung up. The hole in the bucket had been too small.

Four hundred people were in the Sixteenth Street Baptist Church when the cork bobber reached its destination and blew up the rear of the church. On the other side of the wall, eleven-year-old Denise McNair and fourteen-year-olds Cynthia Wesley, Carol Robertson, and Addie Mae Collins were putting on their choir robes. It was their last act.

The explosion gutted the rear of the church, and the concussion even knocked the face of Jesus off the stained glass window.

King, who had been preaching at Ebenezer that morning, rushed to Birmingham when he heard the news. He described the act as "bestial" and despaired of a peaceful solution to such irrational hatred. Things got worse. That night, thirteen-year-old Virgil Ware was shot and killed by two sixteen-year-old whites, and a twenty-year-old black man was arrested for hitting a white motorcyclist with a rock.

Below left:
Now there was nothing left
to do but grieve
(BIRMINGHAM POST HERALD).

(DANNY LYON/MAGNUM)

The black rock-thrower was eventually to serve six months at hard labor: the two whites would get seven months' probation after pleading guilty to manslaughter.

There was a joint funeral service for three of the girls, and King eulogized them as "heroines of a holy crusade for freedom and human dignity. Their death says to us that we must work passionately and unceasingly to make the American dream a reality."

Chambliss was briefly arrested. But Connor would not let state police interview him, and the FBI would not discuss the case with local authorities.

On September 25, two shrapnel bombs exploded in the black section of Birmingham, and FBI files show that Rowe was seen by Birmingham policemen four blocks from the scene. He had called the bureau to report the bombings and get paid for his information. The FBI thought Rowe was valuable. No arrests followed anything he reported, though murder and destruction seemed to follow wherever he went.

When the New Year rolled around, a third of his income would be paid by the FBI as he continued his violent ways around the South.

This was a period of reflection for King. He was writing his third book, this time about the Birmingham campaign, to be entitled *Why We Can't Wait.*

On the afternoon of November 22, 1963, he was in his upstairs bedroom vaguely listening to the television. Suddenly, there was a special bulletin: President Kennedy had been shot during a motorcade in Dallas. His seatmate, Gov. John Connally, was shot also.

He yelled downstairs to his wife, "Corrie, I just heard that President Kennedy has been shot—maybe killed."

Below left:
(DECLAN HAUN/BLACK STAR).

Below, right:
A saddened King eulogized the girls as "heroines of a holy crusade" and lamented the hatred that had cut them down at such an early age. He prayed that they did not die in vain (DANNY LYON/ MAGNUM).

Coretta, who had been chatting with a friend, rushed upstairs to watch the breaking news with her husband. A few minutes later, they were joined by Bernard Lee, King's constant traveling companion.

"This is sick," King said, shaking his head. "You just can't do right and survive in this nation."

Lee said King was visibly shaken, close to tears by the assassination attempt. Then the announcement came that President Kennedy had died, and King, turning to Coretta, said, "This is going to happen to me, also. You know, I don't think I will live to reach forty because this country is too sick to allow me to live."

Coretta was speechless. "I had no words to comfort my husband," she said later. "I could not say, 'It won't happen to you.' I felt he was right."

King was one of twelve hundred people invited to attend the President's funeral in Washington's St. Matthew's Cathedral, wondering where the nation was headed.

The new President, Lyndon Johnson, answered part of that question in his first address to Congress, on November 27, when he said, "No memorial oration or eulogy could more eloquently honor President Kennedy's memory than the passage of the civil rights bill for which he fought so long."

King and other civil rights leaders met with Johnson at the White House December 3. Johnson told them how he had grown up in a poor community and empathized with the pain of the Mexican-Americans and Indians he used to teach. That was his heritage, he said, not the slave-holding South.

He stood up, said Lee, and said, "I'm not going to retreat at all. I am going to introduce legislation that will guarantee civil rights, and Martin, I am going to depend on you to help me."

Johnson, in his earthy way, told the group he was not going to "tiptoe around the issue" of civil rights, but would "pick up where Kennedy left off."

King agreed to do all he could to help, not knowing at the time that it would take one of his bitterest campaigns to spur the legislation through Congress.

The price of freedom in 1964 would be high.

Martin and Coretta at the
Selma march in 1965 (STEVE
SHAPIRO/LIFE MAGAZINE).

Det Norske Stortings Nobelkomite

ALFRED NOBEL

8
WHEN PATIENCE DIES

THE NEW YEAR BEGAN ON A HIGH NOTE.

The January 3, 1964, issue of *Time* magazine announced King as its "Man of the Year," making him the first black American to receive that honor, and only the second black person, after Haile Selassie, to grace its cover.

The rest of the news was disheartening. In Mississippi, Moses and Dennis had decided that this was the year to break the back of that state's fierce resistance to voting rights. Only 6.7 percent of the Mississippi blacks of voting age were registered, the lowest percentage of any Southern state. Across the Confederacy, 38 percent of the eligible blacks had registered, about half the percentage of Northern blacks.

By then, they had organized a statewide network of workers under the COFO banner—though most of the organizers were from SNCC—and planned to put together a statewide Freedom Democratic Party to challenge the seating of the all-white delegation the state party was sending to the Democratic National Convention in Atlantic City, New Jersey, in August.

They made another decision. They would invite thousands of whites from around the country to come to Mississippi and work with SNCC in its campaign. The reasoning was simple, if frightening. More than sixty blacks had been murdered in Mississippi for their involvement in civil rights activities since Moses began organizing there in 1960. There wasn't a ripple of national interest in the killings.

"It was pretty clear to us that we were on our own as far as protection was concerned," said Moses. "The Justice Department was not able to provide any real protection at all."

They knew that if there were large numbers of whites in the state, "the nation would pay more attention. All through sixty-three we had been having cross burnings and church burnings, and part of that reaction in Mississippi was a reaction of the state to the growing importance of the civil rights movement southwide.

"We were powerless. We had no protection for ourselves, and the Lewis Allen murder drove that home. We needed to try something different. If these

The winter of 1964 was slow, giving a tired Dr. King a chance to relax a bit, finish writing his third book, Why We Can't Wait, *and spend some time with his immediate family . . .*
(AP/WIDE WORLD)

. . . who some times accompanied him on short trips. King with daughter Yolanda and son Martin III (BOB ADELMAN).

. . . and his church family (VERNON MERRITT III/BLACK STAR).

He met with Malcolm X and found that the Muslim leader had changed, and their views now were very similar (AP/WIDE WORLD).

kids came down to Mississippi, the country followed them down. It is what the country would not do for us, for the black people who were there working."

It was clear that SNCC would have its hands full that summer.

Inequality in education was becoming a major Northern issue. In New York City, 464,000 blacks boycotted the school system in February and about half that many stayed out through March. Twenty thousand black students boycotted Boston schools; sixty-eight thousand boycotted in Cleveland; and the Chicago boycott was still in progress.

In Washington, Johnson managed to get the civil rights bill through a balky House, but it was stalled in the Senate by the Southern block. It would take something momentous to break through their filibuster.

Something like St. Augustine, Florida.

St. Augustine was America's oldest community, celebrating its four-hundredth anniversary that year. In 1964 it had another distinction besides its age. It was one of the most vicious of Southern cities.

A black dentist named Dr. Robert B. Hayling had begun organizing St. Augustine in the summer of 1963, trying to follow the example set by SCLC's Birmingham campaign. The results were vastly different. Blacks in St. Augustine had no history of resistance, and Hayling could not call on a large core of support the way Birmingham's Reverend Shuttlesworth could. The resistance—in the courts and in the streets—was much stiffer.

Dr. Hayling got teenagers to march in July 1963, and County Judge Charles C. Mathis, Jr., quickly ruled that picketing "was detrimental to the health, morals, and well being of children under seventeen." He had seven teenagers—from fourteen to sixteen years of age—taken from their parents and placed in detention centers for more than four months, pending assignment to foster homes, where he said they could receive better care.

On September 18, 1963, Hayling drove three associates—James Jackson, Clyde Jenkins, and James Howser—down a side road off U.S. 1 to listen to a Ku Klux Klan rally from a distance. Suddenly they were surrounded by armed Klansmen, who took them to the center of the gathering of 450 whites and beat them unmercifully with clubs and chains. Deputy Sheriff Guy Rexford interrupted the proceedings just as the unconscious men were about to be doused with kerosene and burned. The four were charged with assault on two of the Klansmen and were convicted before Judge Mathis that fall.

St. Augustine, Florida, was the oldest city in America . . . and the most lawless . . . and the most violent (AP/WIDE WORLD).

Dr. Hayling had written to President Kennedy and, later, President Johnson asking for help in the lawless town, in which the police actively sided with Klansmen to beat up black protestors. He received no replies. The city had also been in touch with the Johnson administration, and it received $350,000 in federal funds to help with its four-hundredth anniversary celebration. So Hayling wrote his tale of woe to King.

Said C. T. Vivian, "Doc [as the staff referred to King] spotted it as a place that would be good for us to meet head on and deal with the kind of violence that was going on all up and down the coast.

"St. Augustine was the biggest tourist spot, and we had a better chance of winning there than we did in some of the other places. It had a more up front kind of image, and it would have to deal with that."

St. Augustine represented a change. For the first time, King was sending SCLC troopers into a situation not to help the local black population, but to influence developments on the national scene.

Explained Vivian, "Doc felt if we brought out the Klan and all the rest, it would make the way clear for the federal government to make demands on the state government. And one of the major strategies of the civil rights movement at that time was to change the concept of states' rights. We needed to bring a confrontation between states' rights and the federal government.

"It is never to be forgotten that under states' rights the South was able to continually harass, destroy, intimidate, and control black people. We could not move until the federal government came in. We went into St. Augustine to deal with that kind of issue."

King sent Lee, Young, Vivian, and Williams to St. Augustine in early March 1964 to lay the groundwork for a spring campaign. They found a battle zone. Sheriff L. O. Davis ran St. Johns County and was something of a puzzle to St. Augustine's blacks. His father ran a grocery store in the black community, and Davis coached football at both the black and white high schools.

Yet he had more than a hundred deputies. Chief among these was "Hoss" Manucy, who led a group of thugs called the Ancient City Gun Club, which rode around in radio cars with Confederate flags on their antennas. Many of these were also deputized by Sheriff Davis.

"St. Augustine was worse than Mississippi in many ways," said Vivian. "They used guns, chains, lead pipes—the whole works—on black people there."

King spent March and April traveling around the country, raising funds, promoting the stalled civil rights bill, and finishing his book *Why We Can't Wait*, which was to be published in June.

In St. Augustine, the SCLC leaders were teaching the black community how to prepare for nonviolent confrontations, something that had not been tried in the Ancient City yet.

"This was something new," said Henry Twine, then secretary of the St. Augustine NAACP and one of Hayling's advisers. "Blacks had never gotten in the street and marched like that. They had always been afraid. We'd always been taught to run and get under the bed when the police came."

The residents of America's oldest city were "poor as snakes," said Twine, and there were few professionals among them.

As the movement coalesced, Reverend Shuttlesworth and James Bevel came down to help out. Toward the end of May, after an evening workshop on nonviolence, Williams said to Vivian, "You know, I think it's about time."

Vivian answered, "If you think you're ready, come on and let's go."

They launched a two-pronged attack on the city in late May. First, in the mornings, a column of blacks, often lead by Vivian and Shuttlesworth, went to the broad beach. Blacks were allowed to use only one sixteen-hundred-foot stretch of the beach and had been beaten and occasionally drowned for straying out of their zone.

"The Klan would all be out there, and there stood the police," said Williams. "Manucy was their leader, and they would line up with Little League baseball bats. They'd have a line a block or two long on the beach.

"Then, after awhile, Hoss Manucy would give the word 'Charge!' And they would come in the water and beat us with those bats. Nobody ever died, fortunately, but they drew a lot of blood.

"After they whipped us for about five minutes, then the police and the sheriff would move in and arrest everybody for disturbing the peace. It cost us fifty dollars apiece to get out of jail; it cost the Klan two dollars and fifty cents."

On one occasion, when Williams was tied up elsewhere, Vivian turned to Shuttlesworth as they entered the Atlantic Ocean and asked if he could swim.

"Yeah," said the Birmingham minister. "But not in the ocean."

The most disconcerting thing about this campaign, said Vivian, was that "the police force and the Klan were the same thing. Guys who would be beating you in the morning, you would see over at the jail later as deputies.

"I remember seeing a guy step into a police car to change. He was all wet from trying to kill us in the ocean."

The second phase of the plan was then put into effect: the night march.

The first of these was held Tuesday, May 26, and Williams led four hundred blacks on a march—singing and praying as they went—from the First Baptist Church to the old Slave Market in the center of St. Augustine.

"We demanded the right to go into the Slave Market and have a prayer service," said Williams, "and the police didn't want to allow it."

That march was uneventful, but the following night, Davis and St. Augustine Police Chief Virgil Stuart confronted Williams and eight hundred marchers and told them they could not go to the Slave Market because there were not enough police available to protect them in case of violence. At that point, about fifty children in the march were sent back to the church, and the rest continued to the square.

There, they were taunted by about one hundred "armed toughs and hoodlums" who were not searched by police.

Thursday night, May 28, Williams led a group of four hundred from the St. Paul's A.M.E. Church to the Slave Market shortly after 10 P.M. This time the whites attacked, ripping through the center of the line and beating the blacks at will.

"The Klansmen had been storing up bricks all day in the Slave Market," said Clyde Jenkins, "and when the demonstrators approached, they started throwing them. It was really a miracle that no one was killed. The Lord was with us that night."

Not only did the police decline to interfere, they helped the attackers.

Deputy Sheriff W. E. Haynie charged a white reporter named Harry Boyte, beating him and siccing him sixty-pound attack dog on the man. Whites later shot into Boyte's car and shot up the beach house where he and Vivian had been staying. Sheriff Davis would not examine the scene until nearly noon the following day.

King, informed of the attacks, wired President Johnson that "all semblance of law and order has broken down in St. Augustine" and asked for federal assistance.

"They whipped up on us good," said Williams, "and back at the church we would be crying and putting ourselves back together. But there was a lot of pride in being able to stand up under that, and a funny kind of humor developed.

"Somebody would say, 'Hey, did you see Policeman Joe, that big fat one? Boy, he sure could whip some head,' or 'Boy, he sure has a mean left.'

"And we'd talk about the blows we got like they were badges of honor. I guess they were."

King flew to St. Augustine to take charge of the situation and found that the police had secured an injunction against marches after 6 P.M. Andy Young filed a class action suit before Federal District Court Judge Bryan Simpson, of an old-line conservative Florida family.

He began hearings on Monday, June 1, and King and Hayling agreed to postpone further protests until Judge Simpson rendered a decision. The judge was visibly moved by the testimony of Young and Williams and, especially, Dr. Hayling, whose description of his severe beating at the KKK rally and subsequent conviction for assault seemed to be a mockery of justice.

He was appalled to find out that Sheriff Davis had appointed Hoss Manucy, a convicted felon, as one of his special deputies.

He had Manucy put on the stand and demanded to know more about the Ancient City Gun Club. When Manucy pleaded the Fifth Amendment thirty-three times, Judge Simpson declared him in contempt of court and had him placed in jail—with a lot of black prisoners. Thirty minutes later, Manucy gave the judge a list of the members of his special group.

Though the marches stopped for a week, spirits were still high. King addressed a rally and told the crowd, "You know they threaten us occasionally with more than beatings here and there. They threaten us with actual physical death.

"They think that this will stop the movement. I got word way out in California that a plan was underway to take my life in St. Augustine, Florida. Well, if physical death is the price that I must pay to free my white brother and all my brothers and sisters from a permanent death of the spirit, then nothing can be more redemptive.

"We have long since learned to sing anew,
'Before I'll be a slave,
I'll be buried in my grave,
And go home to my Father
And be saved.'"

Judge Simpson did not agonize over his decision long. Though a Southern conservative, he said, "Somebody had to stand in the way of those people. I carried the oath I took when I took the job seriously."

He ruled that the city and police had no right to prevent the marches and granted a preliminary injunction June 9 precluding Sheriff Davis, Police Chief Stuart, and Mayor Joseph Shelly from interfering with the night marches in the future.

The judge also found that St. Augustine and the county had subjected arrested blacks to "cruel and unusual punishment" in their jail treatment, such as cramming twenty-one people into a padded cell only ten feet in diameter, or making them stand in the hot sun until they passed out.

The judge was vilified by whites for ruling against the establishment. Said Judge Simpson, "The world would be so uninteresting if we all thought the same way. Racial views expanded and changed when you really had to face the thing and think it through. I knew I was doing what was right."

King was elated, and he and Abernathy decided to lead a day march to Monson's Motor Lodge, a fiercely segregated resort hotel owned by James and Peggy Brock where they were arrested on June 9.

Brock and a group of whites brought an alligator to the motel's swimming pool and dropped it in to bring a quick end to interracial swimming. King, watching the scene, said, "If they don't think one of those will eat white meat, let one of them get in the pool."

While King was in jail, Williams led four hundred people on another night march, and they were beaten soundly at the Slave Market. King, from his jail cell, called President Johnson to personally complain about the lawlessness and ask for federal protection.

The violence was having an effect in the nation's capital. For the first time, the Senate passed a vote of cloture on a filibuster of a civil rights bill, ensuring its eventual passage.

King and Abernathy were bailed out of jail Wednesday, June 11, and King resumed his speaking engagements while the staff continued putting the pressure on St. Augustine. But there was pressure on the other side, too.

J. B. Stoner, a racist from Marietta, Georgia, whom Detective Little said was "closely connected" with Nacirema, flew into town Friday. In a sense, it was a reunion for Stoner: in June 1958 he was part of a group of Klansmen who blew up Shuttlesworth's Bethel Baptist Church in Birmingham. A Birmingham policeman had approached Stoner about dynamiting the churches of movement leaders for two thousand dollars, and Stoner said he had Shuttlesworth's church blown up the following week "just to show what my boys can do."

Integrating a pool at Monson's Motor Lodge invited a dousing with acid on one occasion, an alligator on another (AP/WIDE WORLD).

King called President Johnson and asked for troops to keep order. But no help was forthcoming from the White House (AP/WIDE WORLD).

(He would pay for that in 1980, when John Yung, the assistant attorney general for Alabama, would say at Stoner's trial that the Klansman was "a professional hater, a cold-blooded bomber, and a bald-faced liar." Stoner would get ten years in jail.)

He exhorted a crowd of Klansmen to resist the pressures of "Martin Lucifer Coon" and led a night march of 170 whites through the black section of town, escorted by sympathetic white policemen and their dogs.

Stoner continued to lead the white hate groups and push for more violence as the confrontations continued on the beaches and at night at the Slave Market. Manucy said during a local television interview that he "did not like coons, Jews, and Martin Luther King."

King returned, and Lee was driving him and Abernathy around one evening when the attacks started on a march, led this evening by Young.

"Some white man hit Andy over the head with a blackjack," said Lee, "and knocked him to the ground. Willie Bolden [Williams's aide from Savannah days] fell over Andy and protected him from some of the blows.

"Then these white guys rushed the car and almost turned it over with us in it. King wanted to get out, but we knew it would be almost suicide for him to lead a march. If anyone had caught him in a situation where they could have eliminated him, they would have done so.

"I said, 'No way will you get out there with those hillbillies and let them kill you. That will prove nothing.'" He jammed the accelerator and roared out of the Slave Market.

On June 25, the historic Civil Rights Act passed, and Stoner led nearly one thousand furious whites out of the Slave Market to brutally beat another group of marchers.

Still the Johnson administration remained strangely silent, sending no federal troops despite repeated pleas from King. The St. Augustine campaign had become a nightmare—one continuous round of beatings and jailings—yet it had achieved its purpose.

"The Civil Rights Act was written in Birmingham," said Williams, "and passed in St. Augustine."

Now, said Williams, "we were looking for an honorable way to bring the movement to a halt."

Judge Simpson provided a way out. He kept judicial pressure on the state and county, giving them orders on how to run the city or be thrown in jail for contempt of court. Under his pressure, Gov. Farris Bryant finally agreed to set up a biracial committee to negotiate an end to the discriminatory practices. At that, SCLC wound down its activities and left June 30.

Two days later, King and other black leaders were at the White House to watch President Johnson sign the Public Accommodations Bill, a part of the Civil Rights Act of 1964. This was a major feat, but there were gaps. The act did not address the problem of voting rights, which were still resisted through much of the South. The act did not address the problem of fair housing. Several states had passed open housing legislation, but it was widely ignored.

And the act did not address the safety of blacks who were seeking to exercise their rights in the South.

After the signing, Johnson met with the civil rights leaders and said that now that the act had passed, there was really no further need for confrontations in the streets. Remedies for injustices could work their way through the court system.

King knew better. In his latest book, *Why We Can't Wait*, which came out during the St. Augustine campaign, King wrote, "The Negro wants absolute freedom and equality, not in Africa or in some imaginary state, but right here in this land today."

That was not possible in 1964. Despite the euphoria of the passage of the Civil Rights Act, Mississippi was about to show it could wear out the patience of the young, and blacks in the North would show that their patience died after the March on Washington.

The violence escalated early. In March, Samuel H. Bowers, Jr., Imperial Wizard of the White Knights of the Ku Klux Klan of Mississippi, decided that something had to be done about the influx of agitators in Mississippi and authorized Klan members in Neshoba County to kill some of them.

The targets of their ire were Michael and Rita Schwerner, New York Jews who had opened a regional COFO headquarters in Meridian along with a local black SNCC volunteer, twenty-year-old James Chaney.

Klan activity and the harassment of volunteers and blacks seeking to register were stepped up in the area, and on June 7, leader Bowers read a "declaration of war" at a KKK rally near Raleigh against "COFO's nigger-Communist invasion of Mississippi." All that was left now was the timing and the method.

On June 21, Michael Schwerner, Chaney, and Andrew Goodman, a twenty-one-year-old Jew attending Queens College in New York, were driving back to Meridian after viewing a church that had been burned to the ground in Longdale when they were stopped by Neshoba County Deputy Sheriff Cecil Price. They were supposedly picked up on a traffic violation, but in reality, Price was part of the Klan apparatus that had planned to make an example of these COFO workers.

The trio was taken to jail in Philadelphia, shortly after 4 P.M., while Klansmen gathered in the nearby Longhorn Cafe. At 10 P.M., the Jackson office of COFO notified the FBI that the three were missing. In reality, they were still

Mississippi summer started on a note of optimism. Hundreds of whites and blacks from the North came to Mississippi to help in a mass voter registration drive. The KKK issued a "declaration of war" against the "nigger-Communist invasion." SNCC workers Schwerner, Chaney, and Goodman were murdered near Philadelphia, Mississippi, June 21, 1964. The summer toll would be 6 murdered, 35 shot, 80 beaten, 1,000 arrested, 30 buildings bombed, and 35 churches burned. Michael Schwerner (AP/WIDE WORLD).

James Chaney (AP/WIDE WORLD).

Andrew Goodman (AP/WIDE WORLD).

in jail, but Price released them a half hour later and told them to get out of town. They did not get far. There followed a high-speed chase by Price and at least seven other men, and the trio was caught about nine miles outside Philadelphia. They were taken to a lonely road, where they were beaten and then murdered. James Jordan shot Chaney in the stomach, the back, and then the head.

There was a pause—the Klansmen weren't all sure they were going to kill the two white men. Then Wayne Roberts shot Schwerner and Goodman in the chest. The three were taken to the site of a new dam on Olen Burrage's farm, six miles southwest of Philadelphia, and buried.

This was the start of the war on COFO that summer. SNCC brought nineteen hundred primarily white volunteers to Mississippi for the project, and before it officially ended August 16, there were one thousand arrests, thirty buildings bombed, thirty-five churches burned, thirty-five shootings, eighty people severely beaten, and six murders.

J. Edgar Hoover, who still hated King for criticizing lax FBI enforcement in Albany two years earlier, announced on June 22 that he was personally directing a massive search for Chaney, Schwerner, and Goodman, who were presumed dead. He flew to Jackson on July 10 to formally open a massive FBI office there, eventually controlling 150 men in the quest for the killers. On July 10, Neshoba County Sheriff Lawrence Rainey received a standing ovation when he addressed a KKK recruitment rally near Meridian.

"Mississippi Summer," said SNCC chairman John Lewis, "really opened things up. It literally brought the country to the realization that something was seriously wrong with American society.

"In Birmingham, you had a drama that people could witness; they saw it on television. But in the Mississippi Summer, you had primarily white people—people from the other America—seeing Americans living on this side of America. The thousands of young people—the doctors, the lawyers, the teachers and other professionals that spent the summer in Mississippi saw this reality with their own eyes. They were participants. They suffered. Some were beaten. Some went to jail. Some of them died."

Mississippi whites weren't the only ones to explode in anger that summer.

On July 18, a white off-duty policeman shot and killed a fifteen-year-old black youth in Harlem. In a matter of minutes, angry crowds gathered and the first of the "long hot summers" began. Thousands of blacks began rioting in the streets of America's most famous black community, burning and looting white-owned stores and battling police.

Before it ended July 23, 1 person was dead, 500 were arrested, and 140 were injured. New York City Mayor Robert Wagner contacted King and asked him to come to New York and try to help quell the violence.

It was a mistake. Local black leaders such as Rep. Adam Clayton Powell and sociologist Kenneth Clark said he had no business coming to Harlem preaching nonviolence without having first conferred with black leaders in the area to find out their side of the story.

"That word nonviolence turned them off," said Lee. "Harlem was a different world for us. They always saw nonviolence as the sissy way out, the weak way out, the do-nothing way out . . . turning the other cheek."

King was stung by the criticism and by charges that he had simply been "used" by Wagner, who had rejected King's suggestion for a civilian police review board. And he was upset by the systematic way in which the Northern system of "integration" brutalized its black population.

It was not the South, but it wasn't right, either.

Violence is contagious. During the next few weeks riots broke out in black communities in Rochester, New York; Jersey City, Keansburg, and Paterson, New Jersey; Philadelphia; and the Chicago suburb of Dixmoor.

The violence was to cause an open split in the fragile working relationship among the six major civil rights organizations. Wilkins was stuffy and indignant at the lawlessness. King, however, said, "If the total slum violations of law by the white man over the years were calculated and were compared with the lawbreaking of a few days of riots, the hardened criminal would be the white man."

President Johnson had just launched a massive, one-billion-dollar "War on Poverty" and appointed Sargent Shriver head of the Office of Economic Opportunity. King, however, viewed this as only a start and wanted the equivalent of a Marshall Plan for America's poor, costing at least fifty times as much.

The riots did not dissuade King from his faith in nonviolence. They did bolster his feeling that eventually, if SCLC were to have real validity, he would have to bring its campaign North—and make it work.

Meanwhile, he returned to the South, launching a hectic People-to-People campaign across Mississippi, in an effort to drum up enthusiasm and support for SNCC's Mississippi Summer Project.

On August 4, 1964, the bodies of Chaney, Schwerner, and Goodman were discovered under fifteen feet of earth in a new dam on Burrage's farm, confirming what SNCC workers already knew. What was equally depressing was that the FBI search for the bodies also turned up three other blacks who had been missing and presumed murdered—a fourteen-year-old boy who was drowned and nineteen-year-olds Charles E. Moore and Henry Dee, who had been beaten to death.

SNCC had fulfilled its purpose and established a statewide voting block, and Moses and SNCC executive director James Forman led the Mississippi Freedom Democratic Party to the Democratic Convention in Atlantic City and challenged the right of the regular, all-white Democratic group to be seated.

Their chances of ousting the entire Mississippi delegation were slim, but King worked hard at lobbying in their behalf. Then there was a split.

Johnson's aides tried to push through a compromise in which the MFDP would get two symbolic seats in the Mississippi section, and the regular delegation would have to sign loyalty oaths. Moses was backing a counterproposal to seat both groups and divide the votes.

"King and the whole liberal wing thought that those two seats were quite an accomplishment," said Moses, and he tried to persuade the delegation to accept it at a tumultuous meeting in a black church near the Atlantic City Convention Center. The UAW's Walter Reuther and Vice President Hubert Humphrey were also pushing the proposal at the meeting.

"SNCC people argued bitterly and strongly against that proposal," said Lewis. "Fannie Lou Hamer said we didn't come this far to get two votes. They wanted to make us honorary guests at the convention, and we said no."

But the MFDP split, essentially on class lines, with the educated blacks from Jackson agreeing to the Johnson plan, and the remainder refusing and picketing the convention. This marked the open break between SNCC and SCLC, its parent organization. It also marked the beginning of the radicalization of SNCC, a radicalization that was to destroy that young group.

"Too much blood had been shed that summer for us to compromise," said Lewis. "That was too little to compensate for all of the suffering. We did not turn away from the philosophy of nonviolence, but there was a change from the early days with the Tuesday sessions. Then, we did not have the attitude of all or nothing.

King worked with SNCC in Mississippi, raising funds and traveling with John Lewis to hear tales of abuse from residents who had tried to vote (BIRMINGHAM NEWS).

Lewis, Moses, and Julian Bond crisscrossed the state trying to get blacks to register (ARCHIE E. ALLEN).

Their Mississippi Freedom Democratic Party challenged the seating of the all-white Mississippi delegation to the Democratic National Convention in Atlantic City, New Jersey (front, left to right) Julian Bond, John Lewis; (back, left to right) Annie Devine, Fannie Lou Hamer.

"If there were degrees of militancy, there was a growing militancy on the part of SNCC. We saw what existed in Mississippi as being radically evil in the extreme. And we shifted in attitude from nonviolence—going limp, for example—to aggressive nonviolence, like physically blocking a door."

After the conventions were over, pressure was put on black leaders to halt all their demonstrations until after the November elections. The feeling was that any violence would help the candidacy of Senator Barry Goldwater, the law and order Republican candidate for the presidency. King agreed with the moratorium and issued a joint statement with Randolph, Rustin, Wilkins, and Young that the Goldwater candidacy threatened "liberal democracy."

Lewis and CORE's Farmer refused to sign the statement. "I just didn't think we should give up the right to protest," said Lewis.

At this point in King's career, he found himself the major figure on the civil rights scene, yet he was estranged from all sides. The youth movement, as embodied by SNCC, which had braved open violence through the Freedom Rides, sit-ins, and voting rights campaigns, criticized King for moving too slowly.

At the other side, the old-line organizations like the NAACP and the Urban League still felt King was an upstart and SCLC was pushing too hard, too fast. Outside the black conflict, the 1964 Gallup Poll said only 10 percent of whites now believed that demonstrations helped blacks get ahead.

King continued charting his course, campaigning that fall for Johnson and traveling extensively to raise funds for the other civil rights groups and raise the hopes of any who called.

SNCC fell into a slump. The emotional toll of watching one colleague after another get beaten, threatened, and, in some cases, murdered was a heavy one. After what they considered a major "loss" at the Democratic Convention in Atlantic City, it was difficult for them to regroup. Many, psychologically worn out, drifted away from SNCC and all civil rights organizing, including the man who is credited with single-handedly organizing the state of Mississippi, Bob Moses.

"People sort of drifted," he said, "and there was a lot of burnout. The Mississippi staff, who had been there in sixty-two, sixty-three, and sixty-four were just kind of sitting around, drinking and being cynical. That was hard to watch.

"The main problem with SNCC was to put SNCC back together again. We could never do that."

Some of the SNCC staff, including Stokely Carmichael, went to Selma to try and revive their voter registration project. SNCC had been in Selma for more than a year, but their drive met more resistance than they could handle in the form of Sheriff Jim Clark and his deputized "posse" of segregationists. In late 1963 Lewis had led more than eight hundred blacks on a voter registration march to the Dallas County Courthouse in Selma, but he and most of the marchers were arrested and only five people were allowed to register.

Now, a year later, SNCC was practically nonexistent in Selma, and local leaders asked SCLC to come in and take over the voter registration effort. According to Hosea Williams, "Jim Clark just beat SNCC out of Selma. He used sticks and cattle prods and anything else. He just whipped them."

There was a serious dispute within SNCC's hierarchy as to whether they should work with whites again. In the end, the budding black nationalist faction

King's selection as the recipient of the 1964 Nobel Peace Prize was greeted joyously throughout black America (LEONARD FREED/ MAGNUM).

His motorcade was mobbed in Baltimore and other cities (LEONARD FREED/MAGNUM).

in SNCC would win out. After the summer of 1964, SNCC was never again a major factor in the civil rights movement.

And what of Mississippi? Sixteen homes and four churches were dynamited in Pike County, around McComb. The FBI charged nine Klansmen with the bombings, and they pleaded guilty to lesser state charges in September. Circuit Court Judge William Watkins gave them suspended sentences, however, saying, "The court understands and appreciates what you have done and the crimes you have committed have been, to some extent at least, provoked and brought about by outside influences."

The FBI did come up with information about the murderers of Chaney, Schwerner, and Goodman, but refused to share it. The district attorney did not have investigative powers and had to rely on either the FBI or the local sheriff's office, which was thought to be responsible for the murders.

A Neshoba County grand jury was empaneled in September, but only issued a report that its investigation had been "curtailed, and in fact stymied by the failure and refusal of agents of the FBI and other federal officials to testify in regard to this matter."

It seemed that Mississippi had gotten away with murder again.

The hundreds of thousands of miles King traveled and the constant pressures eventually took their toll. On October 13, after returning from a European tour with Abernathy, King checked into St. Joseph's Hospital in Atlanta for a checkup and a rest.

The following morning an excited Coretta called him to inform him he had been awarded the 1964 Nobel Peace Prize, making him its third black recipient since its inception in 1895; after Ralph Bunche, the Mideast negotiator, and Albert Luthuli, the leader of the African National Congress.

King immediately announced he would distribute the fifty-four-thousand-dollar prize money to the civil rights movement. He said that this was not a personal honor, "but a tribute to the discipline, wise restraint, and majestic courage of the millions of gallant Negro and white persons of good will who have followed a nonviolent course."

Accolades poured in from around the world, and there were some touching moments. In Atlanta, Archbishop Hallinan of the Roman Catholic archdiocese went to St. Joseph's to offer his congratulations to King.

As he concluded, he said, "May I give you my blessing?" King assented and received the traditional blessing, and the archbishop made the sign of the cross. Then, to King's surprise, the Catholic leader sank to his knees and asked, "May I receive your blessing?" King felt humbled at this sign of religious respect from a Catholic archbishop.

Not everyone was pleased. Hoover, in fact, was livid. He had already launched a quiet smear campaign against King, bugging not only his home but virtually every hotel room he and his staff used when traveling. His men were trying to portray King as a profligate, a charge he never substantiated despite his tapes and that King's staff vehemently denied.

It was a happy time in Oslo, Norway, for the world's leading proponent of peaceful protest (ROLAND MITCHELL).

The family celebrated a singular honor; (left to right) Alberta King, Martin Luther King, Sr., Martin Luther King, Jr., Christine King Ferris, Coretta Scott King, A. D. King (ROLAND MITCHELL).

Above, right: The receipt of the prize (ROLAND MITCHELL).

Right: King said the fifty-four-thousand-dollar prize would be given to the civil rights movement (AP/WIDE WORLD).

Hoover stepped up his campaign of vilification, and his chief aides contacted several representatives of the news media in an effort to get them to listen to tapes purporting to show the black clergyman's indiscretions. Members of the news media, however, were appalled at the FBI's gestapo tactics, disbelieved the tapes, and were disgusted at the trash this venerated law enforcement agency was peddling.

Hoover even had a tape sent to Coretta, accompanied by a threatening, anonymous note. She listened to it along with her husband, Abernathy, Young, Lee, and Lowery.

At first, King was despondent, saying, "They are out to break me. They are out to get me, harass me, break my spirit."

That mood didn't last, however. Hoover had revealed himself as a power-mad, unprincipled individual. King, after days of praying and agonizing with friends and Coretta, decided, "What I do is only between me and my God." He would never again worry about the scurrilous attempts of Hoover.

It was a grand time for SCLC's shock troops. "I had the best voice," said Abernathy (ROLAND MITCHELL).

Not to be outdone, the ladies sang, too . . . (ROLAND MITCHELL).

. . . especially with Coretta as soloist (ROLAND MITCHELL).

Besides, in the court of world opinion, Hoover didn't count. "All of us felt a tremendous sense of pride when King received the prize," said Lee. "I knew from then on that regardless of what white folks said about us, or about the movement, the world community had made its statement, which superceded any of the foolishness and buffoonery that happened in this country.

"There were times when people were talking about you, saying you were taking money, that you were sleeping around; and the world community, through the Nobel Peace Prize, said none of it is true, and none of those comments are important. What was important were your efforts to bring peace to the world. And that gave us a big boost."

So King and an entourage of thirty went to Oslo, Norway, on December 6, and four days later the black man who was the undisputed leader of the second American Revolution was accorded the world's highest honor for his adherence to the principles of freedom, equality, and peace.

(IVAN MASSAR/BLACK STAR).

On that same day, U.S. Magistrate Esther Carter, sitting in Meridian, Mississippi threw out federal charges against Sheriff Rainey, Deputy Price, and nineteen others for depriving Chaney, Schwerner, and Goodman of their civil rights.

They were indicted by another federal grand jury on King's birthday, January 15, 1965, and U.S. District Court Judge Harold Cox tossed them out a month later, saying that, at most, the men could only be charged with misdemeanors. The Justice Department decided to appeal to the U.S. Supreme Court.

SCLC's core staff was working hard trying to organize Selma and prepare for another confrontation with Jim Clark and his posse. Williams had been joined by Bevel and Bernard Lafayette, and Lewis, who was on SCLC's board, lent support from SNCC. Selma had hired a new police chief named Wilson Baker, a professional in the mold of Laurie Pritchett, who felt the city could weather the civil rights onslaught if the sheriff stayed out of the city.

In the beginning, he was relatively restrained. King and John Lewis from SNCC led a joint march with four hundred potential voters to the county courthouse on January 18, 1965, and were met by Clark. The sheriff, following Baker's lead, simply led the group to the courthouse's alley entrance and left them.

Two days later, though, Clark's natural instincts got the better of him, and he and his group roughly handled fifty blacks who were seeking to register. At the mass meeting that night, both SNCC and SCLC jokingly voted to make Clark an honorary member. He became livid when he heard about it.

The following week SCLC obtained a federal court order prohibiting city and county officials from impeding the voter registration, but Clark tried anyway. At one point, Clark assaulted Annie Lee Cooper, and she knocked him down. Then, as three of Clark's posse held her tightly, Clark brutally beat her with his billy club as newspeople and angry black marchers watched.

During the next few weeks there was a stalemate of sorts. There were days when Clark and his posse merely pushed marchers and declined to let them register, and days when he was his brutish, bullying self. On one of these occasions, Bevel was beaten by several of Clark's men. He awakened naked and chained to a bed. He had a concussion and had been doused with cold water. Fortunately, his attorney had him taken to a hospital for treatment.

On the national scene, President Johnson was preoccupied with other matters. He had just ordered the beginning of "Rolling Thunder," the continuous carpet bombing of North Vietnam, and he was preparing to send the first group of Marines to Vietnam as soldiers in the growing Asian war.

On February 10, Clark reached a new low. He and his troopers, in squad cars, used their clubs and cattle prods to force 165 black youngsters on a three-mile run, until they fell, crying, into ditches.

King, who had just returned from Washington, where there was still only a little interest in a voting rights bill, led twenty-eight hundred blacks on a new march the next day and escalated the campaign to the surrounding counties, as well.

Sheriff Jim Clark and his Klan-dominated posse had run SNCC out of Selma, Alabama. Now it was time for a confrontation with SCLC (AP/WIDE WORLD).

There was scattered integration in Selma. A white waitress served SCLC leaders as King chatted with Julian Bond (AP/WIDE WORLD).

The expansion of territory didn't bother Clark, whose posse would go anywhere they had the opportunity to harass blacks. It enabled Al Lingo, the leader of Alabama's state troopers, to get into the act.

On February 18, Lingo's men attacked a group of demonstrators on a night march in Marion, the hometown of Coretta King, Juanita Abernathy, and Jean Young. Twenty-five-year-old Jimmy Lee Jackson saw a trooper beating his mother and ran to help her. He was gunned down in the middle of the street, and he died two days later.

There was a lot of anger in the black community over the killing, and Bevel said it should be "channeled into something constructive."

He suggested taking the body and marching fifty miles to Montgomery and holding a service on the statehouse steps. The idea took hold, but it was eventually decided that King would lead the march on Sunday, March 7, and it would be from Selma to Montgomery, rather than from Marion. They were going to go directly to Governor Wallace and petition him to end the police lawlessness and grant blacks their right to register and vote.

Wallace announced he would not meet with any representatives of the group, banned the march, and ordered Lingo to keep the blacks away from the Cradle of the Confederacy.

King went to Washington to confer with President Johnson. The mercurial Texan still did not think Congress was in a mood to pass another major civil rights bill so soon, but the daily reports of violence and the killing of Jackson was stirring the capital's collective conscience.

The Washington meetings tied up a lot of King's time, and he decided to delay the main march until Monday, March 8, so he could tend to the affairs of his church in Atlanta. Meanwhile, SNCC had had an emergency executive board meeting in Atlanta.

They had been unhappy when SCLC came to Selma, which they regarded as their turf, and took over a movement they had failed to galvanize after more than a year of trying. Lewis had tried his best to smooth over the differences for the sake of the cause—the people of Selma—and he had marched, been beaten, and arrested several times in demonstrations under the SCLC banner.

Many of SNCC's leadership, especially director Forman, were opposed to the march. In their view, said Lewis, "SCLC just wants to go over there and have a march and raise a lot of money and get an ad in the New York *Times.* Meanwhile, a lot of people will get hurt, and a lot of people may get killed.

"I took the position that SNCC people were already there, and that local people had invited SCLC in. If the local people wanted to march, we had an obligation to march with them."

The conclusion was that SNCC members could participate, but as individuals, not as representatives of SCLC. So Lewis and two others got in his car and drove to Alabama on their own.

Brown's Chapel A.M.E. Church was packed that Sunday. Bevel and Williams had gotten hundreds of people to come to a mass meeting, though Williams knew that King had ordered the march postponed until Monday. Williams contacted King and Abernathy in Atlanta and worked out a compromise: he could lead a small march, but they were not to cross the Edmund Pettus Bridge

But most moves toward civil rights ended in confrontations with the law (BOB ADELMAN/MAGNUM).

They called it Bloody Sunday. A line of white people lined the road from the Edmund Pettus Bridge (SPIDER MARTIN).

Major John Cloud, at the helm of Lingo's troops, told Lewis and Williams they had three minutes to disperse the 650 marchers (SPIDER MARTIN).

The state troopers and Jim Clark's posse donned gas masks while checking their watches (SPIDER MARTIN).

Then they moved through the demonstrators, clubbing and gassing as they went (SPIDER MARTIN).

They even rode their horses into a church and tossed a child through a stained glass window showing Christ, the Good Shepherd. (BIRMINGHAM NEWS).

over the Alabama River, which would take them out of city limits, out of the hands of Police Chief Baker, and force a confrontation with Al Lingo and Jim Clark.

Williams disobeyed King, telling Bevel and Young he had gotten the go-ahead, and they drew lots to see who would lead the march. Williams won and Lewis was asked to lead the march with him.

Bloody Sunday was about to commence.

About 650 people headed toward the bridge, with women and children marching in the center.

"We got across the bridge, and we could see a sea of blue," Lewis said. These were Lingo's state troopers, and behind them was Clark's posse, on horse-back. On either side of the road was a line of white people with Confederate flags being held back by the sheriff's men. "We knew what we would be receiving on the other side," Lewis said.

Others were not so sure.

Bevel, who was on the city side of the river, said, "I didn't think Jim Clark would have made that kind of mistake. I wouldn't have jumped on the people with that much news coverage: you had guys in from all over the world, and the day was as bright as any you could imagine.

"If he attacked, he would gain for us the support of onlookers. I thought he would just arrest the people."

He didn't. Major John Cloud, at the helm of the troopers, said, "This is an unlawful march. I am giving you three minutes to disperse and go back to your church."

But they didn't wait that long. As soon as the men had their gas masks on, Major Cloud yelled, "Troopers, advance."

Lingo and Clark vied with each other to be the first to lob tear gas canisters into the midst of the blacks, who had nowhere to go. They were sur-rounded on three sides by angry whites, and the bridge behind them was packed with marchers.

"When they put on the masks," said Lewis, "I turned to Hosea and said, 'Let's stop in a prayerful manner,' and we bowed our heads right there. And they came towards us with clubs and horses and bullwhips and just started beating us. We didn't have much choice. We couldn't go forward because there was a sea of troopers. You couldn't go to the left or to the right. You had to go back. They beat us all the way back to the church."

The posse had charged, riding over people, beating as they went. It didn't matter if they were hitting men, women, or children. They beat anything black they could find. The marchers were choking, crying, falling, as the mounted posse rode through them and the troopers marched over them, beating as they went.

Nor did the enraged Clark and Lingo stop at the city line. They beat the marchers all the way back to the church, even though it was in the midst of a black housing project. The posse beat blacks on the steps of the church, in the front yard, on the streets. Some rode into the church and threw a teenage boy through a stained glass window showing Christ as the Good Shepherd.

At one point, Williams picked up an eight-year-old girl named Sheyann Webb to get her out of the way of the posse.

"I ran with her a couple of steps," Williams said, "and she said, 'Please put me down. You're too slow.' And I put her down and she took off."

Clark was in heaven. His posse was rampaging through the black area of the city, beating at will, oblivious to the fact that blacks who had not been marching, who lived in the area, were coming out onto the streets and throwing bottles and rocks, and some were bringing rifles and shotguns onto the scene.

Andrew Young was frantically running around the streets, collaring everyone black who was armed and telling them to take their weapons back inside. Williams, Lewis, and Bevel were running through it all, picking up the wounded and carrying, pushing, shoving them into the church, then going back into the melee to help some more. Police Chief Baker, who was livid at this lawless display, ordered Clark to take his posse and get out of town. He left.

But the damage was done. When the lawmen were gone, seventy blacks had to be hospitalized, and another seventy were treated for cuts, bruises, tear gas, and other injuries.

Lewis, the normally placid farmboy who had cried over dead chickens, the student leader who had suffered worse beatings in his young life, said, "I remember going back to the church and saying I don't think I have ever been so angry. I couldn't believe what was happening. Some of us came very close to death. Your life just flashed by. The tear gas was so bad—it was more than the pain and violence. You were choking and just couldn't breathe.

"So I stood up to speak, and said I don't understand how President Johnson can send troops to Vietnam and the Dominican Republic, and cannot send troops to Selma, Alabama, to protect black people who want the right to register to vote."

Bevel, the young strategist who wore a yarmulke because he admired the courage and strength of the Hebrew prophets, was elated. Though it pained him to watch such displays of brutality, he had seen many before.

"After the first group was attacked so savagely on the bridge," Bevel said, "we knew we would be able to mobilize people around the country."

He was right.

Gandhi had said decades earlier that nonviolence works only if the conflicting groups share the same moral base. In America, that situation held. The scenes of Bloody Sunday in Selma flashed across the nation and produced anger and revulsion from coast to coast.

ABC television interrupted its Sunday night movie to show a lurid news clip of the assault on the blacks. It was to shake the nation as much as Bull Connor's assault on the children. President Johnson immediately criticized Alabama's violence and lawlessness. Thousands of whites and blacks participated in spontaneous sympathy marches.

King was furious with Williams. Said Lowery, "it just wasn't something we do. We always try to move as a team. He didn't, and that move got a lot of people hurt.

"It was a maverick, a rump thing. It wasn't a decision made by the group.

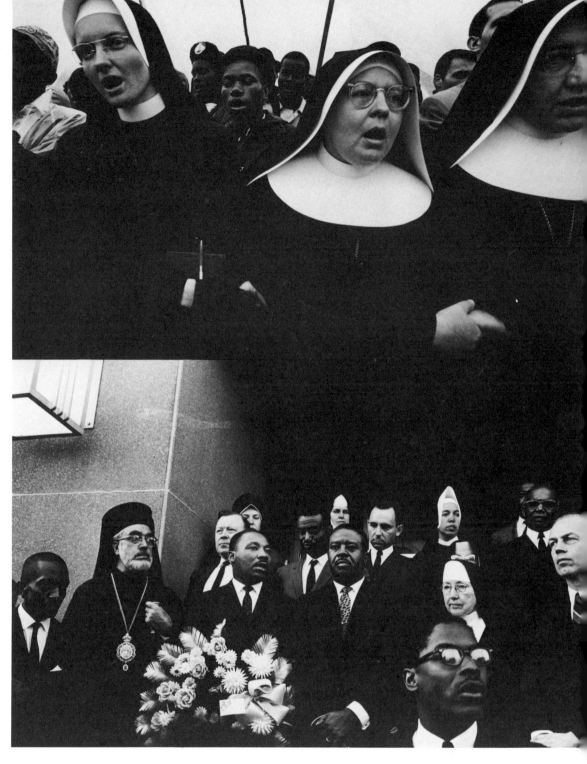

King invited white clergy from around the nation to come to Selma, and they did. Three hundred nuns defied the regional Catholic archbishop and made King the de facto archbishop for the duration of the campaign (BOB ADELMAN/MAGNUM).

One white clergyman, Unitarian James Reeb, was beaten to death for his efforts and eulogized in an interdenominational service (BOB ADELMAN/MAGNUM).

As it turned out, it played an important role in history. But it wasn't a planned, agreed-upon strategy."

King was also despondent because he had not been there when the chips were down. But he had an inspiration. He fired off telegrams to clergymen and ecumenical groups all over the country asking them to join him in a new march on Tuesday, March 9.

On Monday, SCLC attorneys asked U.S. District Court Judge Frank Johnson to issue an injunction preventing anyone from interfering with the march. Instead, Judge Johnson banned the march on Tuesday.

King, Abernathy, and his staff decided to proceed with the march anyway. They remembered the lesson of Albany and were not about to let an injunction kill the momentum of this movement. Tensions were high, and if they were not released on a march, no one knew how they would surface.

So they marched. SNCC was present in full force. Forman and others had chartered a plane to fly over from Atlanta. Scores of clergymen and nuns from around the nation had come to join the pilgrimage.

They were again confronted over the Edmund Pettus Bridge by Major Cloud and the state troopers, backed by Clark and the posse, as the cameras watched. They again knelt in prayer and did not retreat.

This time they were not attacked. Major Cloud ordered his men to clear the road. They did, leaving the way to Montgomery clear.

King did not proceed farther, however.

"We confronted them, we went past the point of the Sunday march, and we proved our point," said SCLC's Lowery. "Then we went back to organize a march."

At that point, no preparations had been made for a march all the way to Montgomery. The logistical side of a demonstration—latrines, food, sleeping tents, medical support, and campsites—had not been worked out. Many of the women on the Sunday and Tuesday marches were in high heels—hardly the garb for a fifty-mile trek.

"There was no intention of going to Montgomery that day," said Lowery. "We were unprepared. We had nothing. We were going to establish our right to cross that bridge—injunction or no injunction—that was the point."

SNCC didn't see it that way. They were furious that the march did not continue Tuesday and challenge Lingo and Clark on the open highway, with or without preparations. They thought King had chickened out.

Moreover, there was jealousy. There was an ad the next day in the New York *Times* showing a picture of the carnage at the march and asking for financial support for SCLC and its efforts.

Said Lewis, "Since I was the chairperson from SNCC and had gotten hurt in the march, they felt they should be able to take full advantage of it."

They insisted that turning back was an act of cowardice rather than prudence, though, Lewis said, "There is nothing wrong with pausing or retreating for a day or a few days to make the long haul."

He added that SNCC had "lost the right" to criticize anything about the march since its board had opposed it and would not participate.

The logic didn't work. Forman left with several SNCC staffers to organize a countermarch to Montgomery. They announced they wouldn't "take any more" and ended the cooperative effort with SCLC. This was the beginning of the nationalist wing of SNCC, which later ousted Lewis and replaced him as chairman with Carmichael, with whom he had shared lodging when they worked as beleaguered teammates during the depressing Mississippi Summer.

There was another casualty after the Tuesday demonstration. Three white ministers went to a soul food restaurant for dinner and were later attacked by a group of club-wielding whites. One of them, Unitarian James Reeb, lapsed into a coma and died in a hospital in Birmingham on Thursday.

SNCC led a counterdemonstration of its own in Montgomery and were beaten by Clark's posse and Lingo's troopers (BRUCE DAVIDSON/MAGNUM).

It took federal troops to protect the march from Selma to Montgomery, though the soldiers' sentiments were obvious on their uniforms (BIRMINGHAM NEWS).

The death overshadowed the week's activities, which had been confined to daily hearings in Judge Johnson's courtroom and a prayer vigil in front of the "Berlin Wall," a rope erected around the church by Chief Baker to prevent any more marches.

America had seen enough. While the death of Jimmy Lee Jackson galvanized only blacks in Alabama, the murder of James Reeb, a white clergyman, was a bit more than it was willing to take.

On March 15, President Johnson went before a joint session of Congress and a nationwide audience and declared that what had happened in Selma was "an American tragedy. It is wrong, deadly wrong, to deny any of your fellow Americans the right to vote."

President Johnson pressed Congress to act to end the frustrating lines of blacks at registration offices . . . (WALKER SANDERS/ LIFE MAGAZINE)

. . . to end the need for America's young to participate in assault workshops . . . (DANNY LYON/MAGNUM)

Johnson was moved as nothing else had moved him. This address, the first before Congress on domestic legislation by a President in nineteen years, was interrupted twice for standing ovations and thirty-six times for applause.

He spoke of his years of privation and his understanding of the dilemma of the poor, stemming from his own impoverished background and his work as a teacher.

"It never occurred to me," said the President, "that I might have the chance to help the sons of those students and people like them all over the country. But now that I have this chance, I'll let you in on a little secret—I mean to use it."

He said, "We have already waited one hundred years and more" for equality to be meaningful to all Americans, and the time for waiting was past. "There must be no delay, or no hesitation, or no compromise" on the urgent need to guarantee the right to vote to all Americans.

"What happened in Selma," said Johnson, "is part of a far larger movement which reaches into every section and state of America. It is the effort of American Negroes to secure for themselves the full blessings of American life. Their cause must be our cause too."

He said he would seek immediate passage of a comprehensive voting rights bill, and he closed with the theme that had followed so many marches and beatings and disappointments: "We shall overcome."

King, watching Johnson on television with Abernathy, his staff, and friends, burst into tears.

The next day, Alabama answered. Clark drove his posse into a group of demonstrators on the steps of the capitol and repeated his Bloody Sunday performance.

On March 17, Judge Johnson granted permission to SCLC to march the fifty-five miles to Montgomery, and ordered Wallace and police officials not to interfere. Some three hundred people were to participate in the march, which was to take three days and end in a huge rally at the site of Jefferson's swearing in —across the street from the Dexter Avenue Baptist Church.

Wallace, a former college classmate of Johnson's, launched a public tirade against the judge and the movement. President Johnson answered by federalizing eighteen hundred Alabama national guardsmen and sending military police and federal marshals to oversee the march and make sure it was not molested again.

The march began with a rally attended by more than three thousand people, though only a tenth of them were going to go the distance. Thousands more were pouring into Montgomery, to meet the marchers and participate in the final rally and meeting on the steps of the state capitol.

On March 25, King led more than twenty-five thousand people through Montgomery to the statehouse, protected by some eight hundred federal troops. It was a joyous occasion, for there was a feeling that they were on the threshold of victory over the forces of racism and violence.

There, on the steps of the Confederacy, they joined in singing "The Battle Hymn of the Republic."

All seemed well. Until it was over.

Then there was the logistics problem of getting home again. A white woman from Detroit named Viola Liuzzo was one of many who had volunteered to help drive people back and forth. As she drove through Lowndes County with a black marcher in her car, another car pulled abreast of hers.

In it were Gary Thomas Rowe and three other Klansmen. They all fired their guns, and Liuzzo's car careened to a halt off the road. She died from a bullet in the head.

That touched off another wave of indignation across the country, and the FBI finally reigned Rowe in. Under a grant of immunity from prosecution, he was to turn on his associates in October and finger them for killing Liuzzo. The FBI then gave him a new life in a new location without delving into his other race-related crimes.

Though Williams and Bevel stayed in Selma, the focus of the movement to secure a voting rights act had shifted to Washington. There were continued demonstrations throughout the rest of the year, and Williams spearheaded a new effort to bring Northern volunteers down to the South to serve as independent poll watchers, to show the need for federal registrars.

It seemed inevitable at that point that they had won: the Voting Rights Act would pass. On June 4, President Johnson told a graduating class at Howard University that he was determined to fight for freedom for all Americans because a declaration of freedom was insufficient.

"You do not wipe away the scars of centuries by saying now you are free to go to where you want and do as you desire and choose the leaders you please. You do not take a person who for years has been hobbled by chains and liberate him, bring him up to the starting line of a race and then say you're free to compete with all the others, and still justly believe you have been completely fair."

Four days later, Johnson authorized sending twenty-three thousand soldiers to fight in Vietnam, aiding the new regime of Gen. Nguyen Van Thieu.

During this period, King was addressing more and more rallies in the North and was becoming convinced that the campaign for freedom had to move into the urban ghettos—if it could work.

The staff was divided on this. Most of them did not want to go. Williams, a maverick anyway, insisted that "moving North was premature. We had not completed the job in the South.

King was in demand all over. He led thirty thousand blacks on a march to Chicago city hall (AP/WIDE WORLD).

"We had used Selma to get a bill through Congress, and that was fine. But we had to continue Selma and elsewhere in the South until the white people came clean with black people. Otherwise, we would be leaving blacks at the mercy of these mean whites, and they would destroy blacks."

For varying reasons, most of the rest of the staff opposed the move North as well. Lowery said flatly, "I'm scared of the North. I wasn't sure we could pull blacks together in a large Northern community the way we did in Montgomery, Selma, or Birmingham. It was a real challenge."

Young felt that if they had to go North, they should try cosmopolitan New York. But King had already been scarred by New York during the riots a year before and was reluctant to enter that maelstrom again.

There were tugs from Chicago. King liked the city. There was an organized group that had been fighting racism in the educational system for more than a year. The crowds there were always warm, large, and enthusiastic. On July

He vowed to work with that Northern city to change conditions for blacks in the ghettos (BURT GLINN/ MAGNUM).

26, he had led thirty thousand blacks on a march to city hall, and black leaders there were entreating him to set up shop in Chicago and help out.

Then there were the people. Chicago's Midwestern blacks had more of a Southern air about them, and the black church was a strong force there: in New York, however, each borough was a different world. Constance Baker Motley, a NAACP attorney, was elected Manhattan borough president that year, but the black community in New York was still a fragmented and—to the Southerners— foreign one. In the end, the majority of the group opposed moving North until the South was set to rights.

"But Martin made the decision to go," said Lowery. "Our leader was moved by the spirit. I thought it was risky, though not necessarily wrong. . . . But Chicago was so big, so difficult to organize. Black folks had so many agendas.

"In Alabama you could pretty much pull the black community in a city together as a unit long enough to make an impact. The economic issues that were raised in Chicago, however, were very complex and did not lend themselves to the kind of solution that the voting or bus or lunch counter moves did."

Then, too, in the South they were not dealing with "the system." They were tackling an old guard trying to hold onto a way of life that didn't exist any more. If they went North, that would not be the case.

"White folks might be prepared to rearrange the furniture," said Lowery, "but they weren't prepared to rearrange the house. They would give us a respectable seat on the porch, but they still owned it."

This was a movement governed by faith, however. If King felt the Lord wanted the movement to go North, then that's what it would do. It was only a matter of time.

In fact, King had done what he set out to do a decade earlier in Montgomery. No, the South had not solved all of its problems. No, it had not eliminated the last vestiges of racism.

But the movement King led had broken the shackles of bondage that had kept blacks subservient for so long. He had shown them a way to combat the system and win, and, more importantly, he had provided the self-respect and the strength necessary to try.

There would come a time in the near future when Jim Clark and George Wallace would kiss black babies at election time and beg for black votes. Wallace would get them; Clark would not. There would come a time when Mississippi would have more black elected officials than any other state, North or South. Blacks in the South could never be sent back now.

But there were still shackles in the North to be dealt with. There were still racist systems to be exposed, hearts and minds to be changed, and spirit and pride infused in people who had long since become used to living at the bottom.

Whether a movement led by Southern Baptist ministers could succeed in the North was anyone's guess. King knew an effort had to be made.

On August 6, 1965, President Johnson capped off a year of record achievement in domestic legislation by signing the Voting Rights Act, which eliminated all qualifying tests for voter registration that tended to discriminate and gave the Attorney General the power to determine the purpose of legitimate tests.

King received the administration's congratulations minutes after President Johnson signed the Voting Rights Act (AP/ WIDE WORLD).

Five days later, a black man named Marquette Frye was arrested for drunken driving in Watts, the black suburb of Los Angeles. A crowd gathered in the afternoon heat. Rumors spread. Tempers flared, and the riot was on. By the thirteenth, it was being called an open rebellion, and thirteen thousand National Guardsmen were called out to put it down. When the last fire was put out, 34 people were dead, 1,032 injured, and 4,000 arrested; two hundred businesses were destroyed, another seven hundred were damaged, and total destruction was estimated at more than $40 million.

Riots are contagious.

Chicago erupted August 12 after a black woman was run over by a fire truck from an all-white firehouse. It took five hundred policemen to quell that two-day disturbance.

During this domestic holocaust, North Vietnamese torpedo boats reportedly attacked the destroyers *Maddox* and *Turner Joy* in the Gulf of Tonkin. An angry President Johnson asked for and got a congressional resolution authorizing him to "take all necessary measures to repel any armed attack against the forces of the United States and prevent further aggression."

By the end of 1965, there would be 184,300 American servicemen in Vietnam, and more on the way. As King pondered his future moves to redress wrongs on the national scene, he began to consider the implications of sending Americans to Asia to fight in an ill-considered war for dubious purposes.

"As we flew around the country," said Lee, "we saw young black troops—sometimes Mexicans, sometimes native Americans—in brand-new uniforms, just out of training. And they were en route to Vietnam.

"Martin shook hands with so many young boys, and there were times he knew that he was shaking their hands for the first and last time because many of them would not return unless they were in a box. We saw them alive on the planes. And later, we saw them unloading bodies from the cargo bays.

"He said, 'They were so doggone young.' With some of them, it was questionable if they were even seventeen."

As he traveled during the end of 1965 he decided these would be the issues he faced in the future.

9
MAKING A DISTINCTION
The Search for Equality

PART ONE: SPREADING THE GOSPEL

"**I** AM EXPERT IN RECOGNITION OF A SIMPLY ELOQUENT truth. That truth is that it is sinful for any of God's children to brutalize any of God's other children."

With that statement in the January 1, 1966, edition of the Chicago *Defender*, King was unalterably committed to opposing the growing war in Vietnam. For the past six months, he had been expressing his disappointment with the war effort, but these comments were off the cuff and erratic. King seemed to have withdrawn because of the opposition his position triggered in the black middle class and across a broad spectrum of civil rights groups.

Leaders of the other major civil rights groups felt King should stick to civil rights and leave other issues alone, especially if it might trigger a backlash that could endanger the diminishing support in Congress for further civil rights legislation.

SNCC had decided in the fall to officially oppose the war in Vietnam, but hadn't issued a public statement to that effect.

King, in his written exposition in the *Defender*, said he had to oppose the notion that "might makes right," a philosophy President Johnson and his advisers had adopted in deciding to seek a purely military solution to the Asian conflict. As an American, King said he and all blacks had an obligation and a right to examine the country's foreign policy and take a stand.

"The Negro must not allow himself to become a victim of the self-serving philosophy of those who manufacture war that the survival of the world is the white man's business alone."

Thursday, January 6, 1966, SNCC issued its formal statement denouncing the war in Vietnam and calling on blacks to contest the draft. Julian Bond, SNCC's publicity chairman, had just won election to the Georgia House of Representatives and was supposed to take his seat the following Monday. Because of the SNCC position, which Bond said he endorsed, the Georgia house voted to bar him from his seat.

King led a SNCC-sponsored demonstration in Atlanta in support of Bond, who would eventually be seated at the order of the U.S. Supreme Court. The furor over Bond's ouster permanently linked King to the budding peace movement, and made him its most prominent spokesman.

King's major effort this year was to be in Chicago, which was a troubled city. It was different from the nation's other major urban centers, in that it was virtually under the complete control of one person—Mayor Richard Daley.

"We had been talking about the logjam in all American cities," said Bevel, "education, poverty, disease. And nobody had been able to break through that. Chicago was unique in that it had a centralized government in Richard Daley, and you can get more done when you have that kind of situation."

There had been efforts to crack Chicago's institutionalized racism. The Coordinating Council of Community Organizations (CCCO), an umbrella for forty groups, was headed by Al Raby and had been fighting a losing battle against the Daley machine. They had tried, initially, to concentrate solely on the issue of inferior education and to force the ouster of school superintendent Benjamin C. Willis. Despite the student boycotts, street marches, rallies, and a 1964 gathering in Soldier Field, where King had addressed more than one hundred thousand people, the policies remained unchanged.

There were marches throughout the spring and summer of 1965, thousands of protesters had been arrested, and Willis was finally replaced. But the policies had not changed, said Raby, "and our movement was exhausted, financially and emotionally and physically.

"I was trying to figure out how to give it another inspirational shot and keep it going. King, at the same time, was trying to figure out how to deal with the riots in a creative way. He found himself continually going to cities where the riots were in progress, and he felt that if the nonviolent movement were in place earlier it could channel those energies in more creative ways."

Because of the infrastructure that existed in Chicago, this was to become the workshop for Northern nonviolent methods. There was a certain amount of naïveté involved in taking the movement North. Their movement had relied on creative tension resulting in massive confrontations with the law enforcement system. It meant filling the jails and putting greater and greater pressures on that system until something cracked.

"But filling the jails in the North," said Lee, "that's more than just a notion. The Cook County jail is as large as some of the cities we worked in in the South. When you talk about filling the jail in New York or Chicago, that is more than a notion. You could fill it, but you are not being realistic at that point, because you are letting your strategy get away from you."

The Northern jails, for one thing, were used to dealing with large numbers of people. They were quite willing to process demonstrators and put them right back on the street. Still, Chicago seemed to have an active, working coalition of black and white churches, organized through the CCCO, and if it was going to work anywhere, it might as well be Chicago.

On January 23 Coretta and Martin moved into a rundown railroad flat in a tenement at the intersection of Sixteenth Street and South Hamlin Avenue, on Chicago's West Side. It had a sitting room, two bedrooms, a kitchen, and a bath —in that order. You had to go through the bedrooms to get a meal or a glass of water.

It had a gas stove that didn't work—though it was fifteen degrees outside —a refrigerator that barely worked, plaster peeling from the walls and ceiling, and a rickety wooden fire escape at the rear. On the corner was a grocery store

It was time to take the movement North. Martin and Coretta rented an apartment in a West Side Chicago slum and prepared for a spring offensive against racism in the ghetto (AP/WIDE WORLD).

"with bad meat and high prices," said Lee, and across the street was a drugstore "which had high prices and was inadequately stocked."

King announced that his presence in the ghetto was to serve notice that he intended to lead a rent strike if the major landlords did not improve their properties. There was a flurry of activity in the building as his landlord mounted a cosmetic war to give the appearance that the building met the city's housing code.

In the ensuing weeks, SCLC's staff—primarily Bevel and Lee—worked hard at organizing tenant groups, evaluating the needs of the nearly one million blacks in Chicago, and preparing for a late spring campaign. Hosea Williams came up to tackle voter registration and to determine how the political system in the city worked and what political pressures might be brought to bear. Their activities were primarily on the West Side. On the South Side, two University of Chicago theology students, David Wallace and Jesse Jackson, had been organizing for the local Kenwood-Oakdale community organization, in the University of Chicago area.

It was a poor area, used to taking whatever was doled out by the Daley machine. "We had to get the head of the Cook County Department of Public Aid to come in and state that people could not lose their welfare payment by voting or protesting," Wallace said. "Their Democratic precinct captains had tried to intimidate them and they had to learn that the precinct captains had nothing to do with welfare at all."

They also found that a large number of the residents "had pictures of Dr. King on their walls" and were looking for help. Like Bevel on the West Side, they had been going door to door, talking to residents about the ability to change their situation if they came together.

"I remember one building that became a model building for us," recalled Wallace. "We went through there and found there were sixty-nine children, and those on the top floor had no water at all in the wintertime. We pulled the parents together in the living room and talked about how their conditions were bad and how they could change it if they came together.

"They organized and put pressure on the landlord. We had a rent strike and got changes made."

For the campaign, SCLC and the CCCO merged into the Chicago Freedom Movement, headed by Raby and King, and prepared for their assault on the city.

Daley, for his part, was not idle. He lost no time in launching a counter-campaign of his own. He announced that the city intended to move against several landlords by stepping up its code enforcement activities. He launched a series of meetings with twenty-five black ministers and invited them to come up with ways life might be improved among the 30 percent of the city that was black. He extended the network of antipoverty programs based in black churches, which had the added benefit of securing the support of black ministers receiving those funds. He moved through the machine-controlled courts against the putative rent strikes.

But this was fencing. The winter of 1966 was so bad that "it practically immobilized everybody," said Raby. It took time for the SCLC staff to decide exactly how and where they wanted to strike. They did not want this campaign to fail, regardless of their individual reservations about the move North.

In the end, they decided to attack the de facto segregation in housing as the root of the city's problem and the one most amenable to resolution through their confrontation methods. This meant going after the real estate agencies, who steered blacks to the ghettos on the West Side or South Side of Chicago.

It meant going after the banks, who redlined black areas and made it nearly impossible to get the funds to improve those communities, and who declined to grant mortgages to blacks who wanted to live elsewhere in the city or, heaven forbid, in the surrounding areas. There were no black banks in the city.

As a result, there was a 1 percent vacancy rate in black areas, and 25 percent of the city's population was confined to about 10 percent of the occupied land. Blockbusting and panic selling in selected areas made realtors rich, while spreading the ghettos and exacerbating conditions.

Jesse Jackson, said Wallace, "developed the image of a quarter and a dime, and to squeeze a quarter onto a dime you had to pervert it and bend it."

That system was not limited to Chicago, of course. In 1966, 53 percent of the nation's blacks lived outside the South. Blacks constituted 26 percent of the population of cities with one million or more people and 20 percent of cities with 250,000 to one million. Only 4 percent of suburban residents were black.

This decision did not mean abandoning Bevel's plan to organize tenant unions to fight slum conditions, but that could no longer be the focus of the campaign. Rev. Al Pitcher, a theology professor at the University of Chicago and Raby's assistant in CCCO, said, "In the long run, tenant unions are about the hardest thing to organize. You have to get so many people in the building to agree, and people move in and out of buildings so frequently. You just don't have any stability."

This decision did not sit well with many who had been working with CCCO for the past two years. Their thrust had been education, and that issue was not being addressed by the movement from the South.

But SCLC had learned its lesson. It was not about to tackle everything in Chicago. They were looking for a way to make a significant change *and* show blacks in the Northern ghetto that they did not have to accept their squalid conditions any more than blacks in the South did.

There was one other problem. Dr. J. H. Jackson, head of the National Baptist Convention, was opposed to King's efforts and pressured his member churches to stay out of the campaign. King was aware of this and the ties many black ministers had to the Daley machine.

Wallace said, "We were convinced—from theory rather than practice—that the church was a foundation where the people were, and that had to be our greatest organizing. While ministers may not be openly supportive of Dr. King, we could at least neutralize them so they did not preach against him."

The Chicago movement began late in the spring, sending in teams of white couples to talk to real estate agents about buying property and then sending in black couples with the same economic profile and seeing what they were shown. The purpose was to compile data on the practices of about sixty major real estate companies.

King had spent the time lecturing and raising funds around the world. As a Nobel laureate, he was more in demand then ever. His opposition to the war in Vietnam had grown, despite outward hostility from President Johnson. On May 1 the war expanded again, when American-led troops began fighting in Cambodia. Before this year ended, Johnson would have 385,300 American troops stationed in South Vietnam, another 60,000 offshore, and 33,000 in Thailand.

That escalation was a mistake. A year earlier, Gen. William Westmoreland had predicted that the war would be won "by the end of 1967." But the high command continually underestimated the Vietcong buildup, though Westmoreland knew he needed many more troops.

The general's requests for troops had grown from 175,000 in June 1965 to 542,000 in June 1966, and Defense Secretary Robert McNamara was telling

King was always traveling, counseling, raising funds for SCLC's campaigns. Airport waiting rooms became common staff meeting places (BOB FITCH/BLACK STAR).

President Johnson that now "there was no reasonable way to bring the war to an end soon." The escalation of the war in Indochina continued.

As the month drew to a close, King accepted the cochairmanship of the Clergy and Laymen Concerned about Vietnam, spearheaded by Rev. William Sloane Coffin and Dr. Benjamin Spock, and his antiwar statement was read at a demonstration at the Washington Monument. King announced he would lead a march on Chicago's city hall on June 26 to begin a "long hot summer" of nonviolent protest against discriminatory housing practices in the city.

On June 6, James Meredith, who had integrated Ole Miss in 1962, was gunned down on Highway 51 during a solitary march from Memphis to Jackson, Mississippi. Meredith's 220 mile "march against fear" was to dramatize the fact that blacks were still not free to move about in Dixie. He didn't get much farther than the Mississippi state line before his point was dramatically made.

King, who was in Atlanta when the shooting occurred, immediately conferred with Rev. Jim Lawson, who had left Nashville and was now organizing demonstrations in Memphis. Lawson assured him that Meredith was still alive in a Memphis hospital and made arrangements for King to see him the next day.

What evolved was a Memphis conference with King and the new directors of two increasingly militant black nationalist organizations: Floyd McKissick of CORE and Stokely Carmichael, who had replaced Lewis at the helm of SNCC. The trio, with Meredith's blessing, agreed to sponsor a joint march to Jackson, taking up where Meredith stopped. There was friction, however. Both McKissick and Carmichael were openly rejecting the nonviolent philosophy that had been prevalent in the movement so far.

The break with the past was especially severe for the suave Carmichael, who had seen one white atrocity too many while working with Lewis in the Mississippi Summer of 1964, and suffering through the abuse of Selma the following year. He had won the chairmanship of SNCC in a fractious, all-night meeting in which Lewis was criticized for his close ties with King—whom they derisively called "de Lawd"—and his strict adherence to nonviolence in an increasingly violent America.

A few weeks earlier, Carmichael had heard Rep. Adam Clayton Powell of Harlem use the phrase "Black Power" in a commencement address at Howard University in Washington, and the idea appealed to him. He insisted that whites be excluded from the coming march.

He was persuaded to back down by King, now joined by Whitney Young and Roy Wilkins. But it was an uneasy alliance. Many of the younger generation of blacks were not interested in walking King's road to freedom.

At the end of one day's march, during the singing of the movement theme song, "We Shall Overcome," many of the voices fell silent when they came to the verse that said "black and white together."

King asked some of the marchers about this and was told, "This is a new day, we don't sing those words any more. In fact, the whole song should be discarded. Not 'We Shall Overcome,' but 'We Shall Overrun.'"

King was stunned. The bitterness coming from the ranks of a movement he led was strange. "I should not have been surprised," he later wrote. "I should have known that in an atmosphere where false promises are daily realities, where deferred dreams are nightly facts, where acts of unpunished violence toward

King, flanked by SNCC's Stokely Carmichael and CORE's Floyd McKissick, announced they were taking up James Meredith's trek from Memphis, Tennessee, to Jackson, Mississippi. Only King favored nonviolence (AP/WIDE WORLD).

It was a hot, tiring, depressing march (VERNON MERRITT III/BLACK STAR).

The younger blacks preferred singing "We shall overrun" to the traditional "We shall overcome" theme song of the movement (DAN MCCOY/ BLACK STAR).

King is flanked by Andrew Young (right) and Floyd McKissick and Stokely Carmichael (left) (CANTON MESSENGER).

Below, left: King and his followers were pushed around by Mississippi police and Klansmen. The SNCC contingent fought back (AP/WIDE WORLD).

The oratory of Hosea Williams and King lost ground to the cries of "Black Power!" "Black Power!" (CANTON MESSENGER).

Negroes are a way of life, nonviolence would eventually be seriously questioned."

The marchers were attacked in Canton and Philadelphia, Mississippi, and the police intervened only when the marchers began actively fighting back. In Greenwood, Carmichael galvanized a group by shouting, "We have been saying freedom for six years and we ain't got nothing. What we gonna start saying now is Black Power!"

From then on, Black Power was the war chant of SNCC and the young, and the trappings of nonviolence disappeared. The phrase, though not new, was seized upon by the media as a harbinger of things to come.

King understood the vehemence behind the chant; a restlessness with the America of 1966. In his last major work, *Where Do We Go from Here: Chaos or Community?*, King wrote that the black power advocates "have watched as America sends black young men to burn Vietnamese with napalm, to slaughter men, women and children; and they wonder what kind of nation it is that applauds nonviolence whenever Negroes face white people in the streets of the U.S., but applauds violence and burning and death when these same Negroes are sent to the field of Vietnam.

"There is nothing essentially wrong with power. The problem is that in America, power is unequally distributed."

The slogan had crystalized the frustrations building up in black America, and it would come back to haunt King repeatedly. He wrote that the only time he was booed at a mass rally was by Black Power adherents in Chicago.

"I went home that night with an ugly feeling. Selfishly I thought of my sufferings and sacrifices over the last 12 years. Why would they boo one so close to them? But as I lay awake thinking, I finally came to myself, and I could not for the life of me have less patience and understanding for those young people.

"For 12 years I, and others like me, had held out radiant promises of progress. I had preached to them about my dream. I had lectured to them about the not too distant day when they would have freedom 'all here and now.' I had urged them to have faith in America and in white society. Their hopes had soared. They were now hostile because they were watching the dream that they had so readily accepted turn into a frustrating nightmare."

He realized, then, that "for the vast majority of white Americans, the past decade had been a struggle to treat the Negro with a degree of decency, not equality. White America was ready to demand that the Negro should be spared the lash of brutality and coarse degradation, but it had never been truly committed to helping him out of poverty, exploitation or all forms of discrimination.

"The outraged white citizen had been sincere when he snatched the whips from the southern sheriffs and forbade them more cruelties. But when this was to a degree accomplished, the emotions that had momentarily inflamed him melted away. White Americans left the Negro on the ground and in devastating numbers, walked off with the aggressor.

"It appeared that the white segregationist and the ordinary white citizen had more in common with one another than either had with the Negro."

The march ended with a jubilant rally in Jackson three weeks after the shooting, but it was obvious that there were few whites marching with them this time. It was a dispirited King who returned to the hot streets of Chicago to

King returned to Chicago, and thirty-five thousand crowded Soldier Field to hear King bring his message of strength and hope North (JOHN TWEEDLE).

(JOHN TWEEDLE).

(JOHN TWEEDLE).

(JOHN TWEEDLE).

There was a lot to be done. He brought hope to kids crowded in deteriorating buildings . . .
(JOHN TWEEDLE)

. . . and led rent strikes to force landlords to clean up their slum property
(JOHN TWEEDLE).

continue the delayed struggle for freedom in the North. This campaign was to do more than just eradicate a bad condition in Chicago. It was to try and prove that there was a better way out than the open confrontations he saw developing.

The Chicago Movement was supposed to begin on Freedom Sunday, July 10, with a giant rally at Soldier Field, followed by a march to city hall. It failed to materialize. Only thirty thousand to thirty-five thousand attended the Movement's opening rally in Soldier Field, far short of the hundred thousand hoped for by the organizers and too few to impress the mayor.

King then led a smaller march to city hall, where he followed the example of his namesake of several centuries before and nailed a set of demands on the door. The Chicago Freedom Movement was seeking an open city and wanted an end to redlining by banks and mortgage companies, construction of public housing outside the ghettos, the restriction of city purchases to firms following fair employment practices, the creation of a civilian complaint review board for the police department, the adoption of a desegregation plan by the city, and the boycotting of discriminatory businesses.

"This day," King said, "we must decide to fill up the jails of Chicago, if necessary, in order to end slums. This day, we must decide that our votes will determine who will be the next mayor of Chicago. We must make it clear that we will purge Chicago of every politician, whether he be Negro or white, who feels that he owns the Negro vote."

The problem, however, was that the Chicago Freedom Movement obviously did not have the bodies to support such a threat. The following day, July 11, King and a delegation from the Movement met with Mayor Daley. It was a short, unproductive session, and King promised to launch a series of boycotts and massive demonstrations until the city changed its ways.

But other events interceded. On July 12 King, Abernathy, and Lee were riding to Mahalia Jackson's home for dinner when they saw several policemen turning off fire hydrants that kids had opened so they could play in the cool water. Later that evening, they heard on the radio that a major altercation had ensued with the police, and "we realized we had seen the beginnings of a riot," said Lee.

Several SCLC staffers took to the streets in an effort to head off an escalation of the riot, but no one in the street was listening. Roving bands of black youths were throwing Molotov cocktails at police in the West Side. By July 14 more than a thousand city policemen admitted that they just couldn't control the growing numbers of angry black youths and asked for reinforcements. Gov. Otto Kerner sent in four thousand National Guard troops the following day. When calm was restored, 2 blacks were dead, 57 injured, and 282 had been arrested.

This was the start of another violent summer for the nation's cities. Gov. James Rhodes of Ohio would declare a state of emergency in Cleveland from July 18 to 20, and send in two thousand National Guardsmen to help local police quell a riot in the black Hough section. When the violence subsided, 4 blacks were dead, 40 injured, 150 arrested, and 50 fires had been set.

In East New York, a section of Brooklyn, two blacks were killed and twenty-nine arrested in a relatively short-lived disturbance. Before the summer ended, there would be violent protests in Omaha, Nebraska; Dayton, Ohio; Waukegan, Illinois; and Benton Harbor, Michigan.

Mayor Daley blamed King for the riot in Chicago, calling him a "trouble-maker" in what had been a peaceful city. But he did meet with King, and later he ordered the installation of sprinklers on hydrants near firehouses, and park police were to permit equal access to Chicago's parks and pools. It was not an auspicious beginning for the assault on the North.

King and Abernathy urged the formation of a Chicago chapter of Operation Breadbasket, an economic self-help concept pioneered by Rev. Leon Sullivan in Philadelphia that sought to pressure companies into hiring and promoting blacks and using black contractors where possible. Jesse Jackson was installed as director, with David Wallace its secretary.

They had some small victories. A boycott of the Country Delight Dairy chain led to an improvement in hiring practices by that firm. It also thrust the young, brash Jackson into the limelight and antagonized some of the older ministers.

Bevel organized a "community hearing" on slum conditions to dramatize the plight of Chicago's poor. One resident after another told of suffering through heatless winters, of regularly finding rotten meat in neighborhood stores, of living with hordes of rats and roaches. Their testimony before King and the news media was at odds with Mayor Daley's robust projections for the city.

The testimony didn't hurt Daley much; the movement was losing momentum. King said, "We've got to do something."

On July 30, they began a series of marches into white communities to demonstrate their closed nature. It was immediately apparent that the residents wanted to keep their areas closed. More than three thousand whites heckled about fifteen hundred marchers led by Andrew Young and Al Raby into the Gage Park area.

"There were a number of cars that had been in a parking lot," said Pitcher. "They were thrown into a lagoon. There were police on hand, but they

A young minister named Jesse Jackson joined SCLC's staff, organizing tenant unions and an economic project called Operation Breadbasket (JOHN TWEEDLE).

Left:
Then they went after the realtors. Albert Raby, head of the Chicago Movement, Revs. Fred Shuttlesworth, Jesse Jackson, and James Bevel held a "pray-in" before the city's hostile real estate board (JOHN TWEEDLE).

Right:
Marches through white Chicago neighborhoods triggered violent outbreaks. King was felled by a rock during a demonstration in Marquette Park on August 5, 1966 (AP/WIDE WORLD).

were not aggressively dealing with the crowd: they didn't interfere with us, but they didn't protect us, either."

When residents did get out of hand, Pitcher said, the police "put them in a paddy wagon, took them a couple of blocks, and let them out."

The following week, August 5, King led another march into Marquette Park, where the hatred broke all around them. They were pelted with rocks, bottles, firecrackers, and epithets. King was hit on the head with a rock and knocked to his knees. He was stunned by the violence of the crowd, saying later, "I have seen many demonstrations in the South, but I have never seen anything so hostile and so hateful as I've seen here today."

They continued marching throughout a summer punctuated by street violence and escalating commentaries on Black Power. Roy Wilkins denounced the idea at his organization's annual convention, saying, "We of the NAACP will have none of this. It is the ranging of race against race on the irrelevant basis of skin color. It is the father of hatred and mother of violence."

Both CORE and the Urban League backed the concept because of its positive aspects of "self-determination" and unity. SNCC's Carmichael and H. Rap Brown, however, drew larger and larger crowds of young blacks to their speeches on Black Power and open cries for an end to nonviolence as a predominant tactic in the quest for freedom.

SCLC was the last bastion of the nonviolent protest. In Chicago, Raby, Bevel, and Jackson led some two thousand marchers into the Belmont-Cragin area, where more than three thousand whites lined the march route, hurling stones and curses over the heads of the police escort and onto the demonstrators.

"We expanded the marches into a variety of neighborhoods to make it obvious that the real estate agencies were not providing services and there was a whole systematic structure which supported that decision," said Raby. "Neither the Human Relations Commission, which had some authority to see that there was equal access to housing, nor the Real Estate Board, which had the authority to lift licenses, were in no way exercising their authority.

"Mortgage companies were not making loans, and there was just violence against people trying to secure housing on an equal basis."

These were not like the large demonstrations King and Abernathy had led in the South.

Said Pitcher, "King was never able to get more than fifteen hundred people on these marches. When we marched downtown we could get forty thousand. But when we went into communities and faced mobs with rocks, firecrackers, bottles—you name it—we never got more than fifteen hundred. And you can't close the city down with only fifteen hundred people."

The marches were causing major problems for the city, however. The predominantly ethnic white police force was stunned by the violence of their neighbors and by being called "nigger lovers" and worse by their ethnic groups.

"There were Catholics in these neighborhoods spitting at the nuns and priests in our marches," said Pitcher. "The diocese was all upset."

The marches upset the mayor. "Daley was horrified and terrified," said Wallace. "These were major ethnic neighborhoods that were a major part of his political base. He was screaming, his aldermen were screaming. They were pulling their hair out, saying, 'How can we deal with this man?'"

King announced he would lead a march into neighboring Cicero, a bastion of racism. There were no blacks in Cicero—the last black family had been burned out in 1951. "It was the symbol of a totally closed community and a closed society," said Wallace. "And whites threatened to kill the niggers if they came in there."

That may not have been an idle boast. During this period, a black man who was walking in Cicero looking for employment was beaten to death.

Archbishop Cody, at the behest of the mayor, called for the Freedom Movement to halt the demonstrations. Daley also secured an injunction that limited the marches severely.

"We could only march between 10 A.M. and 3 P.M.," said Pitcher. "We had to tell him where we were going to march and the exact route. The disruptive effect of our marches was compromised. We didn't have the power to break the injunction, and negotiation became a way out of the situation.

"The movement hadn't grown, and there was no way King could have filled the streets."

It was discouraging, perhaps, to have to seek "an honorable way out." But they had little choice. The support they had expected from Chicago's black churches had never materialized.

"I once went in to see a black preacher who suggested we go see Congressman [Ralph] Metcalf and try to get some help," said Pitcher. "Metcalf opened the safe and said, 'I have here the canceled checks from hundreds of the black preachers that you say you are going to organize.'" They were on the Daley machine's payroll.

There began a series of meetings between the leaders of the Freedom Movement and Chicago's elite—the mayor and leaders of the real estate and business community. The movement had succeeded in exposing the racism in the housing industry and its deleterious effects on Chicago in general and its black residents in particular. Changing that, however, was another matter.

"One of the clear problems with movements," explained Raby, "is a lack of institutional capacity. Movements, by their nature, are temporary. They have the capacity to bring people to the table, but they don't have the capacity to institutionally follow and monitor and keep other institutions accountable."

A series of subcommittees was set up to deal with various issues and thrash out an agreement. "We didn't particularly want to do this," said Raby, "but part of our movement was a moral thrust, a willingness to solve problems. And a need for public support. You couldn't maintain that if people said you made your point and the powers that be have agreed to sit down to talk. We'd had enough demonstrations and enough disruptions in the city."

Unfortunately, Raby added, while the nonviolent movement can force the city's leaders to the negotiating table, "You know that you lose grip on your leverage the moment you go to the table."

They negotiated a ten-point "Summit Agreement" on August 26, in which the city's Commission on Human Rights would ensure that realtors posted Chicago's open housing policy and the city would mount efforts to enforce it.

The Board of Realtors agreed to "withdraw all opposition to the philosophy of open occupancy legislation," but it did not agree to drop its challenge in Cook County Circuit Court against the city's fair housing ordinance. The Cook County Council of Insured Savings Associations and the Chicago Mortgage Bankers Association also pledged to end their redlining and other discriminatory practices.

Of course, there were no assurances that these agreements would be carried out, and the black leadership knew they would probably have to go to the U.S. Supreme Court to make open housing a reality.

At the Summit Meeting, King listened to the city's leaders declare that a new day was coming. He muttered, "Sure, six months and $250,000 down the pike," referring to the slow, costly trek to the nation's highest tribunal.

Daley announced that the agreement signaled a "great day" for Chicago, but the results were not really that rosy.

"I was on a committee that monitored the agreements after the settlement," said Pitcher, "and practically nothing was done."

Black Power advocates in SNCC and CORE denounced the agreement as just a waste of paper and said they would hold their own march through Cicero. This they did on September 4: 205 blacks marched under the guns of 2,700 National Guardsmen and 700 police, through a steady barrage of rocks and bottles.

When SCLC left, the CCCO, which had brought King there, fell apart. "There was such disillusionment," said Pitcher, "and we split over the black-white issue.

"It was difficult for me, since I'm white, to work with Raby, who is black, because if we went out of a meeting at the same time they would accuse Raby of taking orders from me. The Coordinating Council just vanished after King left, though we wobbled on for a couple of months."

Was the trek North a failure? Not really. The fight in the South had been for the right to travel, eat in public places, and vote. Winning success in those areas did not significantly attack the economic and political power of the South. Those changes had to be worked out—locally—long after King and SCLC had left town.

By November, the tenant union, organized primarily by Bevel, who stayed in Chicago, had ten thousand members and was recognized formally by the AFL-CIO. The Chicago Freedom Movement had shown the need to forge a link between the economic and political forces in a city, rather than use one to whipsaw the other, as had been done in the Southern crusades. Operation Breadbasket became a focal point for the city's black businessmen and politicians to jointly attack the city's ills. Two decades later, that would lead to a black mayor in Chicago's city hall and a black candidate for the presidency.

In the short run, though, the trek North was a defeat in that King had given the impression on arrival that this Movement would tear down the walls keeping the black community hemmed into a deteriorating ghetto and debilitating life. That he couldn't deliver.

The Chicago Movement did show that the city's powerful business and political leaders could be forced to step back and negotiate if there was a committed, organized group confronting them. That lesson was not lost.

Center stage was now being taken by a new force and a new philosophy. The rhetoric of the Black Power adherents did not allow for long-term solutions or, for that matter, coalitions that worked for change.

In Atlanta, on September 10, a riot broke out after a white policeman shot and killed a black man. Two more blacks and two policemen were shot before the confrontation ended, and Carmichael was arrested for inciting to riot.

Bevel, worn out from the civil rights wars, took a year's leave of absence from SCLC to go to New York and become director of the National Mobilization Committee to End the War in Vietnam. The Mobilization Committee had sponsored several relatively small antiwar demonstrations during the fall, but it was gearing up for what it hoped would be a series of massive antiwar demonstrations in the spring.

This was to be another period of relative calm for King and SCLC, while they recovered from the physical and emotional rigors of the last campaign and decided what they should do next.

They needed time to consider the movement they had led for the past twelve years and decide if they were still relevant.

"People were being very, very, very vocal in their disbelief in continued nonviolence," said Abernathy. "People were beginning to doubt whether we could win under the banner of nonviolence, and how long we would have to endure nonviolence as a tool.

"We were questioning greatly the validity of nonviolence."

This was not a happy time, for King's star had declined on the national scene and the Chicago Movement had only tarnished the luster. King spent more time working on *Where Do We Go from Here?* and tending to his oft-neglected flock at Ebenezer.

But there was activity in St. Louis involving the Gateway City's high life and low life.

Russel Byers was a hood who had dealt primarily in stolen cars but who had friends and relatives who were on the more violent side of crime. His brother-in-law, John Paul Spica, was sent to Missouri State Penitentiary in 1963 for the contract murder of a local businessman. He shared a cell and became friends with a small-time hood named James Earl Ray.

Ray had little in the way of ideology—he was simply a small-time thief, and money was his sole motivator. He had two brothers, Jerry and John, who were racists. John ran a segregated bar called the Grapevine Tavern in a segregated area of St. Louis. In 1967 the tavern was to become a meeting place and literature distribution center for the American Independent Party, an offshoot of the White Citizens Council, which was to back Alabama governor George Wallace's bid for the presidency.

Byers used to drop his hot cars off in nearby Barnhardt at the Bluff Acres Motel, owned by John Kauffmann. The sixty-two-year-old Kauffmann had purchased the motel in 1960 with proceeds from his legitimate drug company and his earnings as a stockbroker. He also sold drugs illegally and allowed thieves to store hot property at Bluff Acres for a price. Byers had been dropping off cars and other goodies at Kauffmann's place since 1962 and knew him well.

One fall afternoon in 1966, Kauffmann casually asked Byers if he would like to earn fifty thousand dollars.

Byers, surprised, asked what he had to do to earn it and was simply told to come back to the motel at six-thirty. They drove that evening to nearby Imperial, Missouri, to the home of John Sutherland, a prominent patent attorney who was still fighting the Civil War. A year younger than Kauffmann, Sutherland was a Virginia native, the descendant of early colonists and a 1926 graduate of Virginia Military Institute.

He considered himself a diehard Southerner who opposed integration, civil rights, and the U.S. Supreme Court. He was a founder of the St. Louis Citizens Council and officer of the Southern States Industrial Council, an organization of businessmen who fought the "Negro movement."

When he met with Kauffmann and Byers, he wore a Confederate colonel's cap and looked like a throwback to another era, sitting in his den with its large Confederate flag, a rug that was a replica of the Stars and Bars, and walls decorated with Confederate memorabilia.

Sutherland told Byers he was a member of a secret Southern organization that had a lot of money and that Byers could earn fifty thousand dollars by killing Martin Luther King, Jr. Byers said he would think it over, but later dropped both the idea and all contact with Kauffmann. In Byers's view, Kauffmann could get him killed.

It may have seemed strange that a murder contract was offered to a man who had no record of violent crime in the past. But Byers's brother-in-law was in jail for just such a crime, and Kauffmann and Sutherland apparently thought Byers would kill for money or find someone to whom he could subcontract the job.

They were partially right. He wanted no part of it. In the circles in which he traveled, however, word soon got out that "we can always make twenty or thirty thousand if we kill the big nigger for John."

King became the leading figure in the growing antiwar movement, sending an address to a spring mobilization demonstration in Washington . . .
(ROBERT HOUSTON/BLACK STAR)

PART TWO: . . . TO THE MOUNTAINTOP

REV. JIM LAWSON WAS WONDERING WHAT IT WOULD TAKE to change conditions in Memphis for its black city employees, particularly the sanitation workers.

Lawson had been involved in a host of civil rights and labor issues since coming to Memphis, but the sanitation men presented the most vexing problem.

"They were 99 percent black and underemployed," Lawson stated. "They had no benefits whatsoever. If they didn't work on bad days, they didn't get paid. If it started raining while they were on the road, they either continued working or they went home without pay.

"Their white supervisors could sit in the barns on bad days and collect a full day's pay, but the workers themselves had no such benefits. They had no health benefits and were not receiving minimum wages."

They had started an effort to organize in 1966, but it had been bitterly fought by the administration and suspected organizers were summarily fired. "They threatened strikes a couple of times," said Lawson, "but without any luck."

They were just going to have to wait until something happened that angered the thirteen hundred sanitation workers enough to give them the backbone to walk out and take whatever the city decided to throw at them.

In the winter of 1967 Lawson hadn't the faintest idea what that catalyst could be.

King completed *Where Do We Go from Here?* at the end of February. It was a somber work, reflecting the despair of the endgame when one knows the two-minute drill will probably not suffice to salvage a win. He realized the problems of changing an America in which a large part of the economic backbone—factories, hospitals, service industries, and agriculture—depended on the maintenance of a system that economically raped its workers.

In its modern form, the economic system was often little better than its predecessor of three hundred years earlier, when the new colonies were created on the backs of a slave trade. "Black men," King wrote, "the creators of the wealth of the New World, were stripped of all human and civil rights. And this degradation was sanctioned and protected by institutions of government, all for one purpose: to produce commodities for sale at a profit, which in turn would be privately appropriated."

Now there was a time for change—and white America was reluctant to do that. He related how polls showed that 88 percent of white America would object if their teenage child dated a black; 80 percent would mind if a close friend or a relative married one, and 50 percent did not want a black neighbor.

King concluded that blacks and whites weren't even speaking the same language:

"Every civil rights law is still substantially more dishonored than honored. School desegregation is still 90 percent unimplemented. The free exercise of the franchise is the exception rather than the rule in the South; open occupancy laws theoretically apply to population centers embracing tens of millions, but grim ghettos contradict the fine language of the legislation. Despite the mandates of law, equal employment still remains a distant dream."

King lamented the fact that "segregationist obstruction and majority indifference" had conspired to create a climate of confrontation: whites are annoyed with continuing black demands for equality and blacks are angry at the continued delay.

And there was the lament of his own crusade, the slow, painful, bloody trek through Montgomery, Albany, Birmingham, St. Augustine, Selma, and Chicago. It was a crusade led by blacks who sincerely believed that the North would reexamine its conscience and its sociopolitical structures in light of what it saw in the South.

The nonviolent movement "was founded on the belief that opposition in the North was not intransigent, that it was flexible and was . . . at least partially hospitable to corrective influences.

"We forgot what we knew daily in the South: freedom is not given, it is won."

King did not want to seem to be issuing a call for violence or a prediction of one. But, he warned, "it cannot be taken for granted that Negroes will adhere to nonviolence under any and all conditions."

King mused on the events on the world stage. If the nation is to find peace for itself, he said, it must also find peace abroad. In this sense, it was a contradiction in terms for the Johnson administration to talk about peace while enlarging a war.

As King completed his book at the end of February, there was interesting news from Mississippi. A federal grand jury in Jackson had again brought indictments in the murders of Chaney, Schwerner, and Goodman during the Mississippi Summer of 1964. The charges were for depriving the three civil rights workers of their civil rights—not murder—and named eighteen people, including Imperial Wizard Bowers, Sheriff Rainey, and Deputy Sheriff Price. A trial was set for October.

In Washington, President Johnson was not interested in curtailing the war in Vietnam, but he was continuing his war on poverty and his push for civil rights. He asked Congress to pass a new civil rights bill barring discrimination in the sale and rental of housing—a response to King's Chicago campaign—and end discrimination in the selection of juries.

He sent his plea to a conservative-minded Congress, which was in the process of ousting long-term black Congressman Adam Clayton Powell for allegedly misusing public funds and defying New York courts in a defamation suit against him.

As the end of his book indicated, the Vietnam conflict weighed heavily on King's mind during this period. On February 25, 1967, at a rally in Los Angeles, he gave his first speech devoted solely to the war in Vietnam.

"The promises of the Great Society have been shot down on the battlefields of Vietnam," he said. "The pursuit of this widened war has narrowed domestic welfare programs, making the poor, white, and Negro bear the heaviest burdens.

"It is estimated that we spend $322,000 for each enemy we kill, while we spend in the so-called war on poverty in America only about $53 for each person classified as poor. We must combine the fervor of the Civil Rights Movement with the peace movement."

King continued speaking out against the war at rallies across the land, giving a major address in New York's prestigious Riverside Church on April 4, 1967, sponsored by the Clergy and Laymen Concerned About Vietnam. It was a sad, emotional, brilliant enunciation of his own long and, at times, lonely, road to the peace movement. Those who questioned his decision to oppose the war and wondered about his right to get involved in this cause, he said, "have not really known me, my commitment, or my calling. Indeed, their questions suggest that they do not know the world in which they live."

As a preacher, a man of God, he felt there was a connection between his struggle and the battle in Vietnam. In recent times, he said, "it seemed as if there was a real promise of hope for the poor—both black and white—through the Poverty Program.

"There were experiments, hopes, new beginnings. Then came the buildup in Vietnam and I watched the program broken and eviscerated as if it were some idle political plaything of a society gone mad on war, and I knew that America would never invest the necessary funds or energies in rehabilitation of its poor so long as adventures like Vietnam continued to draw men and skills and money like some demoniacal destructive suction tube."

And there was the unfairness of it all. Black Americans were represented in unusually high numbers on the casualty lists, he said. "We were taking the black young men who had been crippled by our society and sending them 8,000 miles away to guarantee liberties in Southeast Asia which they had not found in Southwest Georgia and East Harlem.

"So we have been repeatedly faced with the cruel irony of watching Negro and white boys on TV screens as they kill and die together for a nation that has been unable to seat them together in the same schools. So we watch them in brutal solidarity burning the huts of a poor village but we realize that they would never live on the same block in Detroit. I could not be silent in the face of such cruel manipulation of the poor."

He opposed the war because he was a Christian minister, and he was surprised people didn't fathom such an obvious reason to oppose mass destruction. He was saddened that he had to speak out "against the greatest purveyor of violence in the world today—my own government"; but it would have been hypocritical to have condemned violence everywhere but in Washington.

King called on the United States to end the carpet bombing of Vietnam, declare a unilateral ceasefire, and express a sincere willingness to negotiate a peaceful settlement to the conflict.

The speech may have been masterful, but it unleashed a torrent of abuse on King. President Johnson went so far as to say the comments were "right down the Commie line."

The FBI, which had renewed its interest in King and his growing involvement in the antiwar movement, contacted several media sources to help solicit criticisms of King, including black columnist Carl Rowan. Rowan accepted the FBI's line that Levison and the Communist Party were behind King's antiwar efforts, and in his April 14 column in the Cleveland *Plain Dealer* said, "King is listening most to one man who is clearly more interested in embarrassing the United States than in the plight of either the Negro or the war weary people of Vietnam."

He followed that up with an elaboration for *Reader's Digest,* implying that King was conceited and Communist-influenced, and as a result "persona non grata to Lyndon Johnson."

King was hurt by the criticism. But he said to Coretta, "I know I'm right. I know this is an unjust and evil war. I have made my decision to oppose it, and whatever people say, I am going to stick to my convictions."

In Washington, Defense Secretary Robert McNamara was having increasing doubts about the war and commissioned a secret study of the Indochina conflict—its origins, the crucial decisions that had led to the current state of affairs, and the outlook. The study would run to more than 10 million words and be called the Pentagon Papers.

On April 15 King, Benjamin Spock, and Harry Belafonte led more than

125,000 people in New York City in a massive demonstration against the war—the largest of a series of rallies around the nation sponsored by the Mobilization—while Coretta addressed another 50,000 in San Francisco. King seemed ill at ease with some of the militant rhetoric accompanying the antiwar fervor.

The youths chanting, "Hey! Hey! LBJ. How many kids did you kill today?" and others burning their draft cards went a bit further than he was prepared to go, even if they were nonviolent protests.

For now, though, this was King's cause. As far as he was concerned, the war was morally wrong and, from a practical purpose, economic help would not come to America's poor until the money pouring into Southeast Asia was redirected. It would be his crusade until he found a new campaign to redirect the course of American society.

There was another occurrence during this period, though of little note. James Earl Ray broke out of the Missouri State Prison on April 23. He would come back to St. Louis in July to rob a bank with two associates, and he would do some work in the Wallace campaign out west. Mostly he disappeared into the landscape, with only his brothers to link him to the past.

The fifty-thousand-dollar offer, meanwhile, still stood.

The summer's city violence escalated considerably in 1967.

Stokely Carmichael was arrested in Atlanta for refusing to move at the request of a policeman—an event that triggered a riot. In Cambridge, Maryland, H. Rap Brown told blacks to "burn this town down if this town don't turn around and grant the demands of Negroes." Some people apparently took him literally, and Brown was arrested for inciting to riot.

On July 13, in Newark, New Jersey, a crowd became angry at the way a black taxi driver was treated at his arrest, and began a riot. When it ended six days later, there was 23 dead, 1,200 injured, and 1,300 arrested. Damages exceeded $10 million.

A special commission appointed by Gov. Richard Hughes would conclude a few months later that "excessive and unjustified force" had been used against blacks by Newark police, state police, and the National Guard troops. As a result, innocent bystanders had been gunned down by the law's "indiscriminate" shooting at anyone black.

On July 14 a riot began in Plainfield, New Jersey, and a white policeman was beaten to death by black youths. Governor Hughes declared a state of emergency and ordered National Guard troops to conduct a house-to-house search in black areas for weapons, without search warrants.

The National Guard was called out in Cairo, Illinois, on July 17 after blacks went on a rampage after the hanging of a black soldier in jail for being AWOL.

There were 68 wounded and 205 arrested in Buffalo, New York, and on July 23, as smoke still hung over Newark, a police raid on a black speakeasy in Detroit triggered a riot that lasted till August 6. When it was over, fourteen thousand paratroopers had to support the National Guard and Detroit police in quelling what many termed an open rebellion. There were 43 people dead, 2,000 injured, 7,200 arrested, and more than 1,250 fires set. Damages exceeded $44 million.

Vice President Hubert Humphrey, touring Detroit during the rioting on August 2, said there was a need for a "Marshall Plan" for impoverished areas of the cities, something King had been calling for for more than a year.

There were riots in Chicago and East St. Louis, Illinois; Milwaukee; Grand Rapids, Michigan; New Haven, Connecticut; South Bend, Indiana; Tampa, Florida; Cincinnati, Cleveland, and Toledo, Ohio; Boston; and Winston-Salem, North Carolina. President Johnson tabbed Gov. Otto Kerner of Illinois to head a Special Advisory Commission on Civil Disorders, and New York City's liberal mayor, John Lindsay, became vice-chair.

The forces of nonviolence, at this point, were dormant. Riots and rebellion ruled the land. Whites talked of "backlash" and "law and order." Blacks talked of "Burn, baby, burn!"

And King? He continued to speak out for the needs of the poor. He continued to speak out against the war and its drain on the fiscal resources of society and the ugliness and hatred and violence it was spawning at home. He continued to speak out for the need of everyone to reach out for nonviolent solutions to the crises in American society. But these speeches were less frequent and even less well received.

It was a sad time and, frankly, King's views were just not wanted in many parts of black or white America. He continued to give them anyway.

"He did not get sour," said Abernathy. "He never got bitter. He became disappointed and he was discouraged often and despondent."

He said they would speak of the prophets in times like these, and reflect on how "prophets grew weary and tired and questioned whether they were right and if they should continue. This was nothing new."

The periods might last a few hours or a few days, but they usually ended the same. "We prayed our way out of them," said Abernathy. "We came together and stood together and prayed." Just as they had in Montgomery. Just as they had when their homes and churches were bombed.

And they continued.

By the fall, King knew what he wanted to do. There was time for one last try. One last effort to unify America. One last effort to show that there could be a nonviolent solution to the problems. One last effort to unify poor whites and poor blacks to make all of America deal with the economic racism that had kept the country as a whole from achieving the destiny it deserved.

He wanted to create a Poor People's Campaign, and take three thousand blacks and whites and Chicanos and Indians, camp out in front of the Washington Monument in a tent city, and stay there until the government responded with a massive program for the poor.

The summer riots—and their portent for the future—showed that it was necessary to give it one more try before the country went up in flames.

The staff didn't like it. They thought it too venturesome. The main lesson they had gotten from Chicago was to stay out of the North—pulling together a national campaign seemed extremely far-fetched. But that's what the leader wanted. Badly.

There was good news from Mississippi in October. For the first time, a Mississippi jury had actually convicted whites of killing blacks. Deputy Sheriff

Price, KKK leader Bowers, a gunman Wayne Roberts, and Doyle Barnette, Willy Wayne Posey, Jimmy Arledge, and Jimmy Snowden were convicted of conspiring to violate the civil rights of COFO workers Chaney, Schwerner, and Goodman. Sheriff Rainey, who allegedly participated in the conspiracy but did not accompany the men, and ten others were acquitted. Jordan, the other triggerman, was a key witness for the Justice Department. He pleaded guilty in federal court in Atlanta.

They would eventually get sentences ranging from three to ten years.

There was good news in Washington in October. Thurgood Marshall, the black civil rights attorney who had been instrumental in the historic *Brown v. Board of Education* in 1954, was sworn in as the first black member of the U.S. Supreme Court.

The year's end was not a happy one, however. King publicly announced that SCLC was gearing up for a new spring offensive, and described the Poor People's Campaign to tie up the bureaucracy in Washington until there was action on behalf of the poor.

The reaction to this was as hostile as the reaction to King's continued criticism of the war in Vietnam. President Johnson was particularly incensed that this campaign was, in his view, aimed at him, personally. He let it be known that he had the troops in Washington to deal with any insurgency.

In these times, few people outside SCLC believed that large demonstrations by blacks would remain peaceful. But King faced the New Year with a resolution to try.

James Earl Ray also ended the year in a new frame of mind. He came out of hiding in Los Angeles, briefly, to drive to New Orleans and meet with one of his brothers, who gave him five hundred dollars to live on. A congressional investigation would later say it was highly unlikely that he risked capture for so little money; his brothers regularly mailed him his share of the proceeds from the bank robbery.

In the investigators' view, Ray would only have come to a New Orleans meeting to have a very important talk about his future.

King was in New York at the end of January 1968, relaxing as well as he could during that period at the home of friends in Harlem. They had been talking about black power, and King was troubled, said Lee, that "there was so much more militancy expressed in the black experience than there had been before."

They left the apartment at 4 A.M. and spent the next hour in the predawn cold on Amsterdam Avenue trying to get a cab, always difficult for blacks in Harlem.

"Martin said this was go for broke," said Lee. "We had to put all our chips in it. This would make or break us. All the years of successes we had enjoyed, we had to put all on the line for this one effort."

Lee wanted to be sure he had understood correctly. "Going for broke" implied that if the Poor People's Campaign failed, their movement would be disbanded. Dead.

King turned to Lee and said, "We've got to put it out there. We have got to really win. We have got to have a massive, nonviolent demonstration. We have got to be better than the bogus marches. We can't let them tramp us into the ground.

"Look around here. People need income. They are jobless, and we have to help them. We are going for broke, and if they drive us into the ground, we will be driven into the ground. They will have to beat us in the encampment. We are going for broke."

The SCLC staff had fanned out across the country in January, recruiting support for the coming campaign in selected cities across the South, as well as Baltimore, Philadelphia, Newark, New York, Boston, Cleveland, and Detroit. It was estimated that the campaign would cost at least four hundred thousand dollars, and funds were hard to come by. Black nationalism had dried up many white sources of funds for all civil rights groups, and King's stand on the war had placed an added burden on SCLC's meager coffers.

The war took a significant turn for the worse at this time. The Vietcong, which was supposedly losing a war of attrition to the Americans, launched a coordinated series of attacks all over that divided country, including the South Vietnamese capital of Saigon. The attacks were eventually beaten back—though the human toll was costly on both sides—and Washington proclaimed it a major victory.

In truth, however, Johnson and his advisers were stunned. The Tet offensive showed clearly that the war of attrition was failing and that the Communists had far more resources and had suffered far fewer setbacks than the American high command had believed. Johnson was forced to reevaluate the steadily escalating war in light of the rude lessons of January.

King was frenetically working to raise funds and win support for his campaign for the poor, but it was taking a toll. His depressed periods came more frequently, and some of his sermons had a somber, melancholy air.

There was more talk of death during this period. He would frequently admonish the SCLC staff in general—and his close friend Abernathy in particular—that "if anything happens to me, you must be prepared to continue."

He refused to take precautions against the growing number of death threats against him, saying, "I cannot live in fear. I have to function. If a man has not found something worth giving his life for, he is not fit to live."

A few weeks later, King went to Jamaica for a few days' rest with Coretta and Young and then went on to Acapulco, staying at the El Presidente Hotel with Abernathy.

The campaign was not going well, said Abernathy. "He was very depressed in Acapulco."

He recalls waking up in the middle of the night and not finding King in their suite. He finally located King on the balcony, staring at the waves below. He said he had been restless and couldn't sleep. He turned to Abernathy and said, "Tell me what I'm thinking about.

"Just look out there and tell me what I'm thinking about."

Abernathy didn't know.

"Do you see that rock?" asked King.

"Yes," replied Abernathy. It was a large rock, standing firm as the waves came and went around it and crashed on it. "What about the rock?"

King started singing, "Rock of ages, cleft for me. Let me hide myself in thee."

"I took it to mean that he was saying we shall overcome," said Abernathy, "that the rock represented the power of truth, the strength of truth. We would prevail.

"But there could not be a prevailing without agony."

There was agony in Memphis.

Reverend Lawson and the sanitation workers found their catalyst. During a stormy day early in February, two black sanitation workers took refuge in the back of their huge garbage truck, waiting for the rain to pass. The engine was running, and a malfunction caused the compactor to start, crushing the men.

"That was the vehicle that caused the men to walk out on strike," said Lawson. They demanded recognition as a union and called for compensation to the families of the two dead men. The city said no, and on February 12 the thirteen hundred men walked off their jobs.

Mayor Henry Loeb insisted that the strike was illegal, and he would not negotiate unless the men returned to work. There were still attempts to negotiate, however, and the city council's labor committee held hearings on conditions for the workers. Eventually, they agreed to present a series of recommendations to the full city council.

But Loeb would have none of it, and went to work on the councilmen. On Friday, February 23, the council and the sanitation workers met in Memphis's Civic Auditorium. The meeting was brief. The council voted to leave the settlement of the strike in the hands of Mayor Loeb and adjourned.

The blacks were furious and decided to hold a mass meeting right then and there. They decided to march down Main Street and called Public Safety Director Frank Holloman for permission.

"We agreed to a nonviolent demonstration down Main Street to protest the action of the city council," said Lawson, and Holloman said they could have half the street. It didn't end up that way.

Police cars began crowding the marchers, driving over the yellow line. Finally, one of the cars ran over the foot of a black woman, and men began rocking the police cars. At this, policemen began attacking the marchers with clubs and Mace. The police broke up the march and chased the workers and their supporters back to the black community.

That night, one hundred black preachers met in the Masonic Temple and set up a formal community effort to back the strike. Lawson, the city's ranking activist, was elected chairman of the Strike Strategy Committee.

They decided to have almost daily marches and rallies in support of the sanitation workers. Their major problem was supporting the men financially until the strike ended. They set up a food and clothing bank in the churches and also took up daily, special collections to help pay rents and mortgages.

Lawson called King, told him what was happening, and asked for help. For King, it was just what he needed. The sanitation workers in Memphis were exactly the type of poor people—the underemployed, overworked, and abused— that the Poor People's Campaign was supposed to help.

The need for the Poor People's Campaign had gotten support from a surprising quarter. The Kerner Commission issued a stunning report, laying the blame for the urban riots squarely on "white racism."

It predicted that the United States was "moving towards two societies, one black, one white, separate and unequal," and called for massive federal programs to create jobs and remove discrimination in housing.

President Johnson had no comment on the report.

While the report may have proved the need for the coming campaign, King's staff did not see a need to go to Memphis. "I thought Memphis was a distraction," said Lee. "If we went there, it would commit us. This was a campaign that would get us bogged down."

Others thought it would throw off the timetable for the Poor People's Campaign, which was already way behind schedule.

King had already decided, and told Lawson, "Just let me know as soon as Roy [Wilkins] has gotten there and I'll let you know when I can come to a mass meeting." The NAACP had a large chapter in Memphis and, as a matter of policy, if King was invited to speak there first, Wilkins wouldn't come at all and some of that support would be lost.

King was finally scheduled to come on March 18, the day after James Earl Ray began driving from Los Angeles to Birmingham, where, he told friends in Los Angeles, he was going to meet his brother. It was a leisurely drive, and Ray would get there the following week.

Memphis was moving. There were daily marches, and money for the sanitation workers was beginning to come in from unions and other sympathizers around the country. At one point, said Lawson, there was a settlement, but the mayor changed his mind the next day. At that point, the leaders of the strike decided it was necessary to increase the stakes, so they called for a boycott of the downtown area.

"We mobilized young people to march after school," said Lawson, "and we had double marches—adults in the morning, and young people in the afternoon."

Lawson picked up King, Abernathy, Young, and Lee at the airport and said, "Martin, I told you we were going to have ten thousand people at the rally tonight, but I made a mistake. We are not going to have that.

"His face dropped. It really did. His smile disappeared. Then I said, 'It looks like we are going to have about 25,000 people'—and his face just broke up. He laughed and laughed. He said, 'You're doing in Memphis what I hope to do in the Poor People's Campaign.' "

The Civic Auditorium was a solid sea of humanity that night, and Lawson was glad that King had decided the Poor People's slow march to Washington would now go through Memphis en route. Before the meeting was over, however, Young told King, "We should lead a march here."

Lawson was surprised and pleased. "We hadn't asked for that kind of commitment," he said. "Martin agreed with him, and I said let's settle on a date."

King reclaimed the podium and promised to be back on March 22 to lead a march, and the audience roared its approval.

Lawson and the strike leaders realized that King's coming with his SCLC

The first Memphis march led by King and Abernathy was a disaster. Bands of youths began rioting. It ended with one dead, fifty injured, and the city under martial law (AP/WIDE WORLD).

staff would add backbone to the black community and strengthen the strike. The leadership, therefore, decided to call for a "no work day" the day of the march.

It never did materialize, however, because Memphis was blanketed with a surprise twenty-five inches of snow that day, and the city was paralyzed. He agreed to return March 28.

That was a disaster. One of the problems, said Lee, was that "we didn't have any staff there."

Though Lawson had worked with King and SCLC in nearly all of its campaigns, "he was more of a theoretician" than a strategist, according to Lee. Lee added that "our practice was to have our staff go in prior to Martin's going into a community, so we knew what we were getting into."

What they found, he said, was a "mob of black folks, no order, and no organization for the demonstration."

That may be harsh, but it was evident that there might be plans to disrupt the march and turn it into a violent confrontation, with King in the lead.

"We had a whole rush of young adults," said Lawson, "in the front ranks of the march. He said he felt the march should be held up until the young men were under control, but Young said, 'It will straighten out after we get going.'"

They were mostly high school youths, who were angered over the severe injuries inflicted by police on a black girl that day during a march at Hamilton High School.

They led, then, a motley march. It was not as orderly as King's marches usually were. Suddenly, said Lawson, "I saw young men breaking windows on Main Street already, and up the street I saw police in riot helmets not moving a bit to stop the guys on the same block who were breaking the windows."

He ran to the front of the march and told King he was calling it off because rioting was breaking out and it seemed to him that the police were expecting it and were waiting for an excuse to break up the march. Lee flagged down a passing Pontiac driven by two black women, and King and his associates left the scene. A motorcycle policeman escorted them to the Holiday Inn–Rivermont on the banks of the Mississippi River and personally ordered rooms for the civil rights leader and his staff.

Far left:
King returned to work with
the sanitation employees.
The black-owned Lorraine
Motel became SCLC's
headquarters
(COMMERCIAL APPEAL).

Left:
King was a familiar sight
going up to Room 306 on
the second floor
(COMMERCIAL APPEAL).

The police attacked, making no distinction between the young looters and the rest of the orderly marchers. When it was over, 150 buildings had been set on fire, a sixteen-year-old black youth was shot and killed, fifty people were injured, and three hundred were arrested by police. Martial law was declared and four thousand National Guard troops were called in to restore order.

King was despondent. In their hotel, they called Atlanta and talked to Hosea Williams. King was sure the march had been deliberately disrupted by

The SCLC team—Williams, Jackson, King, and Abernathy—was in a good mood on April 3, 1968, as they got ready to go to dinner, their last together (AP/WIDE WORLD).

black militants who wanted to sabotage his nonviolent movement. Local leaders thought that the march was disrupted by the Invaders, a black group loosely patterned after the Black Panthers. Many of their members had been involved in the disturbance, though none of the leaders had come to the march.

At that point, King and his staff agreed they had to return to Memphis to lead another march to prove that nonviolence could work. They would not do it until there had been some staff planning, however.

But the outbreak of a riot on a march he had led hurt King, and he began questioning the validity of nonviolence. He did not doubt that nonviolence was the proper course to take.

He told Abernathy, "Why don't we just let the violence run its course, because it will not last very long.

"Maybe the good people, the people who believe in nonviolence, should just stand aside until the violence has run its course."

He called his friend Levison in New York and repeated his feelings. Levison couldn't calm him down, either.

"It was the most restless night," said Abernathy. "It was a terrible and horrible experience for him. I had never seen him in all my life so upset and so troubled. I couldn't get him to sleep that night. He was worried, worried. He didn't know what to do. He didn't know what the press was going to say."

The leaders of the Invaders—Charles Cabbage, Calvin Taylor, and Charles Harrington—received a hostile reception from Abernathy the following morning, March 29, when they attempted to meet with King.

They claimed they had not been wholly responsible for the disturbance, but had been kept out of the strike movement by Lawson. Though Lawson vehemently denied that he or the other strike leaders had frozen the Invaders out of the movement, King wanted to have them actively involved in the campaign.

Cabbage said they would need some money to organize; King promised to help them raise it. Lawson didn't like that. The leadership, he said, hadn't rejected offers of help from the Invaders—they had merely rejected demands that they give money to the group to "organize" when the funds were earmarked for buying food and paying rents for the strikers and their families.

But King promised they would have help, and then he, Lee, and Abernathy went back to Atlanta.

Ray was busy that day, as well. He went to the Aeromarine Supply Company in Birmingham and bought a .243 caliber Winchester, using the name Harvey Lowmeyer, who was a man who had been in prison with James's brothers Jerry and John Ray back in the 1950s. Then he went and conferred with Jerry and returned to the store later that afternoon or early the next morning. He told the clerk that his brother suggested he get a bigger bore, and asked for a Remington model 760 .30-06 caliber.

He would later tell his attorney that they decided that the smaller gun was good for "killing small animals," and he needed "a more powerful one that was more likely to kill an individual."

The store clerk told Ray the Winchester could "bring down any deer in Alabama." Ray countered casually that he was hunting bigger game in Wisconsin. A few days later, Ray drove to Memphis.

Lawson led a march in Memphis that Saturday, to show there could be a nonviolent demonstration. "We let the city know in no uncertain terms that we would be on the streets," he said. "We were not going to stop because of that group."

There was an angry staff meeting at Ebenezer Church on Saturday, March 30. Bevel and Jackson were insistent that Memphis be dropped from their plans. The entire staff was angry over the poor planning in Memphis, which had led to the riot.

The two organizers felt it would be a waste of resources to get bogged down in Memphis now, when there was insufficient planning for the Washington march. They were overruled by the others, who felt that once King agreed to lead a march, he was committed. They had to go back.

King had a poignant meeting with his parents. Seated on the porch, he said, "Mother, there are some things I want you to know. There's a chance, Mother, that someone is going to try to kill me, and it could happen without any warning at all.

"Sometimes I do want to get away for a while, go someplace with Coretta and the kids and be Reverend King and family, having a few quiet days like any other American. But I know it's too late for any of that now. And if mine isn't to be a long life, Mother, Dad, well then I respect that, as you've always taught us to respect it as God's will."

There was stunning news Sunday night. President Johnson, convinced that his war effort was not working and was creating too many divisions in his Great Society, announced to a televised audience that he was not going to seek reelection, would scale down the bombing of North Vietnam, and would begin peace talks with the Vietnamese Communists.

By now, half a million Americans were fighting and dying in that country. This was to be the beginning of a slow change in American attitudes toward the war in Vietnam.

By Monday, April 1, Bevel, Jackson, Young, and James Orange were back in Memphis, with Orange and Bevel giving particular emphasis to the Invaders and high school demonstrators to make sure there was no repetition of their riotous behavior.

King returned Wednesday, April 3, and held a series of planning meetings at Lawson's Centenary Methodist Church. During the day, he was served with a temporary restraining order barring any march unless approved by U.S. District Court Judge Bailey Brown. Lawson secured attorneys to represent King and the local leaders at the hearing the following morning.

It was pouring that night, and King really didn't want to go to the rally. Lawson and Abernathy decided to attend and call him if there was a huge crowd. There was, so they called him and Lee drove him over.

"It was eerie," said Lawson. There was thunder and lightning outside, reverberating through the meeting hall, and there was a warm, cozy, family atmosphere inside. King talked about his movement family, calling Lawson a "leading theoretician of nonviolence" and Ralph Abernathy "my best friend."

He reviewed the movement, saying, "Men, for years now, have been talking about war and peace. But now, no longer can they just talk about it. It is no longer a choice between violence and nonviolence in this world, it's nonviolence or nonexistence. . . . If something isn't done, and in a hurry, to bring the colored peoples of the world out of their long years of poverty, their long years of neglect, the whole world is doomed."

He talked to them about patriotism. "If I lived in China or even Russia, or any totalitarian country, maybe I could understand the denial of certain basic First Amendment privileges, because they hadn't committed themselves to that over there. But somewhere, I read of the freedom of assembly. Somewhere, I read of the freedom of speech. Somewhere, I read of the freedom of the press. Somewhere, I read that the greatness of America is the right to protest for right. And so, just as I say, we aren't going to let any injunction turn us around. We are going on.

"Let us rise up tonight with a greater readiness. Let us stand with a greater determination. And let us move on in these powerful days, these days of challenge, to make America a better nation. And I want to thank God, once more, for allowing me to be here with you."

Lawson, sitting in the rear of the hall, thought something was strange. "I kept asking myself why is Martin talking like this? Why is he taking this tack? Some of the phrases in his speech I had heard before in different places, and read others in his book *Strength to Love*. But he had never woven it together like this."

King continued, "I don't know what will happen now. We've got some difficult days ahead. But it doesn't matter with me, now, because I've been to the mountaintop. And I don't mind.

"Like anybody, I would like to live a long life; longevity has its place. But I'm not concerned about that now. I just want to do God's will. And He's allowed me to go up to the mountain. And I've looked over. And I've seen the promised land.

"I may not get there with you. But I want you to know tonight that we as a people will get to the promised land. And I'm happy tonight. I'm not worried about anything. I'm not fearing any man. Mine eyes have seen the glory of the coming of the Lord."

It was a sobering experience for Lawson, but it left King in a buoyant mood. It was a reminder of the inner peace he felt right before his home was bombed, so many years and campaigns and heartaches and triumphs before.

He and Abernathy had a cheerful dinner at the home of Ben Hooks, an NAACP attorney, and then returned to the black-owned Lorraine Motel. There he learned that his brother, A.D., had driven up, and they laughed and talked until nearly sunup.

Ray was moving around, also. He had checked into the New Rebel Motel on the edge of Memphis, but he read a front page article in the *Commercial Appeal* that day about King and his activities. It mentioned that King and his staff were staying at the Lorraine.

He checked out of the New Rebel and moved into Bessie Brewer's rooming house across the street from the Lorraine. Its rear windows faced the motel's Room 306, where King and Abernathy were staying. He waited.

King got up around noon, refreshed and calm. Young and Lawson had been in court all morning, and Judge Brown had not rendered a decision. King had been cheered by his meeting with his brother and had spent an hour on the telephone with his mother.

"You know," he said to Abernathy, "she's always so happy when A.D. is with me. I wish you had been here where you could have talked with her."

They were going to have dinner at Rev. Billy Kyle's house, and the minister's wife was pulling out all the stops for King and his staff. There was roast beef and chitlins, and pig feet, and sweet potato pie, and lots of greens. Young, Lee, and Bevel were in the courtyard, waiting for King and Abernathy to finish shaving, and Jackson was on the balcony. King started outside. Their driver, Ben Branch, said, "You better put your coat on, Doc. It will be cold tonight."

Then they heard a shot.

Lee, who had been in the military, said, "I knew it was a rifle shot. If I never heard anything else, I knew what that was. I looked around and couldn't figure out what was going on. Then this lady screamed, and we looked and she was looking up. There we saw Martin's feet protruding off the balcony."

He and the others rushed upstairs and found Abernathy cradling his long-time friend's head. "Martin, this is me. This is Ralph. This is Ralph, and you have nothing to worry about. Don't, don't worry. It's going to be all right." King looked at his friends, and his lips quivered, but he could not speak.

Young said, "Oh my God, my God, it's all over!"

"No, Andy!" snapped Abernathy. "Don't you say that. Don't say that."

Reverend Kyle threw himself across the bed, screaming.

Police were running everywhere, though no one was on the next street to see Ray leave the rooming house, without the rifle, and drive away.

Abernathy rode with his friend in the ambulance. He and Lee accompanied King into the operating room and refused to leave.

They backed out of the way to let the doctors work. Lee was asked to take King's watch off.

"I went around to take that off. His tissue was still soft, but he was lifeless," said Lee. "And then that monitor just went dashes—just a long blur like on the movie screen. And the doctor walked over to us and said, 'He's gone.'"

It was 7:05 P.M.

Coretta had just returned from a shopping trip with the children when the telephone rang in her bedroom. It was Jesse Jackson saying, "Doc just got shot. You better catch the first thing smoking."

He tried to spare her, implying that King was just badly wounded. But she knew better.

"All of a sudden," she said, "the children were inside my room, and the commentator on the TV was talking. Yolanda [who was twelve at that time] looked at it and screamed and ran out.

"Then Andy called and said, 'Coretta, did you hear about Martin? Well, it's real bad. You better come right away.' He said Martin was still alive, but in a way that let me know that he probably wasn't going to make it."

Young told her to bring Dora McDonald, King's long-time secretary, with her because she was a strong woman and could take care of whatever Coretta needed.

Mayor Ivan Allen of Atlanta provided transportation to the airport, but

Coretta was paged before she got on the plane. The mayor went off to find out what the call was all about, just as McDonald arrived and said, "Let's get some-place where we can sit down."

"I knew then that he had expired," Coretta said. "We went into the ladies room near the gate, and Mayor Allen followed us in there. Dora and I just embraced each other and held each other. And the mayor said, 'Your husband is dead.'

"I knew that, but hearing the words had a sad finality. So I said we should go home because I needed to take care of the children."

The King home was awash with friends and family, all mourning and supporting each other. Jean Young saw Yoki praying behind the living room curtain, saying, "Lord, please take care of my mommy and make her strong."

When she had finished praying, she went up to the bedroom and asked her mother if she should hate assassins.

"I told her no," said Coretta. "Your daddy wouldn't want you to do that. She said, 'Well, Momma, I'm not going to cry then. I'm not going to cry because my Daddy's not really dead and I'm going to see him again in Heaven.'

"I put my arms around her and said, 'Your daddy would be so proud of you.'

"I haven't seen her cry, really, since that day."

In Memphis, Lawson made the rounds of the newspapers and television stations, appealing for calm and stating that the demonstrations would continue. Plans were made for a march the following day, and a memorial march on Monday, April 8.

The FBI was busy as well. It turned all its attention to finding the assassin. They found the Remington in the room where Ray had fired the fatal shot, as well as the April 3 issue of the Memphis *Commercial Appeal*, and Ray's fingerprints were on the front page article about King.

A warrant was put out for his arrest.

The black communities around the nation reacted to the murder of the man of nonviolence in a blaze of violence. Rioting erupted in 125 cities and burned from April 4 through April 11. Around the country 68,887 troops were called out to quell the disturbances, in which 46 people were killed, 3,500 injured, and 20,000 arrested.

In the nation's capital, 711 fires were set, causing $15 million worth of damage, 7 people were killed, 1,166 were injured, and 7,370 were arrested. Fifteen thousand troops were needed to quell the riot in Washington, D.C.

President Johnson declared Sunday, April 7, a day of national mourning. He called on Congress to finish Dr. King's program and pass the stalled civil rights bill banning discrimination in housing and the sale and rental of apartments and homes. Congress responded to that call and passed the bill three days later.

Johnson also called Mayor Loeb to say that the strike had to be equitably settled and that he would dispatch Attorney General Ramsey Clark and a labor arbitrator the following week to make sure that it was.

By April 18, they would have their settlement, and the sanitation workers would get everything they asked for: minimum wages, union representation, clothing allowance, and benefits.

On Monday, April 8, Coretta and her three eldest children joined Abernathy in leading thirty thousand people in a memorial march in Memphis for her slain husband. Then they brought the body back to Atlanta, in a jet chartered by Robert Kennedy, now a senator from New York.

The body lay in state in the chapel at Spelman College, and mourners filed by at a rate of more than twelve hundred per hour.

On April 9 Ebenezer Baptist Church was packed with some eight hundred invited guests; outside, in the heat, another hundred thousand people gathered to pay their final respects to the man who had done so much for so many. The funeral brought together many people from different sides of the political spectrum.

King's long-time supporters in the entertainment community—Sammy Davis, Jr., Harry Belafonte, Sidney Poitier, Mahalia Jackson, and Lena Horne—were there. SCLC's staff—Young, Lee, Bevel, Vivian, Williams, Orange, Shuttlesworth, Lawson, and, of course, Abernathy—were there: hurt, shocked, lost.

John Lewis, the pacifist student leader, and Stokely Carmichael, his firebrand successor, were there. Wilkins and Whitney Young and Floyd McKissick and James Forman were there. Ramsey Clark and Richard Nixon and Jacqueline Kennedy and Vice President Hubert Humphrey were there.

The world was drawn to Ebenezer and listened to King's voice once more, as the tape of his own eulogy was played before the sobbing crowd.

"Yes, if you want to say I was a drum major, say that I was a drum major for justice; say that I was a drum major for peace; I was a drum major for righteousness. And all of the other shallow things will not matter. . . .

"I just want to leave a committed life behind. And that's all I want to say. If I can help somebody as I pass along, if I can cheer somebody with a word or a song, if I can show somebody he's traveling wrong, then my living will not be in vain.

"If I can do my duty as a Christian ought, if I can bring salvation to a world once wrought, if I can spread the message as the master taught, then my living will not be in vain."

Then the thousands walked in a slow procession behind a special hearse—a poor person's hearse, a farm cart drawn by two mules—to South View Cemetery. Rev. Martin Luther King, Jr., ended his last march in a marble tomb emblazoned with the words:

"FREE AT LAST, FREE AT LAST,
THANK GOD ALMIGHTY
I'M FREE AT LAST."

Martin Luther King, Jr.,
in state at Spelman Colle
viewed by more than twel
hundred mourners per ho
(CONSTANTINE MANOS/
MAGNUM).

Coretta King at the fune
service on April 9 at
Ebenezer Baptist Church
(BOB ADELMAN/MAGNUM

(AP/WIDE WORLD).

...drew the powerful:
...ichard Nixon, Robert
...ennedy, Francis Cardinal
...ellman, John V. Lindsay,
...ice President Hubert
...umphrey, Nelson
...ockefeller (AP/WIDE
...ORLD).

...d it drew one hundred
...ousand more, who
...lowed Young, Bevel,
...illiams, Lee, Abernathy,
...uttlesworth, Lawson,
...vian, Lewis, and—in a
...ule-drawn wagon—
...artin Luther King, Jr., on
...e last march for peace
...TLANTA CONSTITUTION).

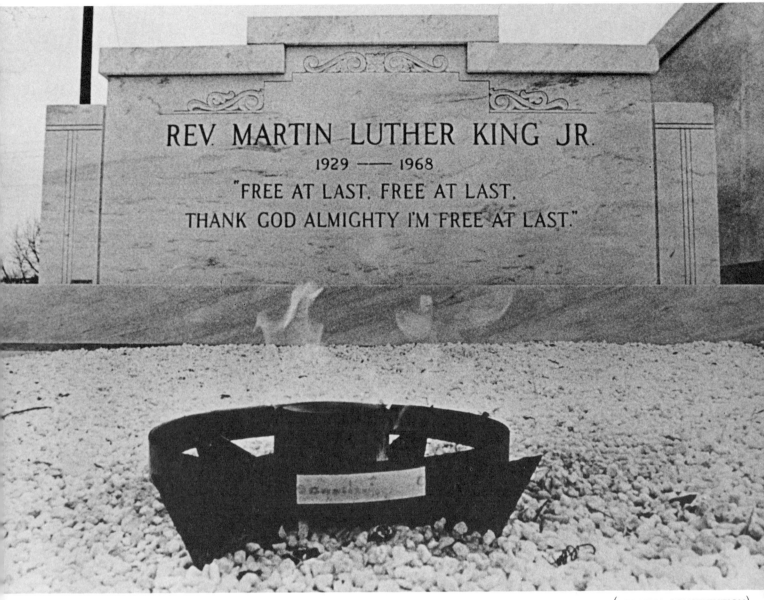

CHRONOLOGY

1929 JANUARY 15. Martin Luther King, Jr., is born in Atlanta, Georgia. His mother is Alberta Christine Williams King. His father is Rev. Martin Luther King, Sr.

1935–1944. King attends David T. Howard Elementary School, Atlanta University Laboratory School, and Booker T. Washington High School. He passes the entrance examination to Atlanta's Morehouse College without graduating from high school.

1941 James Farmer establishes Congress of Racial Equality (CORE) and begins lunch counter sit-ins Chicago.

1947 King is licensed to preach and becomes assistant to his father, who is pastor of the Ebenezer Baptist Church in Atlanta.

1948 FEBRUARY 25. King is ordained to the Baptist ministry.
JUNE. King graduates from Morehouse College with a B.A. in sociology.
SEPTEMBER. King enters Crozer Theological Seminary, Chester, Pennsylvania. After hearing Dr. A. J. Muste and Dr. Mordecai W. Johnson preach on the life and teaching of Mahatma Gandhi, he begins to study Gandhi seriously.

1951 JUNE. King graduates from Crozer with a B.D.

1953 JUNE 18. King marries Coretta Scott in Marion, Alabama.

1954 MAY 17. The Supreme Court of the United States rules unanimously in *Brown v. Board of Education* that racial segregation in public schools is unconstitutional.
OCTOBER 31. King is installed by his father as the twentieth pastor of the Dexter Avenue Church in Montgomery, Alabama.

1955 JUNE 5. King receives a Ph.D. in Systematic Theology from Boston University.
NOVEMBER 17. Yolanda Denise, the Kings' first child, is born.
DECEMBER 1. In Montgomery, Alabama, Rosa Parks, a forty-two-year-old seamstress, refuses to relinquish her bus seat to a white man and is arrested.
DECEMBER 5. The first day of the Montgomery bus boycott. The Montgomery Improvement Association is formed and Dr. King is unanimously elected president of the organization.
DECEMBER 10. The Montgomery bus company suspends service in black neighborhoods.

1956 JANUARY 30. A bomb is thrown onto the porch of the Kings' Montgomery home. Coretta King, Yolanda King, and church member Lucy Williams are in the house: no one is injured.
FEBRUARY 2. A suit is filed in federal district court asking that Montgomery's travel segregation laws be declared unconstitutional.
FEBRUARY 21. Dr. King is indicted with other figures in the Montgomery bus boycott on the charge of being party to a conspiracy to hinder and prevent the operation of business without "just or legal cause."
JUNE 4. A United States district court rules that racial segregation on city bus lines is unconstitutional.
OCTOBER 30. Mayor Gayle of Montgomery instructs the city's legal department to find a legal means to stop the operation of car pools, the transportation system used during the boycott.
NOVEMBER 13. The United States Supreme Court affirms the decision of the district court in declaring unconstitutional Alabama's state and local laws requiring segregation on buses.
DECEMBER 20. Federal injunctions prohibiting segregation on buses are served on bus company officials. Injunctions are also served on city and Alabama state officials.
DECEMBER 21. Montgomery buses are integrated.

1957 JANUARY 27. An unexploded bomb is discovered on the Kings' front porch.
FEBRUARY. The Southern Christian Leadership Conference (SCLC) is formed. Dr. King is elected its president.
MAY 17. Dr. King delivers a speech at the Prayer Pilgrimage for Freedom in Washington, D.C. The pilgrimage was held on the third anniversary of the Supreme Court's desegregation decision.

SEPTEMBER. President Dwight D. Eisenhower federalizes the Arkansas National Guard to escort nine black students to an all-white high school in Little Rock, Arkansas.

SEPTEMBER 9. The first civil rights act since Reconstruction is passed by Congress, creating the Civil Rights Commission and the Civil Rights Division of the Department of Justice.

OCTOBER 23. Martin Luther III, the Kings' second child, is born.

1958 JUNE 23. Dr. King, Roy Wilkins, A. Philip Randolph, and Lester Granger meet with President Eisenhower.

SEPTEMBER. Dr. King's book *Stride Toward Freedom: The Montgomery Story* is published.

SEPTEMBER 20. Dr. King is stabbed in the chest by Izola Curry while he is in a New York City department store autographing his recently published book.

1959 FEBRUARY 2–MARCH 10. Martin and Coretta King spend several weeks in India as guests of Prime Minister Nehru, studying Gandhi's techniques of nonviolence.

1960 JANUARY 24. The King family moves to Atlanta. Dr. King becomes copastor, with his father, of the Ebenezer Baptist Church.

FEBRUARY 1. Students in Greensboro, North Carolina launch widely publicized sit-ins which spark a wave of similar protests throughout the south.

FEBRUARY 17. A warrant is issued for Dr. King's arrest on charges that he did not pay his 1956 and 1958 Alabama state income taxes.

APRIL 15. The Student Nonviolent Coordinating Committee (SNCC) is founded to coordinate student protest at Shaw University in Raleigh, North Carolina, on a temporary basis. It becomes permanent in October 1960.

MAY 28. Dr. King is acquitted of the tax evasion charge by an all-white jury in Montgomery.

JUNE 24. Dr. King has a conference with John F. Kennedy, candidate for president of the United States, about racial matters.

OCTOBER 19–27. Dr. King is arrested at an Atlanta sit-in and is jailed on a charge of violating the state's trespass law. That charge is dropped but King is still held on a charge of violating his probation in a traffic arrest case. He is ultimately transferred to Reidsville State Prison, where he is released on a two-thousand-dollar bond.

1961 JANUARY 30. Dexter Scott, the Kings' third child, is born.

MAY 4. The Congress of Racial Equality (CORE) organizes the first group of Freedom Riders. The Freedom Riders, intent on integrating interstate buses, leave Washington, D.C., by Greyhound bus shortly after the Supreme Court has outlawed segregation in interstate transportation terminals.

1962 SEPTEMBER 20. James Meredith makes his first attempt to enroll at the University of Mississippi. He is actually enrolled by Supreme Court order and is escorted onto the Oxford, Mississippi, campus by U.S. marshals on October 1.

OCTOBER 16. Dr. King meets with President Kennedy at the White House for a one-hour conference.

1963 MARCH 28. Bernice Albertine, the Kings' fourth child, is born.

APRIL. Sit-in demonstrations begin in Birmingham to protest segregation of eating facilities. Dr. King is arrested during the demonstration.

APRIL 16. Dr. King writes "Letter from a Birmingham Jail" while imprisoned for demonstrating.

MAY 3, 4, 5. Eugene "Bull" Connor, director of public safety of Birmingham, orders the use of police dogs and fire hoses on the marching protestors.

MAY 20. The Supreme Court of the United States rules Birmingham's segregation ordinances unconstitutional.

JUNE. Dr. King's book *Strength to Love* is published.

JUNE 11. Governor George C. Wallace tries to stop the court-ordered integration of the University of Alabama by "standing in the schoolhouse door" and personally refusing entrance to black students.

JUNE 12. Medgar Evers is assassinated in front of his home in Jackson, Mississippi.

AUGUST 28. In Washington, D.C., the March on Washington is held. Dr. King delivers his "I Have a Dream" speech on the steps of the Lincoln Memorial.

November 22. President Kennedy is assassinated in Dallas, Texas.

1964 Summer. Council of Federated Organizations (COFO) initiates a voter-registration drive run by black and white students called the Mississippi Summer Project.

June. Dr. King's book *Why We Can't Wait* is published.

June 21. Three civil rights workers—James Chaney, Andrew Goodman, and Michael Schwerner—are reported missing after a short trip to Philadelphia, Mississippi. Their bodies are found six weeks later by FBI agents.

July. Dr. King attends the signing of the Public Accommodations Bill, part of the Civil Rights Act of 1964, by President Lyndon B. Johnson in the White House.

July 18–23. Riots occur in Harlem.

August. Riots occur in New Jersey, Illinois, and Pennsylvania.

September 18. Dr. King has an audience with Pope Paul VI at the Vatican.

December 10. Dr. King receives the Nobel Peace Prize in Oslo, Norway.

1965 February 21. Malcolm X is assassinated in New York City.

March 9. Unitarian minister James Reeb is beaten by four white segregationists in Selma and dies two days later.

March 15. President Johnson addresses the nation and Congress, describing the voting rights bill he will submit, and uses the slogan of the civil rights movement, "We Shall Overcome."

March 21–25. Over three thousand protest marchers leave Selma for a march to Montgomery, protected by federal troops. They are joined along the way by a total of twenty-five thousand marchers. Upon reaching the capitol they hear an address by Dr. King.

March 25. Viola Liuzzo is shot and killed while driving a marcher from Montgomery to Selma.

August 6. The 1965 Voting Rights Act is signed by President Johnson.

August 11–16 Thirty-five people die in riots in the Watts area of Los Angeles, California.

1966 January. Dr. King rents an apartment in a Chicago ghetto.

February 23. In Chicago, Dr. King meets with Elijah Muhammad, leader of the Nation of Islam.

March. Dr. King takes over a Chicago slum building and is sued by its owner.

March 25. The Supreme Court of the United States rules that any poll tax is unconstitutional.

May 16. Dr. King agrees to serve as cochairman of Clergy and Laymen Concerned about Vietnam. An antiwar statement by Dr. King is read at a large Washington, D.C., rally to protest the war in Vietnam.

June. Stokely Carmichael and Willie Ricks, both of SNCC, use the slogan "Black Power".

June 6. James Meredith is shot soon after beginning his 220-mile "March Against Fear" from Memphis, Tennessee, to Jackson, Mississippi.

July 10. Dr. King launches a drive to make Chicago an "open city" in regard to housing.

1967 January. Dr. King writes his book *Where Do We Go from Here?* while in Jamaica, West Indies.

March 12. Alabama is ordered to desegregate all public schools.

March 25. Dr. King attacks the government's Vietnam policy in a speech at the Chicago Coliseum.

April 4. Dr. King makes a statement about the war in Vietnam at the Riverside Church in New York City.

July 12–17. Twenty-three people die and 725 are injured in the riots in Newark, New Jersey.

July 23–30. Forty-three die and 324 are injured in the Detroit riots.

July 26. Dr. King, A. Philip Randolph, Roy Wilkins, and Whitney Young, Jr., appeal for an end to the riots.

November 27. Dr. King announces the formation by SCLC of a Poor People's Campaign, with the aim of representing the problems of poor blacks and whites.

1968 February 12. Sanitation workers strike in Memphis, Tennessee.

March 28. Dr. King leads six thousand protesters on a march through downtown Memphis in support of striking sanitation workers. Disorders break out during which black youths loot stores. One person is killed, fifty people are injured.

APRIL 3. Dr. King delivers "I've Been to the Mountaintop" at the Memphis Masonic Temple.

APRIL 4. Dr. King is shot at the Lorraine Motel in Memphis. He dies in St. Joseph's Hospital.

APRIL 4–11. Riots erupt in 125 cities around the country, including the nation's capital.

APRIL 7–9. Dr. King lies in state at Spelman College in Atlanta, Georgia. Mourners file by at the rate of twelve hundred per hour.

APRIL 8. Coretta King, Yolanda King, Martin King III, Dexter King, and Ralph Abernathy lead a memorial march for Dr. King in Memphis.

APRIL 9. The funeral of Dr. King is held at the Ebenezer Baptist Church. He is laid to rest at the South View Cemetery.

REFERENCES

ABERNATHY—Interviews with Ralph David Abernathy by W.R.W., September 1984, in Atlanta; and the Donald H. Smith Oral History Collection, tape no. SMI-6 in the archives of the Martin Luther King, Jr., Center for Nonviolent Social Change in Atlanta, December 1963.

AMSTERDAM NEWS—"What the Nobel Prize Means to Me," by Dr. Martin Luther King, Jr., November 28, 1964.

ANDERSON, N.—Interview with Norma Anderson by W.R.W., Detroit, October 1984.

ANDERSON, W.—Interview with Dr. William Anderson by W.R.W., Detroit, October 1984.

ANDREWS—Interview with Barbara Andrews by W.R.W., Uriah, Alabama, July 1984.

APPEAL—"An Appeal to the President of the United States for National Rededication to the Principles of the Emancipation Proclamation", by Martin Luther King, Jr. (1962), reprinted in *A Martin Luther King Treasury* (Yonkers, N.Y.: Educational Heritage, Inc., 1964).

AZBELL—Interview with Joseph Azbell, former editor of the Montgomery *Advertiser*, by Mary Gaines, Montgomery, September 1984.

BAKER—Interview with Ida Mae Baker by Mary Gaines, Montgomery, Alabama, September 1984.

BAKER, E.—Interview with Ella Baker by John Britton, staff specialist, Civil Rights Documentation Project, Ralph J. Bunche Oral History Collection, Moorland-Spingarn Research Center, Howard University, June 19, 1968.

BARBOUR—Interview with Almanina Barbour by W.R.W., Philadelphia, Pennsylvania, October 1984.

BEASLEY—Interview with Robert Beasley of the First Baptist Church by Mary Gaines, Montgomery, October 1984.

BENNETT—*What Manner of Man: A Biography of Martin Luther King, Jr. 1929–1968*, 3rd rev. ed., by Lerone Bennett, Jr. (Chicago: Johnson Publishing Co., 1968).

BEVEL—Interview with Rev. James Bevel by W.R.W., Chicago, September 1984.

BOMB—Interviews with Atlanta Police Chief Herbert Jenkins, Ret.; Det. Clyde Hanby, Ret.; and Smyrna Police Chief Everett Little by W.R.W., October 1984.

BOND—Interview with Julian Bond by W.R.W., July 1984.

BRINK—*Black and White: A Study of U.S. Racial Attitudes Today,* by William Brink and Louis Harris (New York: Simon & Schuster, 1966).

CHANDLER—Interview with Prof. G. Louis Chandler of Morehouse, from the Donald H. Smith Oral History Collection in the archives of the Martin Luther King, Jr., Center for Nonviolent Social Change in Atlanta, tape no. SMI-10, December 1963.

CHRONICLE—*The Chronological History of the Negro in America,* by Peter M. Bergman and Mort N. Bergman (New York: Harper & Row, 1969).

CORETTA—Interview with Coretta Scott King by W.R.W., October 1983.

CORETTA KING—*My Life with Martin Luther King, Jr.*, by Coretta Scott King (New York: Holt, Rinehart and Winston, 1969).

DADDY KING—*Daddy King: An Autobiography*, by Rev. Martin Luther King, Sr., with Clayton Riley (New York: William Morrow & Co., 1980).

DURR—Interview with Virginia Durr by Mary Gaines, Montgomery, Alabama, September 1984.

EDWARDS—Interview with Eliza Edwards by Diana Clyne, St. Augustine, Florida, July 1984.

FAR—*The Final Assassinations Report*, Report of the Select Committee on Assassinations, U.S. House of Representatives, Louis Stokes, Ohio, Chairman (New York: Bantam Books 1979).

FLORIDA—Florida *Times-Union.*

GARROW—*The FBI and Martin Luther King, Jr.*, by David J. Garrow (New York: Penguin Books, 1983).

HARRIS—Interview with Mildred Harris by Diana Clyne, St. Augustine, Florida, July 1984.

HASKINS—*The Life and Death of Martin Luther King, Jr.*, by James Haskins (New York: William Morrow, 1977).

HOOKS—Interview with Rev. Benjamin Hooks by W.R.W., July 1984.

JACKSON—Jackson *Clarion-Ledger*/Jackson *Daily News.* Perspective section, Special Report, "Freedom Summer: A Generation Later," July 1, 1984.

JENKINS—Interview with Clyde Jenkins by Diana Clyne, St. Augustine, Florida, July 1984.

JONES—Interview with Quillie Jones by Diana Clyne, St. Augustine, Florida, July 1984.

JOURNAL—The Alabama *Journal.*

JURY—Further Presentment of Grand Jury. Grand Jury, Spring Term, 1964, in the Circuit Court, Seventh Judicial Circuit, St. Johns County, Florida.

LACEY—Interview with Dr. Archie L. Lacey, of Dexter Avenue Baptist Church, by W.R.W., Teaneck, New Jersey, July 1984.

LANGFORD—Interview with Alabama State Senator Charles Langford, former attorney for the MIA, by W.R.W., Montgomery, August 1984.

LAWSON—Interview with Rev. James Lawson by W.R.W., Los Angeles, October 1984.

LEE—Interview with Rev. Bernard Lee by W.R.W., Washington, D.C., October 1984.

LEWIS—Interview with Rufus Lewis, of Dexter Avenue Baptist Church, by Mary Gaines, Montgomery, September 1984.

LEWIS, D.—*King: A Biography*, 2nd ed., by David L. Lewis (Urbana: University of Illinois Press, 1978).

LEWIS, J.—Interview with John Lewis by W.R.W., August 1984.

LINCOLN—*Martin Luther King, Jr.: A Profile*, edited by C. Eric Lincoln. American Century Series (New York: Hill & Wang, 1970).

LOWERY—Interview with Rev. Joseph Lowery, chairman, SCLC, by W.R.W., October 1984.

MANN—Interview with Floyd Mann by W.R.W., Montgomery, October 1984.

MOBILE—The Mobile *Register.*

MONTGOMERY—The Montgomery *Advertiser.*

MOSES—Interview with Robert Moses by W.R.W., Cambridge, Massachusetts, October 1984.

NEWS—The Birmingham *News.*

NIXON—Interview with E. D. Nixon by W.R.W., Montgomery, August 1984.

NYT—New York *Times:* "Informer for F.B.I. Suspect in Bombing," by Howell Raines, Sunday, July 9, 1978, pp. 1, 20. "F.B.I. Informant in Klan Asserts He Shot and Killed a Black in '63," by Howell Raines, Tuesday, July 11, 1978, pp. 1, B7.

OATES—*Let the Trumpet Sound: The Life of Martin Luther King, Jr.*, by Stephen B. Oates (New York: Plume Book, New American Library, 1982).

PATTERSON—Interviews with Alabama Supreme Court Justice John Patterson, former governor and former state attorney general, by Mary Gaines and W.R.W., Montgomery, October 1984.

PITCHER—Interview with Rev. Al Pitcher by W.R.W., Chicago, September 1984.

RABY—Interview with Al Raby by W.R.W., Chicago, September 1984.

RACE—Race Relations Law Reporter. Volume 9, 1964. Andrew Young v. L. O. Davis, as Sheriff, etc., et al. 590–597. Federal Jurisdiction. Habeas Corpus, Removal—Florida. Yvonne Johnson et al. v. L. O. Davis, as Sheriff, etc., et al. 814–819.

RAINES—*My Soul Is Rested: The Story of the Civil Rights Movement in the Deep South,* by Howell Raines (New York: Viking Penguin Books, 1983).

RIDDICK—Interview with Rev. Ed Riddick by W.R.W., Chicago, October 1984.

ROBINSON—Interview with Jo Ann Robinson, of Dexter Avenue Baptist Church, by W.R.W., Los Angeles, August 1984.

SCHULKE—*Martin Luther King, Jr.: A Documentary . . . Montgomery to Memphis,* edited by Flip Schulke (New York: W. W. Norton, 1976).

SHUTTLESWORTH—Interviews with Rev. Fred Shuttlesworth by W.R.W., Cincinnati, September 1984; and the Hosea Williams collection, made in November 1969 and donated to the archives of the Martin Luther King, Jr., Center for Nonviolent Social Change in Atlanta.

SIMPSON—Interview with Federal District Court Judge Bryan Simpson by Diana Clyne, St. Augustine, Florida, July 1984.

SMITH—Interview with Dr. Kenneth L. Smith by W.R.W., October 1984. *Search for the Beloved Community: The Thinking of Martin Luther King, Jr.,* by Smith and Ira G. Zepp, Jr. (Valley Forge, Pa.: Judson Press, 1974).

STRENGTH—*Strength to Love,* by Martin Luther King, Jr. (New York: Harper & Row, 1963). Reprinted in *A Martin Luther King Treasury* (Yonkers, N.Y.: Educational Heritage, Inc., 1964).

STRIDE—*Stride Toward Freedom,* by Martin Luther King, Jr. (New York: Harper & Row, 1958). Reprinted in *A Martin Luther King Treasury* (Yonkers, N.Y.: Educational Heritage, Inc., 1964).

TILLMAN—Interview with Dr. N. P. Tillman, David H. Smith Oral History Collection in the archives of the Martin Luther King, Jr., Center for Nonviolent Social Change, tape no. SMI-9, December 1963.

TWEEDLE—*A Lasting Impression: A Collection of Photographs of Martin Luther King, Jr.,* by John Tweedle, edited by Hermene Hartman (Columbia: University of South Carolina Press, 1983).

TWINE—Interviews with Henry and Katherine Twine by Diana Clyne, St. Augustine, Florida, July 1984.

TYSON—Interview with Cora Tyson by Diana Clyne, St. Augustine, Florida, July 1984.

VIVIAN—Interview with Rev. C. T. Vivian by W.R.W., Atlanta, August 1984.

WALKER—Interview with Rev. Wyatt Tee Walker by W.R.W., New York, September 1984.

WALLACE—Interview with David Wallace by W.R.W., Chicago, September 1984.

WHERE—*Where Do We Go from Here: Chaos or Community,* by Martin Luther King, Jr. (Boston: Beacon Press, 1967).

WILLIAMS—Interview with Hosea Williams by W.R.W., Atlanta, September 1984.

WORDS—*The Words of Martin Luther King, Jr.,* selected by Coretta Scott King (New York: Newmarket Press, 1984).

YOLANDA—Interview with Yolanda King by W.R.W., November 1983.

NOTES

PAGE CHAPTER 1

1   tentative offers of . . . future career: Stride, 18–19.
1   Dr. Johns refused . . . "right goddamned here?": Stride, 29.
3   as many professional people: Abernathy.
3   Abernathy kidded . . . neither did I.": Abernathy.
4   "The Three Dimensions . . . not the source": Stride, 19.
4   tragic implications . . . it still hurt: Stride, 20. Coretta King, 96. Oates, 49–50.
4   "I could never . . . listen to you.": Stride, 20–21.
5   rides at night: Stride, 64.
5   dying father asked . . . Mike to his friends: Daddy King, 88.
5   "was a hard worker . . . just on interest.": Chandler.
6   whip him": Chandler. Daddy King, 130–31.
6   heated row . . . complicated.": Daddy King, 141–42.
6   "an inescapable urge . . . could not escape": Smith, 13.
6   "I was well aware . . . noticed it.": Smith, 16–17.
8   theological basis . . . the individual, ends.' ": Stride, 65–66. Smith, 33–34. Strength, 181.
8   Neither did I.": Smith.
8   "His message . . . inflictor of it.": Stride, 68–69.
9   Reverend Barbour and his guests . . . his style": Barbour.
9   Reverend Barbour counseled Mike: Barbour. Lewis, D., 32–33. Oates, 33–34.
9   Maple Shade: Barbour. Lewis, D., 33–34.
10 "It was difficult . . . willing to do it.": Raines, 33.
10 Peoria . . . "get a movement.": Vivian.
10 Gandhi's phrase . . . better to fight": Stride, 71.
10 "The aftermath of nonviolence": Stride, 71–72.
11 few girls from down home.": Coretta King, 53. Lewis, D., 40.
11 lives of her family: Coretta. Coretta King, 27.
13 talking of marriage: Coretta. Coretta King, 55. Oates, 42–43.
13–15 for a few years.": Stride, 21.
    "We had the feeling . . . section of the country.": Stride, 21.

PAGE CHAPTER 2

17 poll tax: Durr.
18 E. D. Nixon . . . in those days.: Nixon. Stride, 30.
19 "high-class church . . . segregation in Alabama.": Robinson.
20 Patterson . . . Southern Strategy: Patterson. Raines, 304–6.
20 "The consensus . . . moral issue at all.": Patterson.
20–21 Robert Patterson . . . in Alabama: Raines, 297–303. Chronicle, 536–37.
21 Rev. George Lee: Chronicle, 542–43. Lee and Gus Courts got a total of 400 of the 16,012 in Humphreys County to register, prompting a wave of economic reprisals and physical terror by the Klan and White Citizens Council of Mississippi. When Courts was wounded on November 25, 1955, his was the only black name remaining on the voter registration role in the county. Statewide, the campaign cut the number of blacks registered from 22,000 to 8,000 in less than a year. The NAACP raised $300,000 to help the blacks who lost their jobs.
21 Emmett Till . . . away with it: Chronicle, 542. Raines, 132–34, 388–89, 392, 393. Oates, 62.
21 Coretta responded . . . minister's wife": Coretta King, 100–1.
22 most outstanding preacher: Abernathy.
22 "We worked with her.": Robinson.
22 Nixon vetoed.: Nixon. Raines, 37–39.
23–24 "I don't think . . . to sit here.": News, May 12, 1974. Raines, 40–41. Montgomery, December 2, 1955.
24 "get her out.": Durr. Nixon. Raines, 39.
24 "We can break the buses.": Nixon. Raines, 44–45.
24 first called Abernathy . . . "telling people to come.": Nixon. Abernathy. Raines, 45.
25 52,000 fliers . . . two hours.: Robinson. Montgomery, December 4, 1955.
25–26 called Joe Azbell . . . front page.: Nixon. Azbell. Raines, 45–46.
26 Reverend Bennett . . . yield the floor.: Abernathy. Stride, 34–35.
26 King was troubled . . . refuse to cooperate.": Stride, 37–38.
26 One black woman . . . something was wrong.": Abernathy.
27 "Martin, come quickly! . . . empty!": Stride, 38–39. Coretta King, 115.
27 Nixon said . . . and walked": Nixon.
27 Nixon protested . . . talk of secrecy.: Nixon. Raines, 48–49. Stride, 45.
28 King spoke . . . veins of civilization.' ": Stride, 48–49. Montgomery, December 6, 1955.
28 Sellers, dumbfounded: Raines, 49–50.

PAGE CHAPTER 3

32 The meeting Thursday . . . parent company: Stride, 74–75.
32 "You are settling . . . altogether.": Lowery. Raines, 66–67.
33 Parks said . . . "We mean this year.": Stride, 76–78. Montgomery, December 9, 1955.
33 King stopped . . . my grandchildren.": Stride, 56.
33 my soul is rested.": Abernathy.
33 car pool: Lewis. Stride, 55–57. Raines, 58–61.
34 "there is no issue . . . good will.": Montgomery, December 11, 1955.
34 King became angry . . . honest and fair.": Stride, 78–79. Montgomery, December 17, 1955.
34–35 religious challenge . . . folkways.": Stride, 79–80.
35 "very unfair" . . . now a waiting game.: Abernathy. Stride, 81–82. Montgomery, December 20, 1955.

PAGE CHAPTER 9

PART ONE: SPREADING THE GOSPEL

pills in 1967 and was free on an appeal bond through April 1968. He and Sutherland are deceased.

PART TWO: TO THE MOUNTAINTOP

INDEX

Ebenezer Baptist Church, 1, 6, 64, 70, 76, 148, 205, 220, 225
Eisenhower, Dwight D., 39, 50, 56, 58, 61, 63, 76, 77, 81
Elliot, J. Robert, 102
Evans, Glenn V., 126
Evers, Medgar, 133, 134

Farmer, James, 10, 82–83, 89, 90, 94, 135, 165; ill., 86
Fauntroy, Walter, 137–38; ill., 138
Federal Bureau of Investigation (FBI), 66–67, 92, 93–94, 104–5, 120, 131, 135–37, 144, 145–49, 160, 162, 163, 166–67, 168, 184, 210, 223
Fellowship of Reconciliation (FOR), 10, 67
Ferris, Christine King, 76; ill., 168
First Baptist Church (Montgomery), 3, 22, 49–51, 86, 88–90, 93
Forbes, Dave, ill., 72
Forman, James, 163, 172, 178, 225
Frazier, Stanley, 34, 35
"Free at last! free at last! thank God almighty, we are free at last!," 143, 225, 228
Freedom Rides, 82–102, 132
French, E. N., 27, 29
Frye, Marquette, 188

Gandhi, Mohandas K., 8, 10, 34, 36, 61, 68, 71, 97, 98, 176
Gaston, A. G. (Gaston's Motel), 112–13, 129, 130, 131
Gayle, W. A. ("Tacky"), 31, 32, 35–36, 37
Georgia Education Commission, 21
Ghana, King in, 52–53
Glasco, R. J., 31
Goldwater, Barry, 165
Gomillion, C. G., 41
Goodman, Andrew, 160–63, 166–67, 170, 209, 213; ill., 161
Graetz, Robert, 31–32, 38, 49
Graham, Billy, 116
Graham, Henry, 90
Grapevine Tavern, 205
Gray, Fred, 31, 33, 38, 55
Greensboro, N.C., 68
Greenville, Miss., 134
Greenwood, Miss., 21, 103, 134, 197
Gregory, Dick, 104, 110; ill., 110
Griggs, Lee, 52
Guyot, Lawrence, 103, 134

Hale, Lloyd, 73
Hall, Grover, 50
Hallinan, Paul J., 167
Hamer, Fannie Lou, 103, 134, 163; ill., 164
Hanby, Clyde, 66
Handy, John, 92
Harrington, Charles, 219
Hartsfield, William, 74, 77–78
Hayling, Robert B., 154–55, 157
Haynie, W. E., 157
Holloman, Frank, 215
Hollowell, Donald, 76
Holt Street Baptist Church, 27, 43
Hood, James, 132
Hooks, Ben, 221
Hoover, J. Edgar, 104–5, 135–37, 144, 162, 167–69
Horne, Lena, 225
Housing discrimination, 53, 109, 191,

192, 194, 199–204, 208, 209, 223; landlords and, 191, 199; rent strikes and, 191, 199; slums and, 199, 200
Howser, James, 154
Hubbard, H. H., 24
Hudson Street Baptist Church, 49
Hughes, Genevieve, 84
Hughes, Richard, 211
Humphrey, Hubert, 163, 212, 225, 227
Hurley, Ruby, 42, 102
Hurok (Sol) Productions, 107

"I Have a Dream" speech, 139–44
India, King in, 61
Indianola, Miss., 21
In Friendship group, 40–41, 47
Ingalls, Luther, 35
"Institute on Nonviolence and Social Change," 45
Intercollegiate Council, 6
Interstate Commerce Commission (ICC), 93, 96
Interstate travel, Freedom Rides and, 82–102, 132
Invaders, 219, 220

Jackson, J. H., 193
Jackson, James, 154, 156
Jackson, Jesse, 191, 192, 200, 201, 220, 222; ill., 201, 202, 218
Jackson, Jimmy Lee, 172, 181
Jackson, Mahalia, 133, 199, 225; ill., 111
Jackson, Miss., 90, 162, 163, 194–97; march from Memphis to, 194
Jemison, T. J., 33
Jenkins, Clyde, 154
Jenkins, Herbert, 63–66
Jenkins, W. A., 119, 123
Johns, Vernon, 1–3
Johnson, Frank M., 38, 42, 177, 181, 183
Johnson, June, 134
Johnson, Lyndon B., 56, 135, 150, 154, 155, 157, 158, 159, 163, 165, 172, 176, 181–84, 212, 216, 223; address to Congress on Selma, 181–83; ill., 187; and King (see under King, Martin Luther, Jr.); and Vietnam, 171, 176, 184, 188, 189, 193–94, 209, 210, 211, 213, 214; and "War on Poverty," 163, 209
Johnson, Mordecai, 8
Jones, Charles, 94, 100, 102
Jones, Clarence, 137
Jordan, James, 161

Katzenbach, Nicholas, 132–33
Kauffmann, John, 205–6
Kennedy, Jacqueline, 225
Kennedy, John F., 63, 74, 76–77, 81, 82, 89, 90, 93, 102, 107, 109, 112, 119, 120, 127, 129, 131, 132, 133, 135–37, 139, 143–44, 149–50, 155; assassination of, 149–50; and civil rights legislation, 133, 135, 138–44, 150
Kennedy, Robert, F., 76–77, 81, 82, 88–90, 105, 112, 116, 132, 135, 136, 137, 138–39, 225; ill., 227
Kerner, Otto, 200; and Commission on Civil Disorders, 212, 216
Khrushchev, Nikita, 90, 107
King, A. D., 6, 114, 120, 130, 131, 132, 221, 222; ill., 168

King, Alberta Williams (mother), 4, 5, 48, 72, 220, 222; ill., 32, 168
King, Bernice Albertine, 113, 230
King, Chevene, 103
King, Christine, 76; ill., 168
King, Coretta Scott, 1, 4, 11–15, 21, 22, 26–27, 28, 36, 37, 39–40, 48, 59, 61, 70, 76, 82, 107, 120, 139, 143, 149–50, 167, 168, 169, 172, 190–91, 210, 214, 220; background, described, marriage to Martin Luther King, Jr., 11–15, 21; and husband's death, 222–26; ill., 12, 19, 32, 39, 59, 65, 77, 106, 152, 168, 191, 224, 226
King, Delia Lindsey, 5
King, Dexter, 82; ill., 224
King, James, 5
King, Lonnie, 73, 78; ill., 72, 74
King, Martin Luther, Sr. ("Daddy"), 4–6, 9, 13, 39–40, 46, 63, 73, 76–77, 78, 220; ill., 18, 32, 64, 168
King, Martin Luther, Jr.: Abernathy and, 3, 4, 22 (see also Abernathy, Ralph David); and Albany Movement, 96–104, 111, 112, 113–16, 119, 129; assassination plot, Ray and, 205–6, 211, 213, 219, 221, 222–28; attempt on his life in Harlem, 60–61; background, family, education, 4–15; and Birmingham campaign, 109–31, 132; and "Birmingham Manifesto," 116; and Black Power movement, 194–97, 201–4, 213; and Chicago Movement, 190–94, 197–205; and children's crusade, 123–31; chronology, 229–32; as copastor of Ebenezer Baptist Church, 1, 64, 70; death, funeral and burial of, 222–28; and Democratic Party Convention in Atlantic City, 163–65; final address in Dexter Avenue Baptist Church, 61–62; and freedom campaign in the urban ghettos (Northern crusade), 184–86, 190–94, 197–205, 209, 212 (see also specific aspects, places); and Freedom Rides, 82–102; and Freedom Walk in Detroit, 132; in Ghana, 52–53; as head of Dexter Avenue Baptist Church, 1–3, 13–15, 17–29, 49, 61–62; and Hoover and FBI, 104–5, 135–37, 144, 162, 167–69 (see also Hoover, J. Edgar); "I Have a Dream" speech by, 139–44; ill., 2, 7, 12, 15, 18, 19, 29, 30, 38, 39, 40, 44, 47, 53, 56, 57, 59, 60, 65, 72, 74, 77, 79, 80, 86, 101, 105, 106, 115–16, 149, 150, 152, 153, 159, 164, 166–69, 171, 173, 177, 181, 185–87, 191, 193, 195, 196, 198, 199, 208, 217, 218; imprisoned in Reidsville, 74–76; and income tax case, 70–71, 73–74; in demand as a preacher, spends three quarters of the year on the road, 101; in India, 61; jailed in Birmingham, 115–16, 120–23; and Johnson, 150, 154, 155, 157–60, 163, 165, 172, 181–84, 187, 193–94, 209, 210, 213, 223 (see also Johnson, Lyndon B.); and Kennedys, 109, 112, 120 (see also Kennedy, John F.; Kennedy, Robert F.); and leadership role, 46–61; "Letter from a Birmingham Jail" by, 121–23, 130,

ABOUT THE AUTHOR

Wm. Roger Witherspoon began his journalistic career at WCBN radio in Ann Arbor, Michigan, in 1966. He has since worked on the staff of NBC-TV in Burbank, California; the Bergen *Record* and the Newark *Star Ledger* in New Jersey; the New York *Daily News;* and the Atlanta *Constitution.* He is a founder of the Association of Black Journalists and has won several journalism awards, including the National Headliners Club Award for column writing and the Media Award for Economic Understanding, given by the Amos Tuck School of Business Administration at Dartmouth College. Since 1982, Mr. Witherspoon has been a free-lance writer, primarily for *Time, Black Enterprise, Essence,* and the Cable News Network.